MW01596588

English —
a curriculum profile for
Australian schools

A joint project of the States, Territories and the
Commonwealth of Australia initiated by the Australian
Education Council

Curriculum
CORPORATION

Published by Curriculum Corporation
St Nicholas Place
141 Rathdowne St
Carlton Vic 3053
Australia

Tel: (03) 639 0699
Fax: (03) 639 1616

National Library of Australia
Cataloguing-in-publication data
English: a curriculum profile for Australian schools.

ISBN 1 86366 207 3.

1. English language — Study and teaching — Australia.
2. Curriculum planning — Australia.
3. Students — Australia — Rating of.
    I. Australian Education Council.
    II. Curriculum Corporation (Australia).
    III. Title: Statement on English for Australian schools.

428.0071094

Designed by Marketing Partners

Printed in Australia by A E Keating (Printing) Pty Ltd

Foreword

This volume is one of a series of documents which together represent the most significant collaborative curriculum development project in the history of Australian education.

National collaboration has produced sixteen documents: a statement and a profile in each of eight areas of learning — English, mathematics, science, technology, languages other than English, health and physical education, studies of society and environment, and the arts. The sixteen documents are published in seventeen volumes, since the mathematics profile is published in two volumes.

In April 1989 the State, Territory and Commonwealth Ministers of Education endorsed ten common and agreed national goals for schooling in Australia. Over the following years, work proceeded on the development of statements and profiles. This work was undertaken at the direction of the Australian Education Council (AEC), the national council of Ministers of Education.

The statements in the eight areas of learning provide a framework for curriculum development by education systems and schools. They are divided into strands which reflect the major elements of learning in each area. Further, they are structured in four bands, roughly corresponding to the stages of schooling: lower primary, upper primary, junior secondary and post-compulsory. The statements do not provide a syllabus. Rather, they provide a foundation for courses which will meet students' needs and reflect advances in our knowledge — both of the learning area to which the statement is related and of how students learn. The statements encourage innovation and experimentation so that students have a positive experience of each learning area.

The profiles are designed to assist in the improvement of teaching and learning and to provide a common language for reporting student achievement. They are divided into strands for each learning area. Within each strand, eight achievement levels have been developed. Overall, the eight levels reflect the full range of student achievement during the compulsory years of schooling (Years 1–10). The Australian Council for Educational Research (ACER) has validated the levels. The profiles have also been subject to intensive trialling in Australian schools.

The project was managed by the AEC Curriculum and Assessment Committee (CURASS), chaired most recently by the New South Wales Director-General of School Education, Dr Ken Boston. CURASS included representation from the Commonwealth, States and Territories, New Zealand, Catholic and independent schools, parents, teachers, the AEC Secretariat, ACER and Curriculum Corporation. CURASS was supported by a secretariat with representation from all States and Territories and the Commonwealth.

Project teams were established to undertake the writing, while specialist staff from States and Territories and the Commonwealth assisted with development. In each learning area consultants were appointed with responsibility for ensuring that gender equity and Aboriginal and Torres Strait Islander perspectives were reflected in the documents. Throughout the writing process, nationwide consultations occurred with groups such as parents, teachers (from both government and non-government sectors), teacher educators, professional associations, subject and discipline specialists, curriculum developers, community groups, employers and unions.

At its meeting in July 1993, the AEC agreed that the publication of statements and profiles shall be the prerogative of each State and Territory. The Board of Curriculum Corporation in accordance with the wish of member systems is publishing, disseminating and marketing these materials developed through national collaborative processes.

David Francis
Executive Director

Contents

List of work samples

Introduction

The States, Territories and the Commonwealth have, since 1989, worked together on a major national educational initiative to produce statements and profiles in eight broad areas of learning:

The arts	English
Health and physical education	Languages other than English
Mathematics	Science
Studies of society and environment	Technology.

The Australian Education Council (AEC), made up of the education ministers of the States, Territories and Commonwealth, commissioned the work.

Statements provide a framework for curriculum development in each area of learning. They define the area, outline its essential elements, show what is distinctive about it and describe a sequence for developing knowledge and skills.

Statements provide an account of the strands and bands of each learning area. Strands are groupings of understandings of a learning area's content, processes and concepts. Bands are the broad stages in a sequence for developing knowledge, understandings and skills in a learning area. Each statement has four bands. Generally, Bands A and B will be covered in primary schooling, C in secondary school to year 10, and D in the post-compulsory years.

Profiles describe the progression of learning typically achieved by students during the compulsory years of schooling (Years 1–10) in each of the areas of learning. Their purpose is twofold: to help teaching and learning and to provide a framework for reporting student achievement. Profiles are divided into strands, usually the same as those in the statement, and into eight levels of achievement.

Profiles and statements are linked. The profiles show the typical progression in achieving learning outcomes, while statements are a framework of what might be taught to achieve these outcomes.

The English profile is built on the description of English as an area of learning provided in *A statement on English for Australian schools* (1994, Curriculum Corporation, Carlton, Vic.).

As well as identifying the aims of the English curriculum in schools, the statement describes the content of English in terms of two interrelated strands, Texts and Language. In the statement, these content strands apply to all language modes in English (speaking, listening, reading, viewing, and writing).

The profile's strands

In the English profile, the language modes have been adopted as the first focus for organisation:

- Speaking and listening
- Reading and viewing
- Writing

This strand structure facilitates the use of the profile as a reporting framework by enabling teachers to make judgements about students' ability to use their English knowledge and skills to speak, listen, read, view and write with purpose and effect.

The profile's strand organisers

The content strands identified in the statement, Texts and Language, are adopted as strand organisers within each strand of the profile.

From the Texts content strand:

1. Texts

From the Language content strand:

2. Contextual understanding

3. Linguistic structures and features

4. Strategies

Each profile organiser offers a different way of looking at a student's performance as a listener to, speaker, reader, viewer or writer of texts. Because they are interdependent, all organisers should be considered when making a judgement about a student's level of achievement in a particular strand.

1. Texts

What the student is doing with what kinds of texts.

This organiser focuses on the range and content of texts and on conceptual, linguistic and cognitive complexity in students' use of texts in English. It deals with what students typically do with texts at a given level and also says something about the texts. The Texts organiser provides a starting point for considering students' level of achievement. This is complemented by reference to the other organiser in the level.

2. Contextual understanding

The understanding about sociocultural and situational contexts that the student brings to bear when composing and comprehending texts.

This organiser focuses on students' learning about the ways in which people's interpretation and use of the English language varies according to the socio-cultural context and the situation in which it is being used. It deals with students' sociocultural knowledge and their awareness of how their own and other people's interpretation of meaning is influenced by this. The organiser also deals with students' knowledge of how language use is influenced by factors such as purpose, audience and subject matter, and how students use their contextual knowledge when speaking, listening, reading, viewing and writing.

3. Linguistic structures and features

How the student uses linguistic structures and features to compose and comprehend texts.

This organiser focuses on students' learning about the linguistic structures and features of the English language (for example, grammar and cohesion, text structure and organisation, and visual texts' codes and conventions). It deals with students' knowledge about linguistic structures and features and how effectively they use them for constructing and shaping meanings, and discussing and analysing spoken, written and visual texts.

4. Strategies

How the student goes about composing and comprehending texts.

This organiser focuses on the strategies students learn for composing and comprehending texts (for example, planning and revising writing, predicting while reading and viewing, and group discussion procedures when speaking and listening). It deals with students' knowledge of these strategies and how effectively they use them to speak, listen, read, view and write.

Key assumptions underlying the English profile

Several key assumptions underlie the English profile. It is assumed that:

1. As students move through the years of schooling, their teachers ensure that the English curriculum provides them with learning tasks and activities involving the content described in the national statement on English. In particular, this includes at all levels:

   - a broad and balanced range of texts as described in the national statement (pp.6–10)

   - a range of purposes and text types for using the English language. As students progress through the levels of achievement, this range should expand from the familiar to the unfamiliar, and from the simple to the complex

   - a range of audiences for using the English language. As students progress through the levels of achievement, this range should expand from familiar people to include more distant, formal, unknown and larger audiences.

2. The sociocultural and situational context in which English is used will always influence a student's performance of a particular learning task or activity. Teachers, therefore, need to make judgements about students' achievement over time and across a range of tasks and activities involving differing purposes, audiences and types of text.

3. Teachers make professional judgements about what is culturally appropriate and familiar content for the students in their classes.

4. Teachers provide students with guidance and support in their learning activities and tasks, and make judgements about students' level of achievement as part of normal teaching and learning activities.

5. For instructional purposes, English teaching and learning programs will usually integrate students' use of speaking, listening, reading, viewing and writing and give attention to each aspect of English described in the profile's sub-strands.

6. Students' experiences with using English and other languages beyond the school are essential considerations for teachers when constructing teaching and learning programs and in order to gain insight into students' abilities. The profile, however, focuses on outcomes and experiences typically available to all students within the classroom and school. Access to texts for study in English, particularly visual texts on film, television and video, will be provided to students in the classroom.

7. Teachers adopt sound pedagogical principles in their teaching. These principles are applicable to all areas of learning and are not, therefore, described separately for English. Sound pedagogy includes particular attention to the following:

   a) Developing in students
   - positive attitudes towards their learning of English
   - confidence in themselves as users of English
   - the ability to reflect on and evaluate their progress in learning and using English
   - a sense of enjoyment and challenge in learning tasks.
   b) Constructing teaching and learning programs that recognise the learning needs of individual students and groups of students in order to make the learning outcomes described in the profile as achievable as possible by all students. This is particularly important for students recognised as having been disadvantaged by the Australian education system – girls, Torres Strait Islander and Aboriginal students, students in poverty, students with disabilities, students from non-English-speaking backgrounds, and students in isolated situations.

8. Some words and phrases in the profile need to be interpreted to include students with disabilities or impairments:

a) Students with disabilities may need specialised equipment such as braillers, closed circuit TV and other magnification aids such as hand-held magnifiers and telescopes for distance work, word processors with spell checks and other computer programs plus peripherals such as voice synthesiser, large print, to help achieve outcomes.

b) Activities such as 'write', 'use a legible handwriting style', 'use a variety of print/script styles', 'proofread', 'punctuate' can all be done using computers or other physical aids such as braillers.

c) Students with marked vision impairment may use a brailler as their main writing tool.

d) Terms such as 'speak', 'ask', 'talk', 'tell', 'explain' etc. are understood to include all forms of verbal and non-verbal communication, for example, signed communication (signed English, Auslan), communication aids (boards, Compic, Canon communicators).

   The term 'listen' includes attending (lip-reading, watching signed language).

e) The word 'oral' includes all forms of communication, for example, sign language, communicators.

f) Students with marked vision impairment may:
   - use a brailler as their main writing tool;
   - require materials/books in alternative formats (brailled, taped, large print, tactile drawings, diagrams).

Elements of the profile

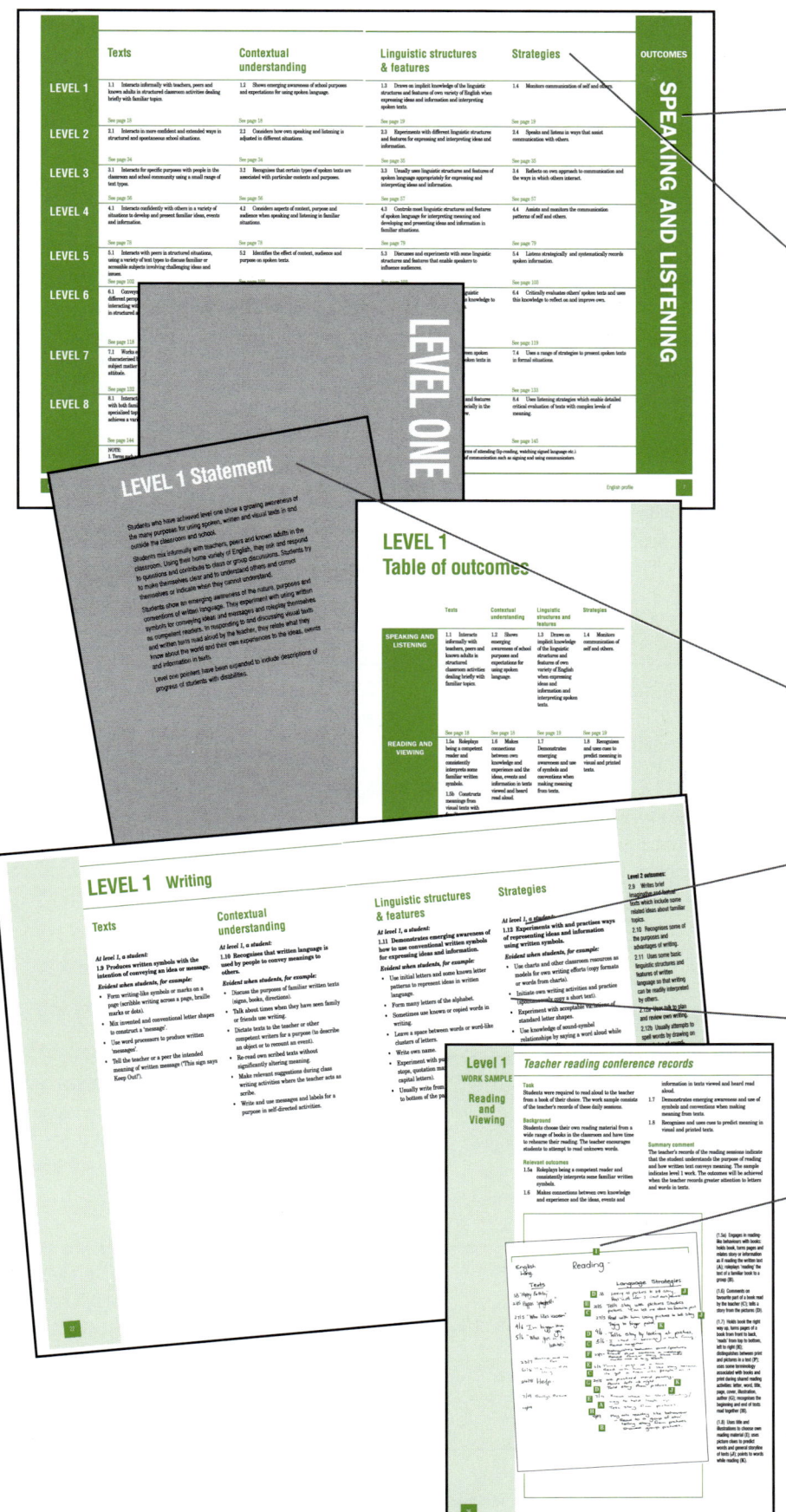

Strand display

Strands are the major organisers of a learning area. They can be groupings of content, process and/or conceptual understanding.

Strand organisers are organisers of content, process and/or conceptual understanding within a strand. There are four strand organisers in the English profile, common to all strands. These are Texts, Contextual understanding, Linguistic structures and features, and Strategies. The strand organiser is indicated by the number after the decimal point in the number sequence before each outcome.

Level display

Levels indicate progression in student learning. There are eight levels covering the compulsory years of schooling (Years 1–10). The level is indicated by the number before the decimal point at the beginning of each outcome.

Level statements are general descriptions of student performance at each of the eight levels within the profile.

Outcomes describe in progressive order the various skills and knowledge that students typically acquire as they become more proficient in an area. They outline the knowledge, skills and processes that are essential and distinctive to the learning area. They are the building blocks of the profile.

Pointers are indicators or signals of the achievement of an outcome. Unlike outcomes, pointers are only examples. Other pointers could also indicate achievement of the outcome. Bracketed sections are examples which further develop pointers. The brackets indicate a sample from a larger set of items.

Annotated work samples show student work which demonstrates the achievement of one or more outcomes at a level. The samples are annotated to show the reasons for this judgement.

	Texts	**Contextual understanding**
LEVEL 1	1.1 Interacts informally with teachers, peers and known adults in structured classroom activities dealing briefly with familiar topics.	1.2 Shows emerging awareness of school purposes and expectations for using spoken language.
	See page 18	See page 18
LEVEL 2	2.1 Interacts in more confident and extended ways in structured and spontaneous school situations.	2.2 Considers how own speaking and listening is adjusted in different situations.
	See page 34	See page 34
LEVEL 3	3.1 Interacts for specific purposes with people in the classroom and school community using a small range of text types.	3.2 Recognises that certain types of spoken texts are associated with particular contexts and purposes.
	See page 56	See page 56
LEVEL 4	4.1 Interacts confidently with others in a variety of situations to develop and present familiar ideas, events and information.	4.2 Considers aspects of context, purpose and audience when speaking and listening in familiar situations.
	See page 78	See page 78
LEVEL 5	5.1 Interacts with peers in structured situations, using a variety of text types to discuss familiar or accessible subjects involving challenging ideas and issues.	5.2 Identifies the effect of context, audience and purpose on spoken texts.
	See page 102	See page 102
LEVEL 6	6.1 Conveys detailed information and explores different perspectives on complex issues through interacting with known social groups, principally peers, in structured and unstructured situations.	6.2 Identifies ways in which listeners' sociocultural backgrounds, knowledge and opinions influence the meaning they obtain from spoken texts.
	See page 118	See page 118
LEVEL 7	7.1 Works effectively with others in situations characterised by complexity of purpose, procedure and subject matter and a need for formality in speech and attitude.	7.2 Considers the inter-relationships between texts, contexts, speakers and listeners in a range of situations.
	See page 132	See page 132
LEVEL 8	8.1 Interacts responsively, critically and confidently with both familiar and unfamiliar audiences on specialised topics in formal situations, and consistently achieves a variety of purposes in speech.	8.2 Shows sophisticated understanding of the power and effect of spoken language when speaking and listening.
	See page 144	See page 144

NOTE:
1. Terms such as 'speak', 'ask', 'talk', 'tell', 'explain' are intended to include forms of communication such as signing and the use of communication aids (boards, Compic, Canon communicators etc.).

Linguistic structures & features

Strategies

1.3   Draws on implicit knowledge of the linguistic structures and features of own variety of English when expressing ideas and information and interpreting spoken texts.

1.4   Monitors communication of self and others.

See page 19

See page 19

2.3   Experiments with different linguistic structures and features for expressing and interpreting ideas and information.

2.4   Speaks and listens in ways that assist communication with others.

See page 35

See page 35

3.3   Usually uses linguistic structures and features of spoken language appropriately for expressing and interpreting ideas and information.

3.4   Reflects on own approach to communication and the ways in which others interact.

See page 57

See page 57

4.3   Controls most linguistic structures and features of spoken language for interpreting meaning and developing and presenting ideas and information in familiar situations.

4.4   Assists and monitors the communication patterns of self and others.

See page 79

See page 79

5.3   Discusses and experiments with some linguistic structures and features that enable speakers to influence audiences.

5.4   Listens strategically and systematically records spoken information.

See page 103

See page 103

6.3   Experiments with knowledge of linguistic structures and features, and draws on this knowledge to explain how speakers influence audiences.

6.4   Critically evaluates others' spoken texts and uses this knowledge to reflect on and improve own.

See page 119

See page 119

7.3   Uses awareness of differences between spoken and written language to construct own spoken texts in structured, formal situations.

7.4   Uses a range of strategies to present spoken texts in formal situations.

See page 133

See page 133

8.3   Analyses how linguistic structures and features affect interpretations of spoken texts, especially in the construction of tone, style and point of view.

8.4   Uses listening strategies which enable detailed critical evaluation of texts with complex levels of meaning.

See page 145

See page 145

2. The term 'listen' is intended to include all forms of attending (lip-reading, watching signed language etc.).
3. The term 'oral' is intended to include forms of communication such as signing and using communicators.

	Texts	**Contextual understanding**
LEVEL 1	1.5a Roleplays being a competent reader and consistently interprets some familiar written symbols. 1.5b Constructs meanings from visual texts with familiar content, particularly texts designed to be viewed in segments. See page 20	1.6 Makes connections between own knowledge and experience and the ideas, events and information in texts viewed and heard read aloud. See page 20
LEVEL 2	2.5 Constructs and retells meanings from: – short written texts with familiar topics and vocabulary, predictable text structures and frequent illustrations, and – visual texts with predictable narrative structures. See page 36	2.6 Understands that texts are constructed by people and represent real and imaginary experience. See page 36
LEVEL 3	3.5 Interprets and discusses some relationships between ideas, information and events in: – written texts with familiar content and a small range of unfamiliar words and linguistic structures and features – visual texts designed for general viewing. See page 58	3.6 Identifies simple symbolic meanings and stereotypes in texts and discusses their purpose and meaning. See page 58
LEVEL 4	4.5 Justifies own interpretation of ideas, information and events in texts containing some unfamiliar concepts and topics and which introduce relatively complex linguistic structures and features. See page 80	4.6 Explains possible reasons for people's varying interpretations of a text. See page 80
LEVEL 5	5.5 Discusses themes and issues in accessible texts with challenging structures and ideas, and constructs responses interpreting these. See page 104	5.6 Recognises that texts are constructed for particular purposes and to appeal to certain groups. See page 104
LEVEL 6	6.5 Explores different perspectives on complex issues through reading and viewing a range of texts, and constructs written and spoken responses relating these perspectives to personal understandings of the contemporary world. See page 120	6.6 Considers the contexts in which texts were or are created and how these are reflected in texts. See page 120
LEVEL 7	7.5 Constructs meanings from a range of texts, including those characterised by complexity of construction and subject matter, and justifies these with detailed and well-chosen evidence from the text. See page 134	7.6 Considers a variety of interrelationships between texts, contexts, readers or viewers and makers of texts. See page 134
LEVEL 8	8.5 Analyses and criticises in a lucid way texts produced for a range of purposes and audiences, including popular texts and linguistically demanding texts which may involve varied narrative perspectives and subtle subtexts. See page146	8.6 Analyses texts in terms of the sociocultural values, attitudes and assumptions that they project and reflect. See page 146

NOTES:
1. Resources include braille texts and tactile books.
2. Information can be recorded on computers or with tools such as braillers.

Linguistic structures & features

Strategies

1.7   Demonstrates emerging awareness and use of symbols and conventions when making meaning from texts.

1.8   Recognises and uses cues to predict meaning in visual and printed texts.

See page 21

See page 21

2.7   Recognises and interprets basic linguistic structures and features of texts.

2.8 a Uses basic strategies for interpreting written and visual texts and maintains continuity in understanding when meaning is disrupted.
2.8 b With teacher guidance, selects own reading material, and gathers and sorts information on a topic from a variety of sources.

See page 37

See page 37

3.7   Identifies and uses the linguistic structures and features characteristic of a range of text types to construct meaning.

3.8 a Integrates a variety of strategies for interpreting printed and visual texts.

3.8 b With teacher guidance, uses several strategies for identifying resources and finding information in texts.

See page 59

See page 59

4.7   With teacher guidance, identifies and discusses how linguistic structures and features work to shape readers' and viewers' understanding of texts.

4.8 a Selects, uses and reflects on strategies appropriate for different texts and reading or viewing purposes.
4.8 b   With peers, identifies information needs and finds resources for specific purposes.

See page 81

See page 81

5.7   Draws on knowledge of linguistic structures and features to explain how texts are constructed.

5.8 a   Uses knowledge of principal conventions of narrative texts to construct meaning from a range of text types.
5.8 b   Systematically finds and records information.

See page 105

See page 105

6.7   Compares linguistic structures and features of texts to highlight their similarities and differences in form and meaning.

6.8 a   Draws on a repertoire of strategies to maintain understanding through dense or extended texts.
6.8 b   Gathers, selects and organises information effectively for specific purposes.

See page 121

See page 121

7.7   Identifies and comments on the impact of techniques intended to shape readers' and viewers' interpretations of and reactions to texts.

7.8   Uses reading and viewing strategies that enable detailed critical evaluation of texts.

See page 135

See page 135

8.7   Analyses how linguistic structures and features influence interpretations of texts, especially in the construction of tone, style and point of view.

8.8   Uses reading and viewing strategies that enable detailed critical evaluation of texts which may have complex levels of meaning.

See page 147

See page 147

3. The term 'view' includes 'attends to' for vision impaired students.
4. The term 'texts' includes taped materials.

	Texts	Contextual understanding
LEVEL 1	1.9 Produces written symbols with the intention of conveying an idea or message. See page 22	1.10 Recognises that written language is used by people to convey meanings to others. See page 22
LEVEL 2	2.9 Writes brief imaginative and factual texts which include some related ideas about familiar topics. See page 38	2.10 Recognises some of the purposes and advantages of writing. See page 38
LEVEL 3	3.9 Experiments with inter-relating ideas and information when writing about familiar topics within a small range of text types. See page 60	3.10 Recognises that certain text types and features are associated with particular purposes and audiences. See page 60
LEVEL 4	4.9 Uses writing to develop familiar ideas, events and information. See page 82	4.10 Adjusts writing to take account of aspects of context, purpose and audience. See page 82
LEVEL 5	5.9 Uses a variety of text types for writing about familiar or accessible subjects and exploring challenging ideas and issues. See page 106	5.10 Identifies the specific effect of context, audience and purpose on written texts. See page 106
LEVEL 6	6.9 Conveys detailed information and explores different perspectives on complex, challenging issues through writing for specific and general audiences. See page 122	6.10 Predicts some of the likely characteristics and expectations of particular audiences and tries to accommodate or resist these expectations as appropriate. See page 122
LEVEL 7	7.9 Writes sustained texts characterised by complexity of purpose and subject matter and a need for formality in language and construction. See page 136	7.10 Selects text type, subject matter and language to suit a specific audience and purpose. See page 136
LEVEL 8	8.9 Writes convincingly and expressively on specialised topics and complex, often abstract, ideas, and consistently achieves a wide variety of purposes in writing for both specific and general audiences. See page 148	8.10 Makes critical choices of tone and style to suit different purposes and to influence audiences. See page 148

NOTES:
1. Students with disabilities will need specialised equipment such as braillers, word processors with spell check and other computer programs to help meet outcomes.
2. Activities such as 'write', 'use a legible handwriting style', 'use a variety of print/script styles', 'proofread' and 'punctuate' can all be done using computer assisted learning.
3. Students with marked vision impairment may use a brailler as their main writing tool.

Linguistic structures & features

Strategies

1.11 Demonstrates emerging awareness of how to use conventional written symbols for expressing ideas and information. See page 23	1.12 Experiments with and practises ways of representing ideas and information using written symbols. See page 23
2.11 Uses some basic linguistic structures and features of written language so that writing can be readily interpreted by others. See page 39	2.12a Uses talk to plan and review own writing. 2.12b Usually attempts to spell words by drawing on knowledge of sound-symbol relationships and of standard letter patterns. See page 39
3.11 Controls most basic features of written language and experiments with some organisational and linguistic features of different text types. See page 61	3.12a Experiments with strategies for planning, reviewing and proofreading own writing. 3.12b Consistently makes informed attempts at spelling. See page 61
4.11 Controls most distinguishing linguistic structures and features of basic text types such as stories, procedures, reports and arguments. See page 83	4.12a When prompted, uses a range of strategies for planning, reviewing and proofreading own writing. 4.12b Uses a multi-strategy approach to spelling. See page 83
5.11 Controls the linguistic structures and features necessary to communicate ideas and information clearly in written texts of some length and complexity. See page 107	5.12 Draws on planning and review strategies that assist in effectively completing particular tasks. See page 107
6.11 Uses and experiments with a range of linguistic structures and features designed to influence audiences. See page 123	6.12 Revises own writing for meaning and effectiveness. See page 123
7.11 Controls spelling, syntax and text structures to meet the demands of most expository and imaginative writing. See page 137	7.12 Critically evaluates others' written texts and uses this knowledge to reflect on and improve own. See page 137
8.11 Manipulates linguistic structures and features for specific effect so that meaning is conveyed expressively and concisely. See page 149	8.12 Revises writing of self and others for cohesion, impact and meaning. See page 149

LEVEL ONE

LEVEL 1 Statement

Students who have achieved level one show a growing awareness of the many purposes for using spoken, written and visual texts in and outside the classroom and school.

Students mix informally with teachers, peers and known adults in the classroom. Using their home variety of English, they ask and respond to questions and contribute to class or group discussions. Students try to make themselves clear and to understand others and correct themselves or indicate when they cannot understand.

Students show an emerging awareness of the nature, purposes and conventions of written language. They experiment with using written symbols for conveying ideas and messages and roleplay themselves as competent readers. In responding to and discussing visual texts and written texts read aloud by the teacher, they relate what they know about the world and their own experiences to the ideas, events and information in texts.

LEVEL 1
Table of outcomes

	Texts	Contextual understanding	Linguistic structures & features	Strategies
SPEAKING AND LISTENING	1.1 Interacts informally with teachers, peers and known adults in structured classroom activities dealing briefly with familiar topics.	1.2 Shows emerging awareness of school purposes and expectations for using spoken language.	1.3 Draws on implicit knowledge of the linguistic structures and features of own variety of English when expressing ideas and information and interpreting spoken texts.	1.4 Monitors communication of self and others.
	See page 18	See page 18	See page 19	See page 19
READING AND VIEWING	1.5a Roleplays being a competent reader and consistently interprets some familiar written symbols. 1.5b Constructs meanings from visual texts with familiar content, particularly texts designed to be viewed in segments.	1.6 Makes connections between own knowledge and experience and the ideas, events and information in texts viewed and heard read aloud.	1.7 Demonstrates emerging awareness and use of symbols and conventions when making meaning from texts.	1.8 Recognises and uses cues to predict meaning in visual and printed texts.
	See page 20	See page 20	See page 21	See page 21
WRITING	1.9 Produces written symbols with the intention of conveying an idea or message.	1.10 Recognises that written language is used by people to convey meanings to others.	1.11 Demonstrates emerging awareness of how to use conventional written symbols for expressing ideas and information.	1.12 Experiments with and practises ways of representing ideas and information using written symbols.
	See page 22	See page 22	See page 23	See page 23

TOWARDS LEVEL 1

In TOWARDS LEVEL 1, level 1 pointers have been supplemented with additional pointers to show progress of students with disabilities. Level 1 outcomes and pointers start on page 18.

Speaking and Listening

Texts
Towards level 1, students:

- Respond to environmental sounds and stimuli and familiar people.
- Respond to communication with others.
- Initiate communication.
- Use conversation conventions (turn-taking, listening).

Contextual understanding
Towards level 1, students:

- Express needs, wants and feelings in appropriate ways at school.
- Request assistance or information.

Linguistic structures & features
Towards level 1, students:

- Participate in language experience activities involving repetition of language, its patterns and vocabulary.
- Convey likes and dislikes.
- Interpret facial expressions, gestures, volume, pitch and intonation.
- Use words and phrases in response to simple questions.

Strategies
Towards level 1, students:

- Communicate comprehension difficulties, ask 'what?'.
- Self-correct words, pronunciation and signals in familiar contexts.

Reading and Viewing

Texts
Towards level 1, students:

- Demonstrate reading like behaviour, such as: hold book correct way up, demonstrate that story is presented from front to back, turn single pages in order, tracks from left to right.
- Maintain focus when looking at books, advertising material, magazines.
- Request stories.
- Listen, watch and enjoy a story when given a choice.
- Indicate main idea of a picture.
- Match words with pictures.

Contextual understanding
Towards level 1, students:

- Identify familiar features in pictorial texts.
- Indicate connections between features in texts and own experience.

Linguistic structures & features
Towards level 1, students:

- Demonstrate understanding of language associated with reading (look, listen, read, front, back, upside down, right way up, book).
- Sequence pictures and objects.
- Recognise and interpret familiar logos (fast food signs).
- Recognise elements of print from personal experience (Steve looks at stop sign and says, referring to 'S', "That's my name").

Strategies
Towards level 1, students:

- Predict events in daily routine.
- Predict coming events and enjoyable activities and say what it is that they enjoy.
- Request favourite stories and give reasons for their preference.
- Identify main features of a story.

Writing

Texts

Towards level 1, students:

- Demonstrate fine motor control (reach for and grasp objects, manipulate objects and develop grip).
- Perform tasks that require eye-hand coordination (join dots and follow patterns).
- Establish hand dominance.
- Make meaningful marks to represent letters.
- Reproduce symbols that may include curved, intersecting or straight lines that simulate letters.
- Produce written symbols in response to cues.

Contextual understanding

Towards level 1, students:

- Identify written texts in own environment (signs, books).
- Imitate writing when they see others writing (in a bank or on a bank form).
- Participate in the production of class materials (teacher-made books using pictures of people, objects and things).

Linguistic structures & features

Towards level 1, students:

- Write some letters from own name.
- Use a 4 and a 7 to convey meaning.

Strategies

Towards level 1, students:

- Use photographs or pictures to make choices, represent ideas, express feelings.
- Identify that a written phrase or sentence has been recorded.
- Use words when paired with pictures.

LEVEL 1 Speaking and Listening

Texts

At level 1, a student:

1.1 Interacts informally with teachers, peers and known adults in structured classroom activities dealing briefly with familiar topics.

Evident when students, for example:

- Use appropriate greetings, introductions and farewells.

- Join in poems, action verse and refrains recited by class or read by the teacher.

- Tell jokes, riddles and anecdotes to peers.

- Follow, one step at a time, short, simple instructions (for playing a game, completing a classroom task).

- Attempt to give directions and instructions to others.

- Recount personal experiences and discuss experiences shared with adults and peers.

- Report briefly to a group on personal knowledge about a topic (describe aspects of favourite pastimes, pets, television programs, people).

- Ask and answer questions seeking information or clarification.

- When prompted, make relevant contributions in class and group activities and discussions.

Contextual understanding

At level 1, a student:

1.2 Shows emerging awareness of school purposes and expectations for using spoken language.

Evident when students, for example:

- Understand purpose and their own roles in routine classroom activities involving speaking and listening.

- Attempt to observe agreed rules in structured classroom situations (raise hand to speak, take turns, answer questions, listen attentively, offer ideas and opinions).

- Cooperate with others on tasks.

- Use talk to establish relationships with others in the classroom.

- Ask, accede to and refuse requests in agreed ways.

- Compare greetings and farewells used at home and at school and discuss those appropriate to different situations ('Good morning' to a teacher in the classroom, 'See ya' to other students in the yard).

- Make connections between first or home language (including signed language) and school English, recognising that all languages serve a communicative function.

Linguistic structures & features

At level 1, a student:

1.3 Draws on implicit knowledge of the linguistic structures and features of own variety of English when expressing ideas and information and interpreting spoken texts.

Evident when students, for example:

- Sequence ideas in speech in intelligible ways.
- Use 'and', 'then', 'but' to link ideas in their speech.
- Interpret and use simple statements, commands and questions.
- Attempt to adopt appropriate tones of voice and intonation patterns to convey meaning.
- Pronounce most sounds clearly.
- Speak audibly on most occasions.
- Interpret and respond to non-verbal cues in ways appropriate to their own culture (facial expression, gesture, silence, pause).

Strategies

At level 1, a student:

1.4 Monitors communication of self and others.

Evident when students, for example:

- Anticipate stages in familiar spoken texts (predict next part of teacher's directions for an activity).
- Stay on the general topic and ask and respond to questions when discussing shared experiences with teachers and peers.
- Listen to a speaker and contribute some relevant comments to a conversation or discussion.
- Usually indicate when something is not understood (through facial expressions and body language, asking questions).
- Demonstrate attentive listening in non-verbal ways appropriate to their own culture.
- Self-correct to clarify meaning ('Then she runned ... ran', 'The monster was scared ... no, I mean ... He was scared of the monster').

Level 2 outcomes:

2.1 Interacts in more confident and extended ways in structured and spontaneous school situations.

2.2 Considers how own speaking and listening is adjusted in different situations.

2.3 Experiments with different linguistic structures and features for expressing and interpreting ideas and information.

2.4 Speaks and listens in ways that assist communication with others.

LEVEL 1 Reading and Viewing

Texts

At level 1, a student:

1.5a Roleplays being a competent reader and consistently interprets some familiar written symbols.

Evident when students, for example:

- Engage in reading-like behaviour (hold book, turn pages and relate story or information as if reading the words).

- Mimic teacher's role in a shared book session by pointing to and 'reading' the text of a familiar big book largely from memory.

- Point to text on signs and provide a relevant meaning according to context.

- Recognise the meaning of familiar print (advertising logos, labels, classroom signs, street and traffic signs, names and labels on classroom equipment).

- Recognise own names.

1.5b Constructs meanings from visual texts with familiar content, particularly texts designed to be viewed in segments.

Evident when students, for example:

- Take part in class discussion about possible interpretations of a picture (stories that can be inferred from a newspaper photograph).

- Discuss television programs (express reasons for preferring certain programs; offer some reasons for a character's actions).

- Discuss favourite aspects of films and videos and identify features that appeal to them (action segments, scary parts, particular characters).

Contextual understanding

At level 1, a student:

1.6 Makes connections between own knowledge and experience, and the ideas, events and information in texts viewed and heard read aloud.

Evident when students, for example:

- Compare personal knowledge and experience with information in texts (make comments such as, 'That's like ...'or 'When I did that I ...'or 'My silkworms didn't look like that ...').

- Express personal views about a character's actions and speculate on their own behaviour in a similar situation ('If I were ... I would have ...').

- Reflect on their own experiences compared with those in texts viewed or heard read — through talking, drawing, roleplay, craft (draw a picture showing when they felt the way a character did).

- Compare the way familiar people live with those in visual and printed texts (how the families represented are like or unlike their own).

- List and discuss new things learned or questions raised through viewing or listening to a text read aloud (new information gained through shared reading of an informational book).

Linguistic structures & features

At level 1, a student:

1.7 Demonstrates emerging awareness and use of symbols and conventions when making meaning from texts.

Evident when students, for example:

- Hold book or other text the right way up, turn pages of a book from front to back, 'read' from top to bottom, left to right.

- Use terms associated with books and print during shared reading activities (letter, word, title, page, cover, illustration, author).

- Recognise some words in texts.

- Recognise full stops, capital letters and spaces between words in printed texts.

- Recognise and name some letters of the alphabet and show some awareness of letter-sound relationships (the sounds represented by initial and final letters in words).

- Recognise the beginning and end of texts viewed or heard read (identify the beginning and end of a television program by the theme music, sound effects, titles, graphics).

- Recognise familiar media narratives as belonging to program categories (news, cartoons, quiz shows, sport programs).

Strategies

At level 1, a student:

1.8 Recognises and uses cues to predict meaning in visual and printed texts.

Evident when students, for example:

- Use title and illustrations to predict what a text might be about ('That book is about koalas').

- Draw on personal experience or knowledge of a topic or context to predict events and information during shared book activities or when viewing a short film or video with the class.

- Use picture clues, patterns of language or initial letters/sounds to narrow possibilities in predicting words in texts during shared book activities.

- Point to words while reading.

- Use knowledge of the structure of familiar television programs with regular characters, settings and segments to predict who will appear and what might happen next.

- Predict plot development based on cause-and-effect relationships in texts (in a television program, 'The bank robbers stole the money and now the police have to catch them').

Level 2 outcomes:

2.5 Constructs and retells meanings from:

- short written texts with familiar topics and vocabulary, predictable text structures and frequent illustrations, and

- visual texts with predictable narrative structures.

2.6 Understands that texts are constructed by people and represent real and imaginary experience.

2.7 Recognises and interprets basic linguistic structures and features of texts.

2.8a Uses basic strategies for interpreting written and visual texts and maintains continuity in understanding when meaning is disrupted.

2.8b With teacher guidance, selects own reading material, and gathers and sorts information on a topic from a variety of sources.

LEVEL 1 Writing

Texts

At level 1, a student:

1.9 Produces written symbols with the intention of conveying an idea or message.

Evident when students, for example:

- Form writing-like symbols or marks on a page (scribble writing across a page, braille marks or dots).

- Mix invented and conventional letter shapes to construct a 'message'.

- Use word processors to produce written 'messages'.

- Tell the teacher or a peer the intended meaning of written message ('This sign says Keep Out!').

Contextual understanding

At level 1, a student:

1.10 Recognises that written language is used by people to convey meanings to others.

Evident when students, for example:

- Discuss the purposes of familiar written texts (signs, books, directions).

- Talk about times when they have seen family or friends use writing.

- Dictate texts to the teacher or other competent writers for a purpose (to describe an object or to recount an event).

- Re-read own scribed texts without significantly altering meaning.

- Make relevant suggestions during class writing activities where the teacher acts as scribe.

- Write and use messages and labels for a purpose in self-directed activities.

Linguistic structures & features

At level 1, a student:

1.11 Demonstrates emerging awareness of how to use conventional written symbols for expressing ideas and information.

Evident when students, for example:

- Use initial letters and some known letter patterns to represent ideas in written language.
- Form many letters of the alphabet.
- Sometimes use known or copied words in writing.
- Leave a space between words or word-like clusters of letters.
- Write own name.
- Experiment with punctuation marks (full stops, quotation marks, lower case and capital letters).
- Usually write from left to right and from top to bottom of the page.

Strategies

At level 1, a student:

1.12 Experiments with and practises ways of representing ideas and information using written symbols.

Evident when students, for example:

- Use charts and other classroom resources as models for own writing efforts (copy formats or words from charts).
- Initiate own writing activities and practice (spontaneously copy a short text).
- Experiment with acceptable variations of standard letter shapes.
- Use knowledge of sound-symbol relationships by saying a word aloud while trying to write it.
- Ask a peer or the teacher to read writing efforts.
- Ask someone to act as scribe.
- Ask for help to express ideas.

Level 2 outcomes:

2.9 Writes brief imaginative and factual texts which include some related ideas about familiar topics.

2.10 Recognises some of the purposes and advantages of writing.

2.11 Uses some basic linguistic structures and features of written language so that writing can be readily interpreted by others.

2.12a Uses talk to plan and review own writing.

2.12b Usually attempts to spell words by drawing on knowledge of sound-symbol relationships and of standard letter patterns.

Beware of aunts

Task

Students were required to comment on the book *Beware of the Aunts* by Pat Thomson after having it read to them. The teacher asked the students to draw four different aunts to illustrate the book, talk about any surprises in the way the author writes about aunts, and look at the book from the point of view of an aunt.

Background

The class found that a lot of children's books have aunts as characters. They were looking at the ways writers represent aunts when one student commented that aunts in books were often mean. The teacher chose to read aloud *Beware of the Aunts* because it was funny, new, and by a popular writer.

Relevant outcomes:
Speaking and listening

1.1 Interacts informally with teachers, peers and known adults in structured classroom activities dealing briefly with familiar topics.

1.2 Shows emerging awareness of school purposes and expectations for using spoken language.

1.3 Draws on implicit knowledge of the linguistic structures and features of own variety of English when expressing ideas and information and interpreting spoken texts.

1.4 Monitors communication of self and others.

Reading and viewing

1.6 Makes connections between own knowledge and experience and the ideas, events and information in texts viewed and heard read aloud.

Summary comment

The transcript extract and the teacher's observations indicate level 1 achievement of Speaking and listening outcomes. The transcript also clearly indicates achievement of Reading and viewing outcome 1.6.

Work sample
Brief extract from transcript of teacher-class discussion as below.

Teacher: OK. Here's the next question. You are an aunt.
STUDENT: I'm not an aunt. **F** **O** **P**
Teacher: Pretend (over quiet hubbub about pretending to be an aunt) that you are an aunt. How would you feel about the way Pat Thomson's written about you, about people like you in the book? Can we have hands up for answers. A? **G** **H** **E**
STUDENT: She says that aunts are mean, she says that they don't let her [do things], like the aunt that says that children aren't allowed in her special room! It's not **J** **K** **I** **D** **I**
B fair. My aunts aren't like that! **A** **L** **M**
C **N**

(1.6) Compares own knowledge and experience with information presented in texts: 'My aunts aren't like that!' (**A**); expresses own view about the representation of characters in texts: 'It's not fair!' (**B**); comments on own experiences compared with those in texts viewed or heard read aloud (**C**); compares the qualities of the aunts in the text with own aunts (**D**).

(1.1) Reports briefly on personal knowledge about a topic: gives an opinion about the representation of aunts in the text (**E**); responds to the teacher's questions (**F**); makes relevant contributions in a structured class discussion (**G**).

(1.2) Observes agreed rules in structured classroom situations: raises hand to speak, takes turns, answers questions, listens attentively, offers ideas and opinions (**H**).

(1.3) Orders ideas in speech in meaningful ways: lists ways in which aunts are represented in the book and then comments on them (**I**); interprets and uses simple statements and questions (**J**); adopts appropriate tone of voice and intonation patterns to convey meaning (stressed the words, 'It's not fair!') (**K**); pronounces most sounds clearly (**L**); speaks audibly (**M**).

(1.4) Stays on the general topic and asks and responds to questions during the class discussion (**N**); listens to a speaker and contributes relevant comments to the discussion (**O**); indicates when something is not understood: 'I'm not an aunt.' (**P**).

Discussion of TV program

Task

The student engaged in a conversation with the teacher about plans for the weekend.

Relevant outcomes: Speaking and listening

1.1 Interacts informally with teachers, peers and known adults in structured classroom activities dealing briefly with familiar topics.

1.2 Shows emerging awareness of school purposes and expectations for using spoken language.

1.3 Draws on implicit knowledge of the linguistic structures and features of own variety of English when expressing ideas and information and interpreting spoken texts.

1.4 Monitors communication of self and others.

Reading and viewing

1.5b Constructs meanings from visual texts with familiar content, particularly texts designed to be viewed in segments.

Summary comment

The transcript and the teacher's observations indicate level 1 achievement of Speaking and listening outcomes (level 2 achievement would be indicated by the student giving more extended responses or volunteering more information). The transcript also indicates achievement of Reading and viewing outcome 1.5b (a fuller account or description of the television program would have pointed towards level 2 achievement).

(1.1) Describes aspects of a favourite television program (**A**); responds to questions seeking information or clarification (**B**); makes relevant contributions to the conversation (**C**).

(1.2) Participates in the discussion with the teacher (**D**).

(1.3) Orders ideas in speech in meaningful ways (**E**); interprets and uses simple statements and questions (**F**); adopts an appropriate tone of voice and intonation patterns to convey meaning (**G**); pronounces most sounds clearly (**H**); speaks audibly (**I**).

(1.4) Stays on the general topic and responds to teacher's questions (**J**); listens to the teacher and contributes relevant comments to the conversation (**K**); demonstrates attentive listening by maintaining eye contact with the teacher while speaking (**L**).

(1.5b) Recalls and briefly describes some aspects of a favourite television program (**M**); comments on parts of television programs aimed at a general viewing audience (**N**); discusses television programs viewed at home (**O**).

Work sample

Transcript of a brief conversation between teacher and student.

> **Teacher:** What are you going to do on the weekend?
> **Student:** Stay home. **B** **C**
> **Teacher:** What do you like to do at home?
> **Student:** Watch a video.
> **Teacher:** What kind of video?
> **Student:** About Harry and the Hendersons. It's on TV on a Monday, Tuesday and Wednesday and we video it and watch it on Saturday and Sunday.
>
> **Teacher:** Who are the Hendersons? **B** **C** **M**
> **Student:** A family.
> **Teacher:** Who is Harry? Is he a dog?
> **Student:** No, he's a Big Foot. Well, actually he's like a gorilla. The Hendersons found him in the jungle. That's where he lived and the Hendersons took him home to live with them. **A** **M**
>
> **Teacher:** Does he like living with the Hendersons? **M**
> **Student:** Yes. He likes Ernie.
> **Teacher:** How does Harry talk?
> **Student:** Well, actually he doesn't talk properly. He just says, "Harry, Harry." **B** **C** **M**

(margin bracket labels: **D E F G H I J K L N O**)

Teacher reading conference records

Task

Students were required to read aloud to the teacher from a book of their choice. The work sample consists of the teacher's records of these daily sessions.

Background

Students choose their own reading material from a wide range of books in the classroom and have time to rehearse their reading. The teacher encourages students to attempt to read unknown words.

Relevant outcomes

1.5a Role plays being a competent reader and consistently interprets some familiar written symbols.

1.6 Makes connections between own knowledge and experience and the ideas, events and information in texts viewed and heard read aloud.

1.7 Demonstrates emerging awareness and use of symbols and conventions when making meaning from texts.

1.8 Recognises and uses cues to predict meaning in visual and printed texts.

Summary comment

The teacher's records of the reading sessions indicate that the student understands the purpose of reading and how written text conveys meaning. The sample indicates level 1 work. The outcomes will be achieved when the teacher records greater attention to letters and words in texts.

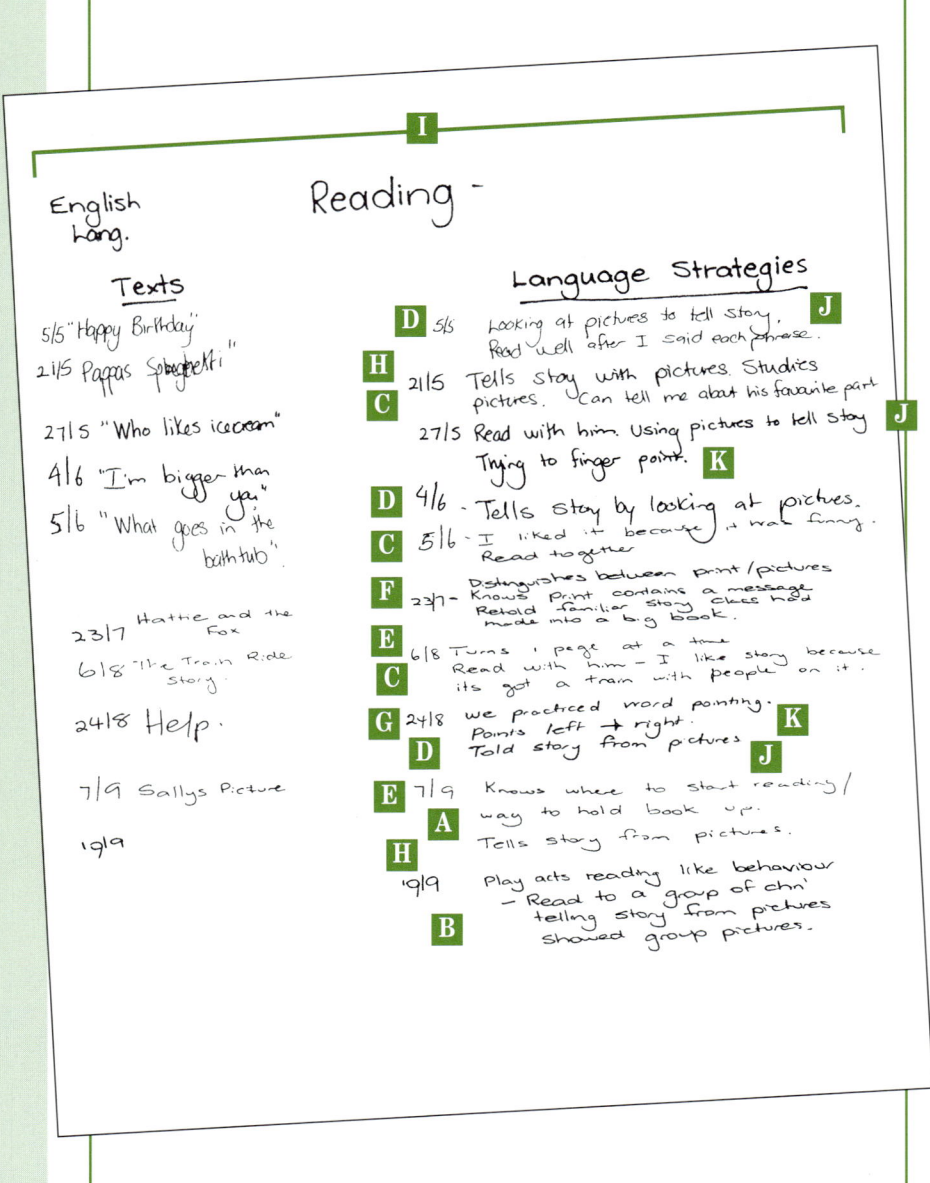

(1.5a) Engages in reading-like behaviours with books: holds book, turns pages and relates story or information as if reading the written text (**A**); roleplays 'reading' the text of a familiar book to a group (**B**).

(1.6) Comments on favourite part of a book read by the teacher (**C**); tells a story from the pictures (**D**).

(1.7) Holds book the right way up, turns pages of a book from front to back, 'reads' from top to bottom, left to right (**E**); distinguishes between print and pictures in a text (**F**); uses some terminology associated with books and print during shared reading activities: letter, word, title, page, cover, illustration, author (**G**); recognises the beginning and end of texts read together (**H**).

(1.8) Uses title and illustrations to choose own reading material (**I**); uses picture clues to predict words and general storyline of texts (**J**); points to words while reading (**K**).

I went to the shop

Task

Students were required to write a recount.

Background

The class started the day with a news-telling session. The teacher then demonstrated on the easel how to write a recount. The children read the text as the teacher wrote. The children were asked to write their own accounts of their weekend activities. The class talked about writing strategies or things to remember when writing (such as spaces between words, listening to identify sounds in words, especially the beginning sound, and trying to relate sounds to the associated letter). The student wrote a recount and read it to the teacher, who scribed under the student's work and asked the student to copy the writing. The student then illustrated the work.

Relevant outcomes

1.9 Produces written symbols with the intention of conveying an idea or message.

1.10 Recognises that written language is used by people to convey meanings to others.

1.11 Demonstrates emerging awareness of how to use conventional written symbols for expressing ideas and information.

1.12 Experiments with and practises ways of representing ideas and information using written symbols.

Summary comment

The text shows awareness of the purposes and uses of written language conventions and symbols.

(1.9) Uses conventional letters (**A**), invented letter shapes (**B**) and other known symbols (**C**) to represent meaning; tells the teacher the intended meaning (scribed below student's text) of written symbols (**D**).

(1.10) Selects appropriate subject matter by recounting a weekend activity (**E**); reads own text (**F**).

(1.11) Writes own name (**G**); forms conventional letters of the alphabet (**H**); writes from left to right and from top to bottom of the page (**I**).

(1.12) Experiments with variations of standard letter shapes (**J**); repeats known letters to sustain writing (**K**).

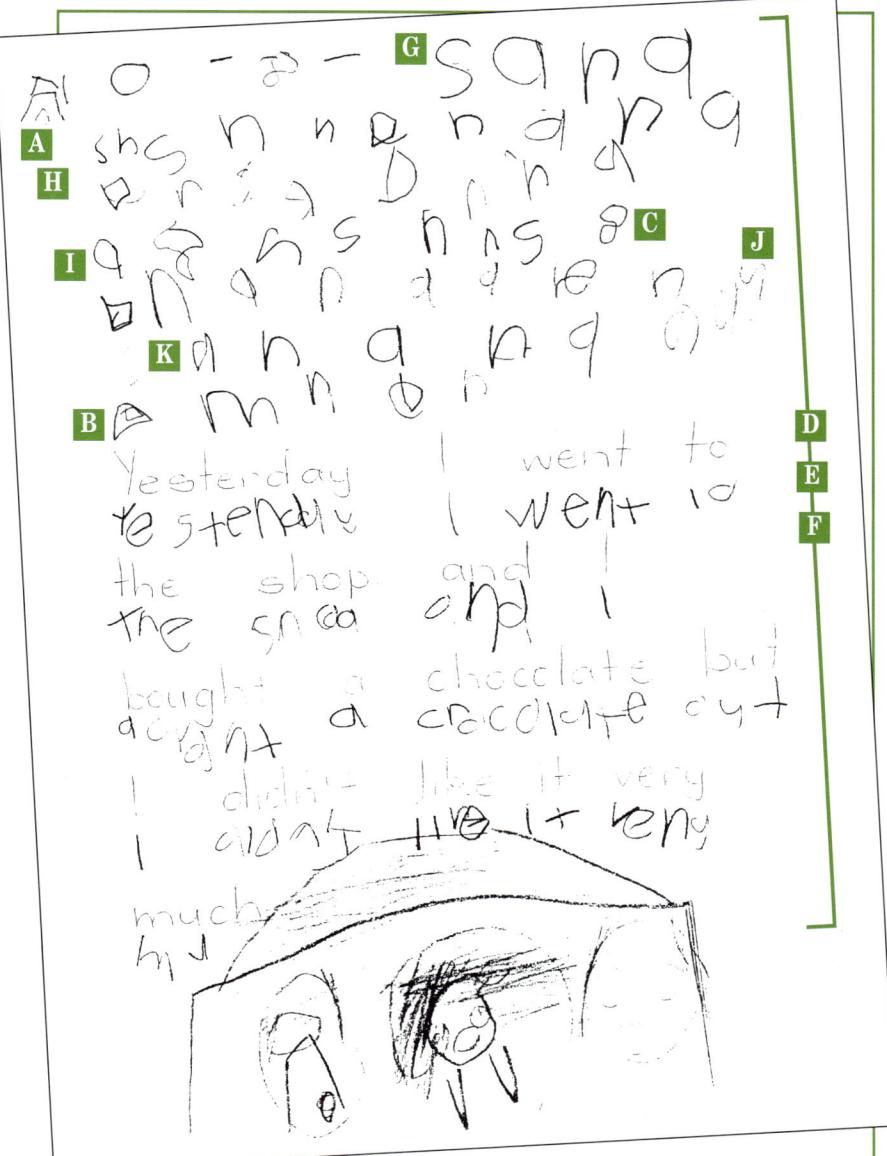

'Translated' text

Yesterday I went to the shop and I bought a chocolate but I didn't like it very much.

Recipe for jelly

Task

Students were required to write a recipe for jelly as an example of procedural writing.

Background

Over a few weeks, class activities such as making pancakes and playdough, playing games and tying shoelaces had led on to the class writing procedural texts. This activity called for each student to write a recipe for jelly.

Working in groups, the students followed instructions to make jelly. They were encouraged to vocalise each step. They then discussed the ingredients and the process and how a recipe would need to be written for someone to be able to follow it. Aspects of this text type discussed were the need for headings, writing in point form and organisation. Students then worked on a first draft of their own jelly recipe.

Relevant outcomes

1.9 Produces written symbols with the intention of conveying an idea or message.

1.10 Recognises that written language is used by people to convey meanings to others.

1.11 Demonstrates emerging awareness of how to use conventional written symbols for expressing ideas and information.

1.12 Experiments with and practises ways of representing ideas and information using written symbols.

Summary comment

The sample shows a beginning writer's effort to adopt the features of a recipe demonstrated by the teacher. Attention has been paid to layout and the use of the imperative form, as well as to the challenges of conveying a message through use of letter formation, spelling, spacing and punctuation.

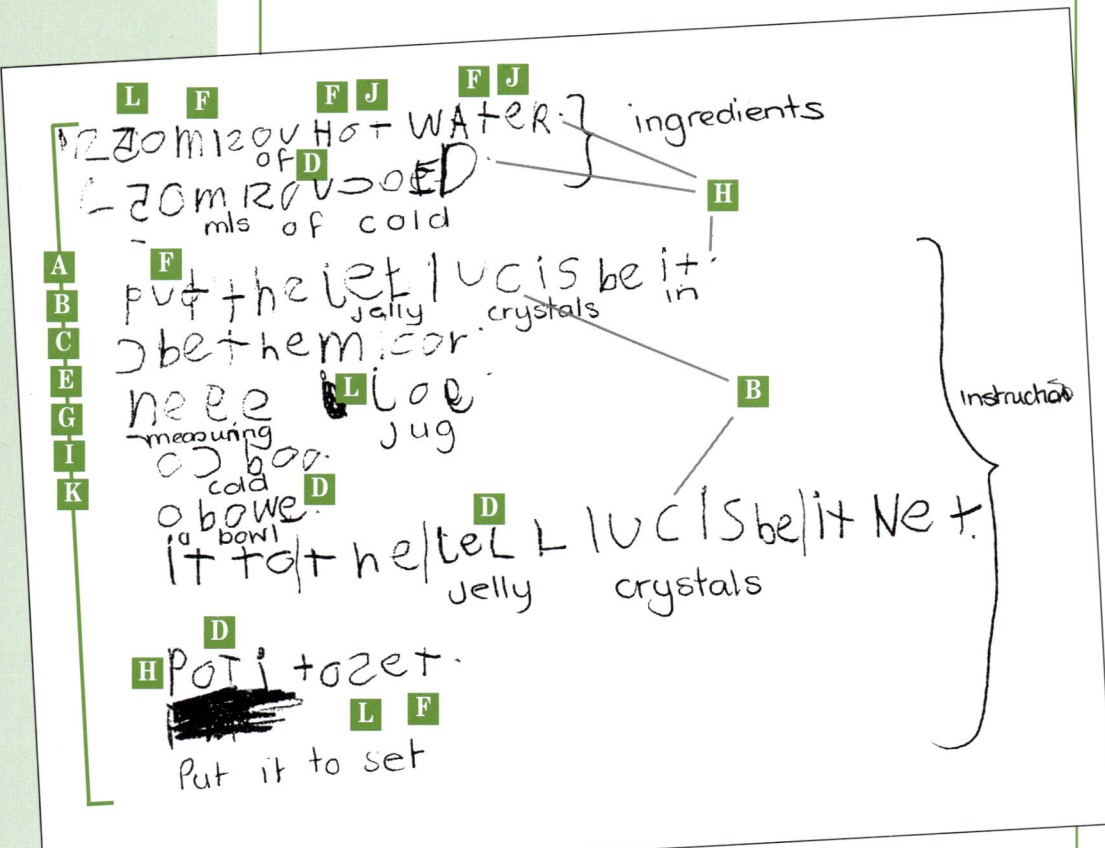

(1.9) Forms writing-like symbols on the page for a specific purpose (**A**); uses conventional letter shapes and letter clusters to construct meaning (**B**).

(1.10) Layout and text reflect recognition that the purpose of a recipe is to instruct others (**C**).

(1.11) Uses initial letters and some known letter patterns to represent words (**D**); forms many letters of the alphabet correctly (reverses some) (**E**); spells known words such as the, it, to and copied words such as water, mls, put (**F**); leaves a space between most words or word-like clusters of letters (**G**); uses full stops at the end of lines and experiments with capital letters (**H**); writes from left to right and from top to bottom of the page (**I**).

(1.12) Copies words from blackboard, peers (**J**); uses recipe format demonstrated by the teacher (**K**); experiments with acceptable variations of standard letter shapes such as letter reversal (**L**).

'Translated' text
50 mls of Hot Water.
50 mls of cold .
put the jelly crystals in.
Beat them pour
measuring jug
cold
a bowl
into the jelly crystals in it
Put it to set.

The jigaree

Task

Students were required to prepare a written response to a shared text.

Background

After reading a shared book called *The Jigaree*, the students were asked to imagine that they had a Jigaree and to write about what they would do with it. The student read this text to the teacher, matching spoken words with word-like letter clusters.

Relevant outcomes

1.9 Produces written symbols with the intention of conveying an idea or message.

1.10 Recognises that written language is used by people to convey meanings to others.

1.11 Demonstrates emerging awareness of how to use conventional written symbols for expressing ideas and information.

1.12 Experiments with and practises ways of representing ideas and information using written symbols.

Summary comment

The sample is a good example of level 1 achievement because it shows a number of outcomes.

(1.9) Uses conventional letter shapes and word-like clusters to write her message (**A**)

(1.10) Student responded appropriately to the task and read the text to the teacher (**B**).

(1.11) Uses initial letters and invented letter patterns to represent words (**C**); forms letters of the alphabet clearly (**D**); uses known words (I, it) and copied (Jigaree) words in writing (**E**); leaves a space between words or word-like clusters of letters (**F**); writes a complete sentence and uses a full stop at the end of it (**G**); writes from left to right and from top to bottom of the page (**H**).

(1.12) Copies the word 'Jigaree' from the shared book cover (**I**); experiments with lower- and upper-case letters (**J**); uses knowledge of letter sound relationships to attempt to spell unknown words ('wld', 'afa') (**K**).

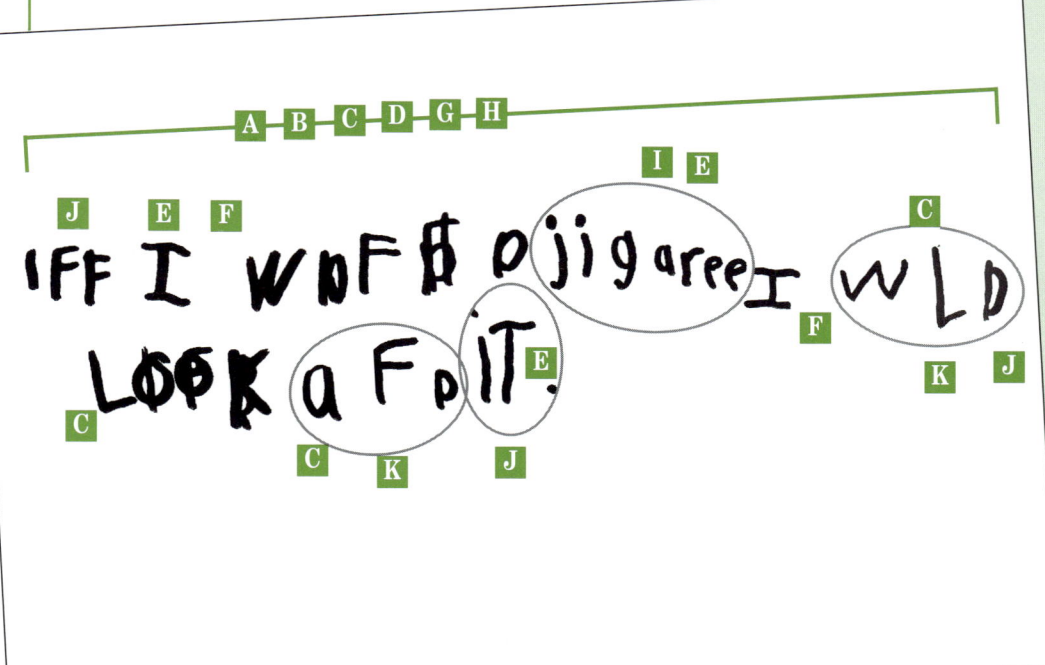

'Translated' text
If I had a jigaree I would look after it.

Teacher's notes

Task

Over two weeks, the teacher took notes on one student's interactions with peers, teachers and other adults in the classroom. Structured situations included:

- the 'Good morning folder' activity, where students take part in the morning administrative tasks;
- class meetings in which students take turns to be organiser, chairperson, observer, timekeeper and recorder;
- interviews, for which students compile a list of questions to interview a partner, publish this information and present it on video to be viewed by the whole class.

The work sample consists of the teacher's notes collected on a proforma based on the draft English profile. The comments have been rearranged for easier annotation.

Background

The student observed has a congenital disability that severely limits his speech. He has been involved in a communication program to develop his speech and integrated into the classroom with gesture and signing as his means of communication. The student had been introduced to Makaton sign language to assist development of his vocabulary.

Relevant outcomes

1.1 Interacts informally with teachers, peers and known adults in structured classroom situations dealing briefly with familiar topics.
1.2 Shows emerging awareness of school purposes and expectations for using spoken language.
1.3 Draws on implicit knowledge of linguistic structures and features of own variety of English when expressing ideas and information and interpreting spoken texts.
1.4 Monitors communication of self and others.

Summary comment

The teacher's notes provide evidence of achievement of all level 1 outcomes for Speaking and listening and some evidence that in class activities the student is beginning to work within level 2.

(1.1) Joins in poems, action verse and refrains recited by class or read by the teacher (**A**); follows, step at a time, short, simple instructions (**B**); attempts to give directions and instructions to others (**C**); recounts events from personal experiences and discusses shared experiences with adults and peers (**D**); reports briefly in a group on personal knowledge about a topic: describes aspects of favourite pastimes, pets, television programs, people (**E**); asks and responds to questions seeking information or clarification (**F**); makes relevant contributions in structured class and group activities and discussions (**G**).

(1.2) Understands purpose and own roles in routine classroom activities involving speaking and listening (**H**); attempts to observe agreed rules in structured classroom situations: raises hand to speak, takes turns, answers questions, listens attentively, offers ideas and opinions (**I**); cooperates with others

to undertake tasks (**J**); uses talk to establish and build relationships (**K**); makes connections between signed language and school English (**L**).

(1.3) Sequences ideas in sign, gesture and sound in intelligible ways (**M**); interprets simple statements, commands and questions in dealing with others and responds using signs, gesture and sounds (**N**); adopts appropriate tones and intonation patterns to convey meaning (**O**); interprets and responds to non-verbal cues: facial expression, gesture, silence, pause (**P**).

(1.4) Stays on the general topic and asks and responds to questions when discussing shared experiences with teachers and peers (**Q**); listens to a speaker and contributes relevant comments to a conversation or discussion (**R**); demonstrates attentive listening in a variety of non-verbal ways (**S**).

Teacher's observation notes

Showed me a picture of a chair in a picture book and reproduced it in his activity book. Signed and said 'chair'.

Gestured and used signing and made vocal sounds to express that the rain had stopped. He used a picture dictionary to indicate 'rain'.

Had a go at sharing news today. He showed the Lego he had brought to school. The children asked questions and A pointed to children and used gestures and signs.

Works with another child to complete maths task—making six-sided shapes. Makes sounds to indicate how polydrons fit together. Replies, 'Yes', when asked by S if he needs help.

Discussed train and track he had made during activity time. Used gesture and sound to indicate that he had made a round track. I signed my response to his gestures.

Joined circle and sat legs crossed, eyes on speaker, for duration of meeting (15 minutes). Put his hand up to consent to idea of a JP disco.

Used the picture dictionary to assist him during writing.

Uses non-verbal cues to organise children's borrowing in the library. Uses sign, gesture and sounds to communicate procedures for borrowing.

Joined in singing and dancing when we played 'Ricky and Pete' tape.

Listened and joined in repetitive phrases of text in the big book, 'The sunflower that went flop'—made sounds and gestures in response to the text.

Attends in class meeting and 'good morning folder'—admin news; shares and responds in class meeting.

Gestures affirmation of ideas during brainstorm on 'Feeling safe' during Child Protection Week; raised hand and suggested a question for tomorrow's Police visit.

Participates in skill streaming session with school counsellor, role playing conflict resolution situations, demonstrating school rules.

Ricky and Pete Performance: sits and looks at performers; attended to video on Kangaroo Creek Gang—looks, listens and signs to child next to him.

Participated in recording our videos of interviewing a partner—he listened to directions and followed instructions to record information and share on video camera.

Working with Special Ed teacher: communicates a story about a car he has made using gesture, picture dictionary and responding to questions. He attempts to record this.

Attends and participates in big book sharing; is eager to be leader, he indicates willingness to follow text with a ruler and turn pages—joins in signing text.

Participates in vote for Landcare representative. Records name and gestures in discussion. Nominates child for success time.

Responds to Ricky and Pete performance. He makes attempts to record a letter to performers and illustrates this.

Listens and attends in group situations. Sits still on the mat and keeps eyes on the speaker. Able to attend for periods up to 15 minutes.

LEVEL TWO

LEVEL 2 Statement

Students who have achieved level two use English in ways that reflect their beginning knowledge of conventions, codes and symbols for using spoken, written and visual texts.

Through their familiarity with using English for school purposes, students mix with others in more confident and complex ways. They are developing some awareness of how they and other people adjust their speaking and listening to suit their purposes and audience. Students draw on what they are learning about language to experiment with their own speaking and listening. They also adopt new ways to improve their communication with others.

Students can now interpret and discuss the meanings they find in short written texts and visual texts with predictable narratives. They understand that texts are produced by people and that they represent real and imaginary experience in different ways.

Students produce brief written texts understood by others and which include related ideas and information about familiar topics. They are aware that writing can be planned, reviewed and changed and can discuss these things.

LEVEL 2
Table of outcomes

	Texts	Contextual understanding	Linguistic structures & features	Strategies
SPEAKING AND LISTENING	2.1 Interacts in more confident and extended ways in structured and spontaneous school situations.	2.2 Considers how own speaking and listening is adjusted in different situations.	2.3 Experiments with different linguistic structures and features for expressing and interpreting spoken ideas and information.	2.4 Speaks and listens in ways that assist communication with others.
	See page 34	See page 34	See page 35	See page 35
READING AND VIEWING	2.5 Constructs and retells meanings from: – short written texts with familiar topics and vocabulary, predictable text structures and frequent illustrations, and – visual texts with predictable narrative structures.	2.6 Understands that texts are constructed by people and represent real and imaginary experience.	2.7 Recognises and interprets basic linguistic structures and features of texts.	2.8 a Uses basic strategies for interpreting written and visual texts and maintains continuity in understanding when meaning is disrupted. 2.8 b With teacher guidance, selects own reading material, and gathers and sorts information on a topic from a variety of sources.
	See page 36	See page 36	See page 37	See page 37
WRITING	2.9 Writes brief imaginative and factual texts which include some related ideas about familiar topics.	2.10 Recognises some of the purposes and advantages of writing.	2.11 Uses some basic linguistic structures and features of written language so that writing can be readily interpreted by others.	2.12a Uses talk to plan and review own writing. 2.12b Usually attempts to spell words by drawing on knowledge of sound-symbol relationships and of standard letter patterns.
	See page 38	See page 38	See page 39	See page 39

LEVEL 2 Speaking and Listening

Level 1 outcomes:

1.1 Interacts informally with teachers, peers and known adults in structured classroom activities dealing briefly with familiar topics.

1.2 Shows emerging awareness of school purposes and expectations for using spoken language.

1.3 Draws on implicit knowledge of the linguistic structures and features of own variety of English when expressing ideas and information and interpreting spoken texts.

1.4 Monitors communication of self and others.

Texts

At level 2, a student:

2.1 Interacts in more confident and extended ways in structured and spontaneous school situations.

Evident when students, for example:

- Explain familiar procedures or give simple instructions to peers showing awareness of the steps required (tell someone how to order lunch, tell a new classmate how things work and where things are, explain to the class how to make something).

- When prompted, extend the contributions of others in group and class discussions (compare their experience of and reactions to an issue with those of others, speculate about other people's reactions in a particular situation, reflect on their own knowledge).

- Listen attentively to and converse with others for a purpose (speak to a teacher about how the use of play equipment is organised, speak to a peer about the habits of snakes or frogs, talk to visiting authors about their books).

- Describe real or imagined events in logical sequence (retell scenes from stories heard, read or viewed; tell anecdotes about personal experiences; retell a short story, attending to main elements of its plot).

- When prompted, include key information in a short spoken recount of an experience or event (where, when, who, what), for instance, when giving a morning talk to the class.

- Present information on a known topic to a group or the class with some attention to adequacy and relevance of information.

- Listen to and comment positively on the contributions of others in group and class discussions.

Contextual understanding

At level 2, a student:

2.2 Considers how own speaking and listening is adjusted in different situations.

Evident when students, for example:

- Discuss the effects different audiences and topics can have on a speaker (compare talking to a friend about a shared experience with talking to the whole class or the principal about the same experience).

- Discuss the reasons for class rules on speaking and listening (those relating to turn-taking, loudness, asking questions).

- Compare ways in which spoken dealings with familiar people vary (roleplay buying something from a shopkeeper, making a special request of a parent, arguing with a sibling, chatting with a friend; consider differences such as tone, pace, pronunciation and body language).

- Consider occasions when they adjust their voice volume according to purpose and situation (telling a secret to a friend, attracting a friend's attention in the playground or library).

- Demonstrate ways to use non-verbal cues such as gestures and facial expressions to show emotions and responses (interest and lack of interest, excitement, shyness, fear).

- Discuss ways in which different kinds of talk can affect other people (calling people by their correct names, encouraging and praising people, being negative or abusive).

Linguistic structures & features

At level 2, a student:

2.3 Experiments with different linguistic structures and features for expressing and interpreting spoken ideas and information.

Evident when students, for example:

- Understand and use some familiar and appropriate idioms ('you're a star', 'hang on a minute').

- Sometimes use similes to make speech more effective when explaining or describing ('It was just like...').

- Understand and, in speech, experiment with more complex grammatical connectives such as 'because', 'if' and 'after' to sustain a topic and to express ideas.

- Experiment with varying voice tone, volume and pace of speech to indicate emotions, to create excitement, and to emphasise meaning.

- Recognise the beginning and end of a spoken text and try to organise their own speech effectively.

- Try out and interpret sound effects used with spoken texts.

- Experiment with rhyme, rhythm and word play to create humorous effects.

- With teacher guidance, compare grammatical alternatives for expressing similar meanings (compare standard and non-standard constructions).

Strategies

At level 2, a student:

2.4 Speaks and listens in ways that assist communication with others.

Evident when students, for example:

- Identify a speaker's topic and ask questions seeking explanations or more information ('Where do they live?', 'Do you mean we should ...?').

- Ask questions and make comments that expand ideas during one-to-one, small group and class discussions.

- Seek clarification when something is not understood.

- Clarify comments by rephrasing ('What I meant was ...' and 'When I think about ...').

- Plan spoken descriptions, recounts and reports (identify the main ideas or information to be presented to a group or the class).

- Attend to responses of others and review or elaborate on what has been said (answer questions from listeners, repeat or rephrase ideas and information, try to give explanations).

- Observe procedures for class activities (taking turns, asking questions, interrupting speakers).

Level 3 outcomes:

3.1 Interacts for specific purposes with people in the classroom and school community using a small range of text types.

3.2 Recognises that certain types of spoken texts are associated with particular contexts and purposes.

3.3 Usually uses linguistic structures and features of spoken language appropriately for expressing and interpreting ideas and information.

3.4 Reflects on own approach to communication and the ways in which others interact.

LEVEL 2 Reading and Viewing

Level 1 outcomes:

1.5a Roleplays being a competent reader and consistently interprets some familiar written symbols.

1.5b Constructs meanings from visual texts with familiar content, particularly texts designed to be viewed in segments.

1.6 Makes connections between own knowledge and experience and the ideas, events and information in texts viewed and heard read aloud.

1.7 Demonstrates emerging awareness and use of symbols and conventions when making meaning from texts.

1.8 Recognises and uses cues to predict meaning in visual and printed texts.

Texts

At level 2, a student:

2.5 Constructs and retells meanings from:
– short written texts with familiar topics and vocabulary, predictable text structures and frequent illustrations, and
– visual texts with predictable narrative structures.

Evident when students, for example:

- Read and respond to texts for beginning readers (comment on own interpretation of stories, informational texts, rhymes, songs, student-made texts).

- Interpret accurately familiar short classroom and home texts (notes, messages, signs, charts and lists, classroom rules).

- Retell ideas from an informational text for beginning readers; comment on things learned or questions raised by reading.

- Relate the story of a picture book, providing some supporting detail from the text and offering an opinion about the story or aspects of it (opinion of a character's actions).

- Follow simple written instructions (instructions for using the classroom computer, a short recipe).

- Talk about own interpretation of information provided in print media advertising (sale catalogues, billboards, signs, magazine and newspaper advertisements).

- Retell and comment on incidents from a short children's film with attention to plot elements such as setting, character, conflict and resolution.

- Make inferences about characters' qualities, characteristics and motives in visual texts based on features such as facial expressions, body language, gesture and clothing, and the ways in which other characters respond to them.

Contextual understanding

At level 2, a student:

2.6 Understands that texts are constructed by people and represent real and imaginary experience.

Evident when students, for example:

- Refer to the author and illustrator of a book, commenting on other books produced by them.

- Recognise that visual texts such as films are produced by many people, including actors, directors, cinematographers, producers, scriptwriters.

- Distinguish between the character in a television program and the actor (between Humphrey Bear and the person who plays that part).

- Consider, on the basis of personal knowledge and experience, how likely are the events, behaviour, settings and outcomes found in texts.

- Discuss the ways different groups of people are represented in texts (the different activities in which males and females or older and younger people engage).

- Recognise that texts could have been written or produced differently (change aspects of plot or characterisation and list one or two possible consequences).

Linguistic structures & features

At level 2, a student:

2.7 Recognises and interprets basic linguistic structures and features of texts.

Evident when students, for example:

- Point out and explain the purpose of some organisational features of written informational texts (headings, diagrams and indexes).

- Recognise relationships in written sentences signalled by conjunctions such as 'because', 'and', 'but'.

- Maintain noun-pronoun and subject-verb links across simple and compound sentences when reading (understand that 'it' refers to the cat in 'The cat has long black fur. It chases mice.').

- Have a bank of known sight words recognised automatically in printed texts.

- Recognise letters and letter combinations which represent sounds in words.

- Usually interpret statement, question and command structures and their punctuation markers when reading texts aloud.

- Recognise regular formats and characteristics of popular television programs (the basic format of quiz shows: host/hostess, contestants, competition for prizes of commercial value).

- Identify elements of setting in visual texts (objects, clothing, sound effects, music and dialogue).

- Recognise features (characters' dress, actions, gesture and dialogue) to identify heroes and villains in visual and printed texts.

- Discuss the role of the presenter in television programs (while viewing a program, list the various things the presenter does).

Strategies

At level 2, a student:

2.8a Uses basic strategies for interpreting written and visual texts and maintains continuity in understanding when meaning is disrupted.

Evident when students, for example:

- Use picture clues to predict a text's content and make connections between illustrations and written text.

- Draw on knowledge of letter-sound relationships when trying to identify unknown words ('sound out', attempt to break words into syllables).

- Make substitutions or omissions which maintain meaning when reading.

- Attempt to self-correct when meaning is disrupted while reading (pause or repeat words or phrases to maintain meaning).

- Use knowledge of media narrative structures to predict likely endings (for cartoons, make predictions based on knowledge of program length, experience that a resolution will be reached and expectation that main characters overcome difficulties in order to return to the next episode).

2.8b With teacher guidance, selects own reading material, and gathers and sorts information on a topic from a variety of sources.

Evident when students, for example:

- Choose texts from a range provided, for enjoyment or information on the basis of interest area, book cover, title, illustrations, print size, and recommendations of others.

- Compare pre-selected resources on a topic, deciding which are more appropriate and making decisions using simple scanning techniques involving cover, title and illustrations.

- Gather information from first-hand experience, people, concrete objects and secondary sources such as books, pictures and AV materials.

- Report events, facts and ideas in a list, chart or brief written text.

Level 3 outcomes:

3.5 Interprets and discusses some relationships between ideas, information and events in:

– written texts with familiar content and a small range of unfamiliar words and linguistic structures and features

– visual texts designed for general viewing.

3.6 Identifies simple symbolic meanings and stereotypes in texts and discusses their purpose and meaning.

3.7 Identifies and uses the linguistic structures and features characteristic of a range of text types to construct meaning.

3.8a Integrates a variety of strategies for interpreting printed and visual texts.

3.8b With teacher guidance, uses several strategies for identifying resources and finding information in texts.

LEVEL 2 Writing

Level 1 outcomes:

1.9 Produces written symbols with the intention of conveying an idea or message.

1.10 Recognises that written language is used by people to convey meanings to others.

1.11 Demonstrates emerging awareness of how to use conventional written symbols for expressing ideas and information.

1.12 Experiments with and practises ways of representing ideas and information using written symbols.

Texts

At level 2, a student:

2.9 Writes brief imaginative and factual texts which include some related ideas about familiar topics.

Evident when students, for example:

- Reflect briefly on an aspect of a personal experience including two or more relevant ideas ('We went to the zoo and the lion looked scary.').

- List several items of information about a topic or describe a few characteristics of a familiar person, place, animal or object ('My dog is black. She eats meat and chases our cat.').

- Write an imaginary story with two or more events in sequence.

- Create poems using the structure of a familiar poem as a guide (find substitutes for key words from a familiar poem to generate a different meaning).

- Write simple directions or instructions for a known procedure involving a few steps in sequence.

- Explain in writing one or two reasons for a common phenomenon, personal action or opinion.

- Devise an advertisement for a real or imaginary product including several product details.

- Write a short note or letter to a friend giving a few items of information.

Contextual understanding

At level 2, a student:

2.10 Recognises some of the purposes and advantages of writing.

Evident when students, for example:

- Discuss some of the advantages of writing to record information and ideas (shopping lists, reference books and data bases).

- Discuss examples of how writing enables people to communicate over time and distance (letters to distant friends, stories from long ago).

- Discuss familiar examples of how writing gives information to many people (newspapers, magazines, school newsletters, safety signs).

- Discuss some of the different purposes for which people write (stories to entertain, instructions to direct, signs to warn of danger).

- Initiate writing for particular purposes (reminders, notes, signs, stories).

Linguistic structures & features

At level 2, a student:

2.11 Uses some basic linguistic structures and features of written language so that writing can be readily interpreted by others.

Evident when students, for example:

- Always write from top to bottom, left to right, and leave spaces between words.
- Usually use correct word order in sentences.
- Link ideas in writing by using pronouns to refer to preceding nouns ('My goats have soft fleece and they are my pets.').
- Link ideas using conjunctions such as 'and', 'then', and sometimes indicate relationships between events and ideas using conjunctions such as 'because' or 'but'.
- Adopt grammatical patterns demonstrated by the teacher (imperative form in instructional writing).
- Use some punctuation markers accurately in their own writing and experiment with others (use capital letters to begin names, sometimes mark common contractions — such as can't, I'm — with an apostrophe).
- Spell some common words accurately in their own writing (common sight words, friends' names, words relating to topics of personal interest).
- Form most letters of the alphabet correctly and try to write clearly in straight lines, using letters of uniform size, shape, slope and spacing.

Strategies

At level 2, a student:

2.12a Uses talk to plan and review own writing.

Evident when students, for example:

- Give purpose and intended reader before writing ('I am writing a get-well card to cheer up my sick friend.').
- Tell key ideas or events to teacher or a peer, or share ideas for writing in a group before writing.
- Make organisational decisions before writing ('I'll start here so it will fit.').
- Contribute ideas to brainstorming sessions before group or class writing activities.
- Discuss ideas for writing when dictating for a scribe.
- Read their own writing aloud and make some corrections to clarify meaning (cross out or add a letter).
- Read writing to the teacher or a peer and respond to questions seeking elaboration or clarification.

2.12b Usually attempts to spell words by drawing on knowledge of sound-symbol relationships and of standard letter patterns.

Evident when students, for example:

- Attempt spelling by matching sounds within words with known phonic letter patterns.
- Use knowledge of familiar letter patterns when attempting to spell unknown words (use suffixes such as -ed, -ing, -s).
- Use letters or letter combinations to represent most syllables in words.
- Immediately self-correct some words which do not look right when first written.
- Identify possible spelling errors after completing writing (by circling or underlining doubtful words).
- Use a variety of resources to find correct spelling of an unknown word (their own dictionary, wall charts, spell checkers).

Level 3 outcomes:

3.9 Experiments with inter-relating ideas and information when writing about familiar topics within a small range of text types.

3.10 Recognises that certain text types and features are associated with particular purposes and audiences.

3.11 Controls most basic features of written language and experiments with some organisational and linguistic features of different text types.

3.12a Experiments with strategies for planning, reviewing and proofreading own writing.

3.12b Consistently makes informed attempts at spelling.

School assembly presentation

Task

Students were required to plan, present, and rehearse the fortnightly R-7 school assembly, and then to evaluate the task.

Background

1. The whole class listed tasks to prepare for the assembly.

2. In pairs, students prepared notes for a brief persuasive class talk outlining the tasks they thought they or peers would be best suited to do.

3. Each student delivered a brief talk. Tasks were then allocated by teacher and class consensus.

4. Suitable wording for introducing assembly items was discussed and suggestions written on the blackboard.

5. In pairs, students wrote a draft of their assembly item introduction.

6. This was dictated to the teacher, who produced a version on the computer.

7. Students practised reading their introduction aloud to a partner, then to the class, and then in the assembly hall, using the microphone. The teacher and class members provided comment and encouragement about volume, clarity and speed of delivery.

Steps 1 to 7 took about 90 minutes.

8. The assembly was recorded on video.

---

a. Transcript of extract from whole class discussion (Step 1) showing student's extended exchange.

C **Q**

Teacher: Assembly preparation. what are the things we've got to decide about?

Student: We've got to decide who's going to read out the things at assembly.

Teacher: Before we decide who is going to do things at assembly, what do we have to decide?

S **T**

Student: The writing on pieces of paper that people have to read out at assembly ...

Teacher: What other jobs do we have to do?

Student: We have to write up the big list of what is going to go first, second, third, fourth....

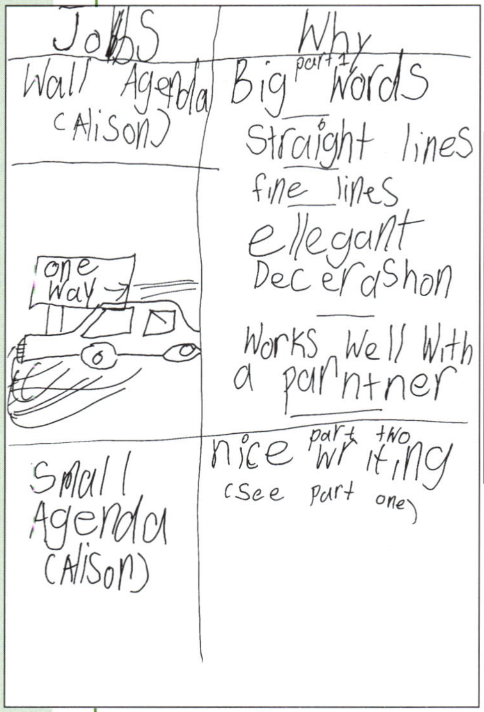

Handwritten notes:
Jobs / Why part 1 / Wall Agenda (Alison) / Big words / Straight lines / fine lines / ellegant / Decerashon / Works well with a parntner / one way / nice writing part two (see part one) / Small Agenda (Alison)

---

b. Student's notes for persuasive talk to class.

Insert original work sample (Translation below)

Jobs	Why
	part 1
A Wall agenda	Big words
R (Alison)	Straight lines
	Fine lines
	Elegant decoration
	Works well with a partner
Small agenda	
(Alison)	Part 2
	Nice writing
	(See part 1)

---

c. Transcript of student's persuasive talk to the class.

Teacher: OK who's going to be next to tell us which job they should do in assembly? R? OK Come on out.

P

B

Student: Well, I think, Alison and I think that we should do the poster saying what the items are at the Assembly. What order they're going to be in. Um... 'cos, um... we can work together well. Alison is excellent at printing. I can say what the spelling should be. For the agenda that has to go on the wall we decided we need to put big words so that kids can read it. And we have to write in straight lines. We want to put elegant decorations on the poster so it looks really good. **N**

(2.1) Gives attention to adequacy and relevance of reasons in support of an opinion (persuasive talk plan) (**A**); attempts to persuade others in the class to select a peer for assembly tasks, giving a few reasons (**B**); makes an extended contribution to the class discussion in response to the teacher's questions (**C**); consults and collaborates during pair discussion (**D**); prepares and presents a brief spoken text in formal assembly performance (**E**); when prompted, includes key information in evaluation of own performance during assembly (**F**); listens to and comments positively on the contributions of others in group and class discussions (**G**).

(2.2) Considers effects of different audiences and topics on a speaker's own feelings of self-confidence and behaviours when talking to a friend, to the whole class and at the formal assembly (**H**); considers need to adjust style of language, volume and speaking pace according to purpose and situation (**I**); demonstrates ways to use non-verbal cues such as gestures and facial expressions to assist communication at assembly performance (**J**); adapts well to the use of the microphone (**K**).

9. The class viewed the videotape. Students evaluated their performances by listing their strengths and suggesting improvements.

The work samples illustrate one student's part in the speaking and listening activities before and after the assembly.

Relevant outcomes

2.1 Interacts in more confident and extended ways in structured and spontaneous school situations.
2.2 Considers how own speaking and listening is adjusted in different situations.
2.3 Experiments with different linguistic structures and features for expressing and interpreting spoken ideas and information.

2.4 Speaks and listens in ways that assist communication with others.

Summary comment

The work samples provide evidence of ability to speak and listen effectively in a variety of classroom situations with teacher guidance and support. The work indicates achievement of the level 2 outcomes because it shows use of speaking and listening to explore and extend ideas with others and to present them with some confidence. The persuasive talk sample also shows ability to prepare more complex spoken texts, providing evidence that the student is beginning to work within level 3.

(2.3) Experiments with formal tone, manner and style of assembly introduction (**L**); understands and in own speech experiments with more complex grammatical connectives such as 'because' to sustain a topic and to express ideas (persuasive talk) (**M**); experiments with varying own voice elements such as tone, volume and pace to emphasise meaning (**N**); organises own speech effectively and recognises the beginning and end of a spoken text (**O**).

(2.4) Asks relevant questions and makes comments to extend ideas during one-to-one, small-group and class discussions (**P**); with teacher guidance, plans and prepares spoken texts, identifying the main arguments for persuasive talk, preparing script for introduction to assembly segment (**Q**); attends to responses from others and reviews or elaborates on what has been said: answers questions from listeners, repeats or rephrases ideas and information, attempts to give explanations (**R**); observes agreed procedures in class activities for taking turns, asking questions, interrupting speakers (**S**).

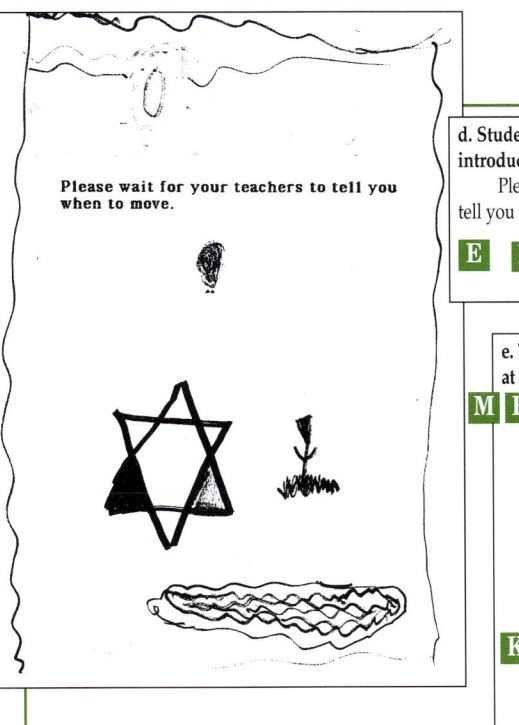

Please wait for your teachers to tell you when to move.

d. Student's assembly segment introduction script.
Please wait for your teachers to tell you when to move.

E **R**

e. Transcript of student's actual introduction at the assembly.

M **E** The last assembly item has been completed and another child has thanked the audience for their participation. The student comes to the centre of the 'stage'.
Loud noise from assembled children.
Please wait.... (continued noise)
Please wait... (louder, against continued noise)

K Student puts up hand as signal to the assembled school and tries again.
Please wait... (Teacher comes onto stage and puts up hand.)
Student puts up hand and waits for assembly to be quiet.
Please wait for your teachers to tell you to move.
Teachers direct their classes to leave.

f. Teacher's observation notes of one student (extract from notes on this task only).
Observations made during assembly task
Preparation
Wrote a plan for his persuasive talk.
Uses persuasive language- spoke fluently and persuasively, tone and delivery quite confident.
Contributes relevant comments and suggestions to class discussion of list.
Consulted, showed and collaborated during pair planning.(takes turns to speak, listens to and considers partner's concerns).
Rehearses presentation.
Speaks audibly and clearly to the class.
Performance
Waited briefly for audience to settle.
Repeated instructions when necessary.
Loud, slow, clear, appropriate tone, manner and language (formal).
OK, confident with the microphone.
Review of assembly videotape
Own evaluation after viewing tape: 'Next time I'll wait 'til they're quiet.' 'I went loud and slow.' 'The words I used were good for an assembly.' Shows awareness of own strengths and weaknesses.

Olympic Games talk

Task

Students were required to prepare a short talk for the class about an Olympic Games sport.

Background

The task involved three stages over three weeks at school and at home.

- Observation and research about the sport (guided by teacher-prepared questions).
- Written preparation of the talk (guided by teacher's model).
- Presentation of the talk to the class (demonstrated by the teacher).

Students were allowed to use their written notes when giving their talks.

Organisational format for talk provided by the teacher

Make a plan!

1. Introduction

   What is your sport? Why did you choose it?

2. Training and equipment

   What special equipment or training would you need to play the sport?

3. Australian participants or famous participants

   Any information you have about people who play the sport.

H

Observation notes

The student began the talk on kayaking reading slowly and carefully from prepared notes. Her tone of voice and style of language were formal ('Introduction: I did not think anybody else would choose it.')

She made eye contact only with the teacher.

When the student had finished, the teacher asked her to talk about kayaking without notes and then asked follow-up questions. When responding, the student used a more informal tone of voice and style of language ('Well, it's like this…').

H

J **I**

The student's speech was soft but clear. She used lots of hand movements to explain how the event operated. She maintained eye contact with the teacher while answering questions but had none with the class.

E

Following the presentation, the teacher discussed with the student how the formal situation made her feel and its effect on such things as her confidence, voice volume and eye contact. The student said she found it easier to talk about her topic to one or two friends, and that answering the teacher's questions wasn't as difficult as giving the talk.

B **C** **D**

```
TRANSCRIPT OF RACHEL'S OLYMPIC TALK

Rachel read from prepared notes

RACHEL: "Introduction. Kayak. I did not think any-body else would
choose it."
```

F   TEACHER: "Is that correct?" [Rachel nods]   **G**

```
RACHEL:" Training and Equipment. You need a fast flowing river, a
kayak, a paddle, a helmet and some gates. Most would start as
teenagers.
       Australian Participants. Danielle Woodward police... is a
policeman [pauses raises eyes ]  oh a policewoman from
Victoria.
       Olympic Games. By time over course. Yes, the medals have
been decided. The gold was won by Germany; Silver was won by
Australia and the Bronze by U.S.A.
       Winning. My view is that if you have done your best it
doesn't matter."
```
G **L** **K**

```
[Once she had finished the talk Rachel maintained constant eye
contact with the teacher but did not look to the audience at
all.]

TEACHER: [takes notes from Rachel] " Without using the notes tell
us a bit about the kayak because you've seen it on TV. Tell us,
for the people who haven't seen it, tell us how it works."

RACHEL: [ stood confidently] "Well you have some green gates and
some red gates and when you go .... You have to go through the
green gates when you're coming down and the red gates going up.
```
B

N

```
Well, it's like this.[ used hand movements to indicate position
of gates]
```
I

K
```
Just say there was a green gate here and a red gate here you
could be coming through the green gates and then the red one
would be over here. [ used hand movements to show how kayak moves
through the gates]
You'd go past then come back up and then you'd go back down to
the next one and then ..[ pauses,thinks] If your paddle touches
one of the gates, you'd get penalised 4 seconds."
```
G **K**

```
TEACHER: " And just tell us again how do they decide the winner?"

RACHEL: " By time over course."
```
N

```
TEACHER: " Right. O.K. So what you're saying is that it's the
person who gets through the course in the fastest time."

[Rachel listened intently to the question and nodded in
affirmation as the teacher spoke]

RACHEL: "Yes"
```
N

(2.1) Explains and describes a procedure to peers in logical sequence, showing awareness of the steps needed: how the kayaking event proceeds (**A**); when prompted, includes key information such as, where, when, who, what, in a short spoken recount of an experience or event, presents talk to the class using the framework provided by the teacher, responds to teacher's questions(**B**); presents information on a known topic to a group or the class with some attention to adequacy and relevance of information (**C**).

(2.5) The student obtained most of the information for the talk from television. Retells key information about kayaking, responds to teacher's question regarding the importance of winning (**D**).

(2.2) Discusses some of the effects that different audiences and topics can have on own feelings of self-confidence and behaviours when speaking (**E**).

(2.3) Adopts the teacher's organising framework for the formal part of the talk (introduction, training and equipment, Australian participants) (**F**); chooses specific vocabulary for purpose ('penalised', 'fast

4. Your sport and the Olympic Games

How is the gold medal decided?

Have the medals been decided?

If so, who won the three medals?

If your sport has an Australian competitor who did not win a medal, talk about how that person might feel about not winning.

5. Is winning the first prize the most important thing for athletes at the Olympic Games?

Talk about whether the gold medal is more important than being able to improve on their best performances.

Relevant outcomes:
Speaking and listening

2.1 Interacts in more confident and extended ways in structured and spontaneous school situations.

2.2 Considers how own speaking and listening is adjusted in different situations.

2.3 Experiments with different linguistic structures and features for expressing and interpreting spoken ideas and information.

2.4 Speaks and listens in ways that assist communication with others.

Reading and viewing

2.5 Constructs and retells meanings from: ... – visual texts with predictable narrative structures.

Summary comment

The work sample provides evidence of level 2 achievement in showing the student attempting, with some success, a formal text type for speaking and listening. The student's heavy reliance on the questions and format provided by the teacher distinguishes the work from level 3 achievement.

flowing river', 'by time over course') (**G**); uses formal tone and style for prepared talk and informal speech when answering questions (**H**); uses appropriate gestures, tone of voice (**I**); speaks audibly and clearly (although quietly) throughout entire presentation (**J**); uses grammatical connectives such as 'if', 'and then', 'but', to sustain a topic and to express ideas (**K**).

(2.4) Clarifies and self-corrects comments by rephrasing (**L**); plans for the talk by identifying the main ideas or information to be presented (**M**); attends to responses from others and reviews or elaborates on what has been said (answers questions from listeners, repeats or rephrases ideas and information, attempts to give explanations) (**N**); rehearsed presentation before speaking to the class (**O**).

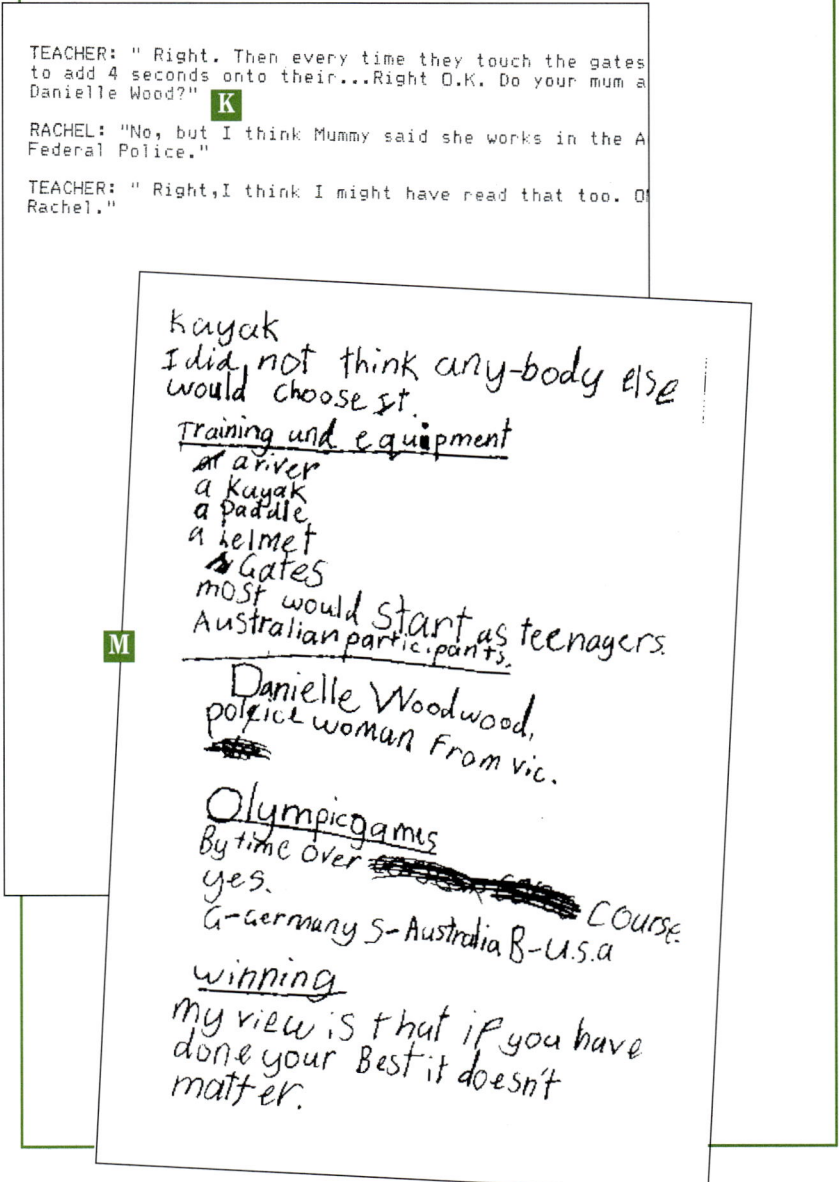

```
TEACHER: " Right. Then every time they touch the gates
to add 4 seconds onto their...Right O.K. Do your mum a
Danielle Wood?"  K

RACHEL: "No, but I think Mummy said she works in the A
Federal Police."

TEACHER: " Right,I think I might have read that too. O
Rachel."
```

kayak
I did not think any-body else i would choose it.
Training and equipment
at a river
a kayak
a paddle
a helmet
Gates
most would start as teenagers.
Australian participants
Danielle Woodwood,
police woman from vic.
Olympic games
By time over _____ course
yes.
G-Germany S-Australia B-U.S.a
winning
my view is that if you have done your Best it doesn't matter.

Real life and fantasy in texts

Task

Students were required to choose a fiction text from the class library, to read it alone or with a partner, and then to list the real-life and fantasy elements in the text under the heading: 'What writers think that children like to read about'. The book chosen was the picture book, *Where Forest Meets the Sea* by Jeannie Baker.

Background

Before the activity, the class took part in a number of activities designed to develop their understanding that people make decisions about what they put into the books they write, and that children's story books include real-life and fantasy elements.
These activities included:

- developing a wall chart listing the things writers decide to have girls and boys do in the books they write for children
- identifying the characteristics of very evil and very good characters in books (for example,

drawing and labelling those in *Fantastic Mr Fox* by Roald Dahl)

- comparing what the child does in the special world created by John Burningham in *Oi! Get Off Our Train* with what children do in their own world.

Relevant outcomes

2.5 Constructs and retells meanings from:
   – short written texts with familiar topics and vocabulary, predictable structures and frequent illustrations…

2.6 Understands that texts are constructed by people and represent real and imaginary experience.

Summary comment

The work sample indicates level 2 achievement because it shows interpretation of an independently read text and growing understanding of the constructed nature of texts.

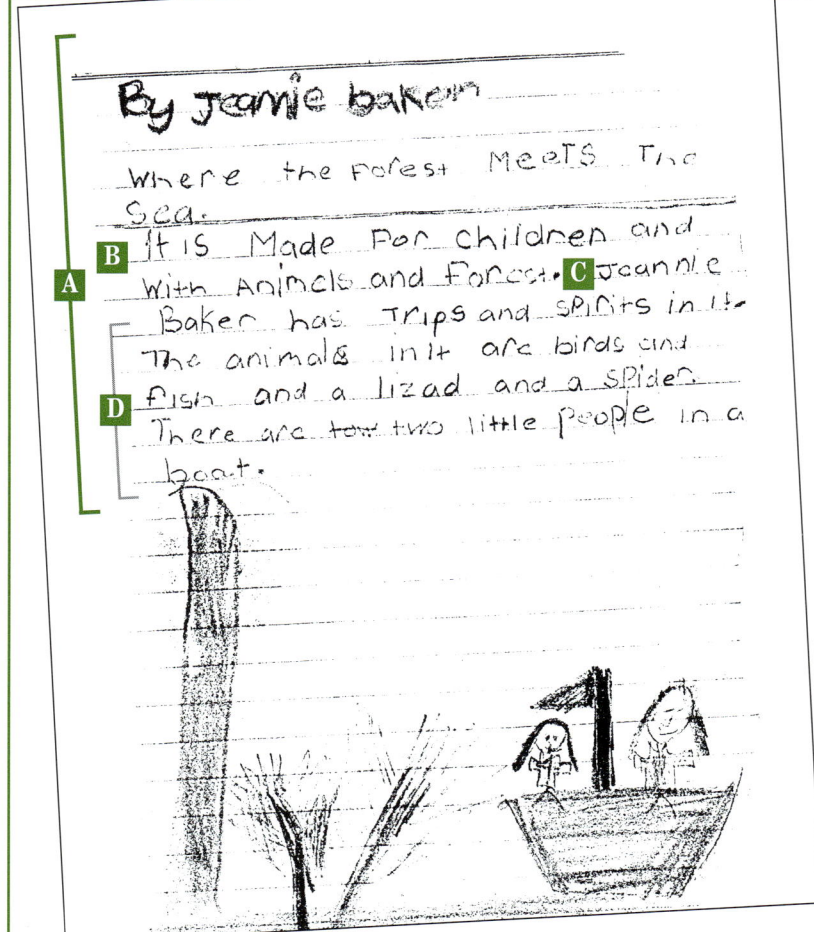

(2.5) Reads the text and responds appropriately to the activity by showing understanding of what has been read (**A**).

(2.6) Shows an understanding that the picture book was written for a particular audience: 'It is made for children…' (**B**); refers to the writer's construction of the text through selection of content: 'Jeannie Baker has trips and spirits in it.' (**C**); recognises and lists real-life and imaginary elements of the story (**D**).

Typed version of text
By Jeannie baker
Where the forest Meets The Sea.
It is Made For children and with Animels and Forest. Jeannie Baker has Trips and spirits in it. The animals in it are birds and fish and a lizad and a spider. There are two little people in a boat.

Reading conference records

Task

Students were required to read aloud to the teacher from a book of their choice.

Background

Students choose their own reading material from a wide range of books in the classroom and have time to rehearse their reading. The teacher encourages students to attempt to read unknown words.

Relevant outcomes

2.5 Constructs and retells meanings from:
– short written texts with familiar topics and vocabulary, predictable structures and frequent illustrations...

2.7 Recognises and interprets basic linguistic structures and features of texts.

2.8a Uses basic strategies for interpreting written and visual texts and maintains continuity in understanding when meaning is disrupted.

Summary comment

The teacher's records indicate achievement of the level 2 Reading and viewing outcomes with short printed texts.

(2.5) Reads and responds informally to a range of texts produced for beginning readers: asks questions, explains appeal of a story, compares main character with self (**A**).

(2.7) Points out and explains the purpose of some organisational features of written informational texts: table of contents (**B**); recognises relationships in written texts signalled by conjunctions such as 'because', 'and', 'but' (**C**); maintains noun–pronoun and subject–verb links across simple and compound sentences when reading (**D**); recognises many words automatically when reading printed texts (**E**); recognises letters and letter combinations which represent sounds in words: Grrr (**F**).

(2.8a) Predicts the ending of a story (**G**); attempts to find the meaning of unknown words by using more than one cue: draws on personal experience or knowledge of the topic or context, uses picture clues and patterns of language, identifies initial letter to narrow possibilities (**H**); points as an aid to reading (**I**); attempts to self-correct when meaning is disrupted while reading (**J**); asks others meaning of unknown

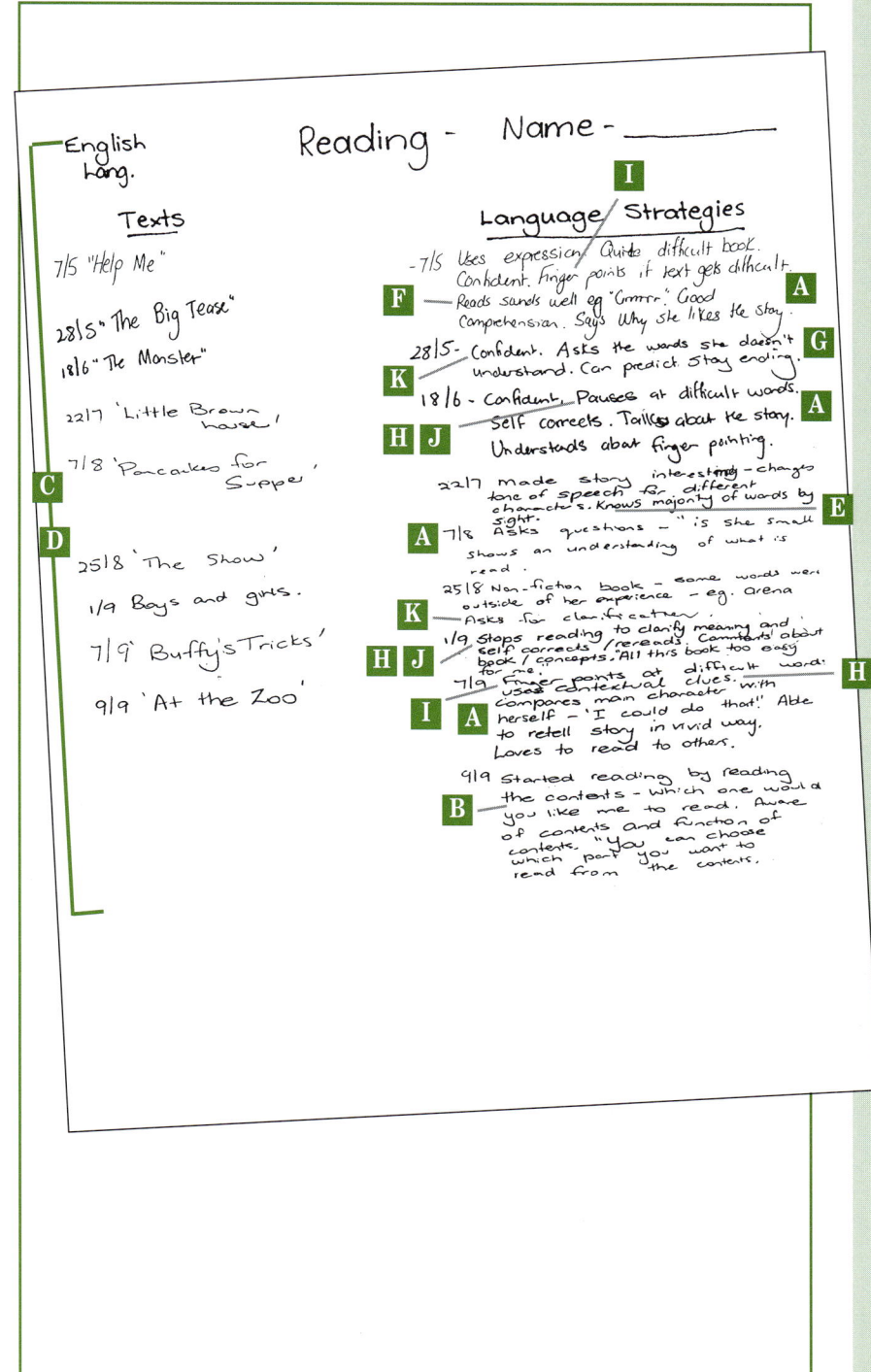

Oral reading and retelling records

Task

The student was required to read *The New Baby Calf* by E. N. Chase & B. Reich aloud to the teacher.

Background

The teacher recorded observations on the student's reading on a typed version of the text. The teacher also kept a cumulative record sheet of notes about all reading sessions.

Relevant outcomes

2.5 Constructs and retells meanings from:
 – short written texts with familiar topics and vocabulary, predictable structures and frequent illustrations...

2.7 Recognises and interprets basic linguistic structures and features of texts.

2.8a Uses basic strategies for interpreting written and visual texts and maintains continuity in understanding when meaning is disrupted.

Summary comment

The teacher's records of the student's reading behaviours and retellings with texts of this difficulty indicate achievement of the level 2 outcomes. Achievement of level 3 outcomes requires competence with more linguistically and conceptually difficult or unfamiliar texts.

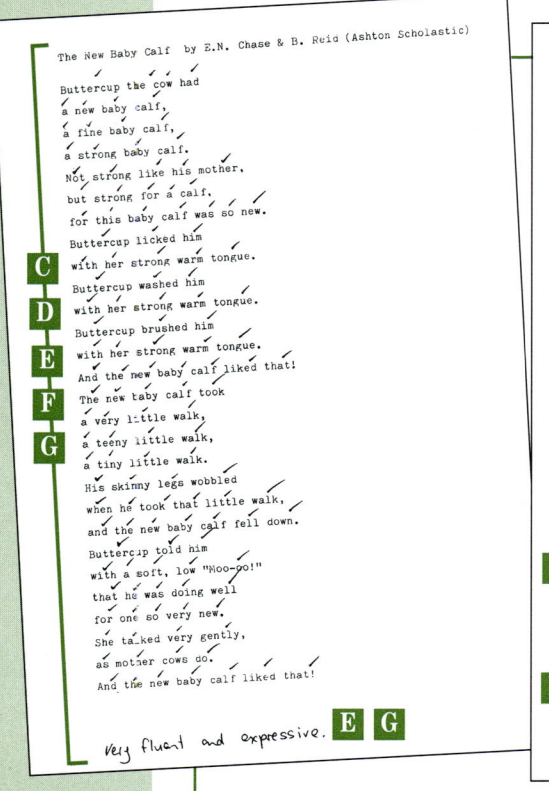

(2.5) Reads and responds to a range of texts produced for beginning readers (**A**); retells the main storyline of texts for beginning readers, providing some supporting detail (**B**).

(2.7) Recognises relationships in written texts signalled by conjunctions such as 'because', 'and', 'but' (**C**); maintains noun–pronoun and subject–verb links across simple and compound sentences when reading (**D**); automatically recognises many words (**E**); recognises letters and letter combinations which represent sounds in words (**F**); attends to statement, question and command structures and their punctuation markers when reading texts aloud: reads aloud fluently and with expression (**G**).

(2.8a) Uses picture clues to predict what a text might be about and makes connections between illustrations and written text (**H**); predicts events (**I**); attempts to find the meaning of unknown words, using more than one cue (**J**); draws on knowledge of letter–sound relationships when attempting to identify unknown words (**K**); points as an aid to reading (**L**); attempts to self-correct when meaning is disrupted while reading (**M**).

Viewed text summaries

Task

Students were required to summarise episodes of the television series *The Colonials*.

Background

The class viewed one episode a day of the series, as a part of their social studies program. After each episode, students briefly discussed the program in groups, then spent about 15 minutes writing individual summaries. The teacher then led a class discussion of the day's episode.

Relevant outcomes

2.5 Constructs and retells meanings from:...
– visual texts with predictable narrative structures.

Summary comment

The work sample provides evidence of ability to identify key information and ideas in a visual text. Comment on the information or storyline of the text would indicate level 3 achievement.
(Note: The work sample also shows level 2 achievement in Writing, with some evidence of working within level 3.)

(2.5) Identifies and records several key items of information from a viewed informational text.

Typed version of texts

1. The Arrival
The Bowman family were very pore in englend, so they decided to go to tasmanea. It took 8 months to get to tasmanea on the boat.

2. Going Bush
The Bowman family got all there supplies and set of in the bush. They made a camp and Ben was bitten by a snake. Jonas Arch, a convict, tried to still some boots and a horse, then he got wipped.

3. Bush Baptism
The Bowman family were going to find a place to live. There naybere was Mr Hains. Mr Hains Had his coat and boots and gun stolen. Then the Bowman family set down to work they bilt there own house it was nice.

Olympic Games report

Task
Written news report about the Olympic Games.

Background
The class were involved in a unit of work focusing on the Olympic Games, and students were asked to write a news report on Australia's participation in the games. The teacher provided key words: Australia, bronze, gold, silver, medals. Only one draft was required.

Relevant outcomes
2.9   Writes brief imaginative and factual texts which include some related ideas about familiar topics.

2.11   Uses some basic linguistic structures and features of written language so that writing can be readily interpreted by others.

2.12b Usually attempts to spell words by drawing on knowledge of sound-symbol relationships and of standard letter patterns.

Summary comment
The sample clearly demonstrates achievement of some level 2 outcomes. Lack of cohesion between ideas in the text distinguishes it from level 3 work, although there is evidence that the student is moving towards this by attempting to interrelate ideas, as in, 'Australia has six medals. The first... the second... the other one... and the three bronze medals...'

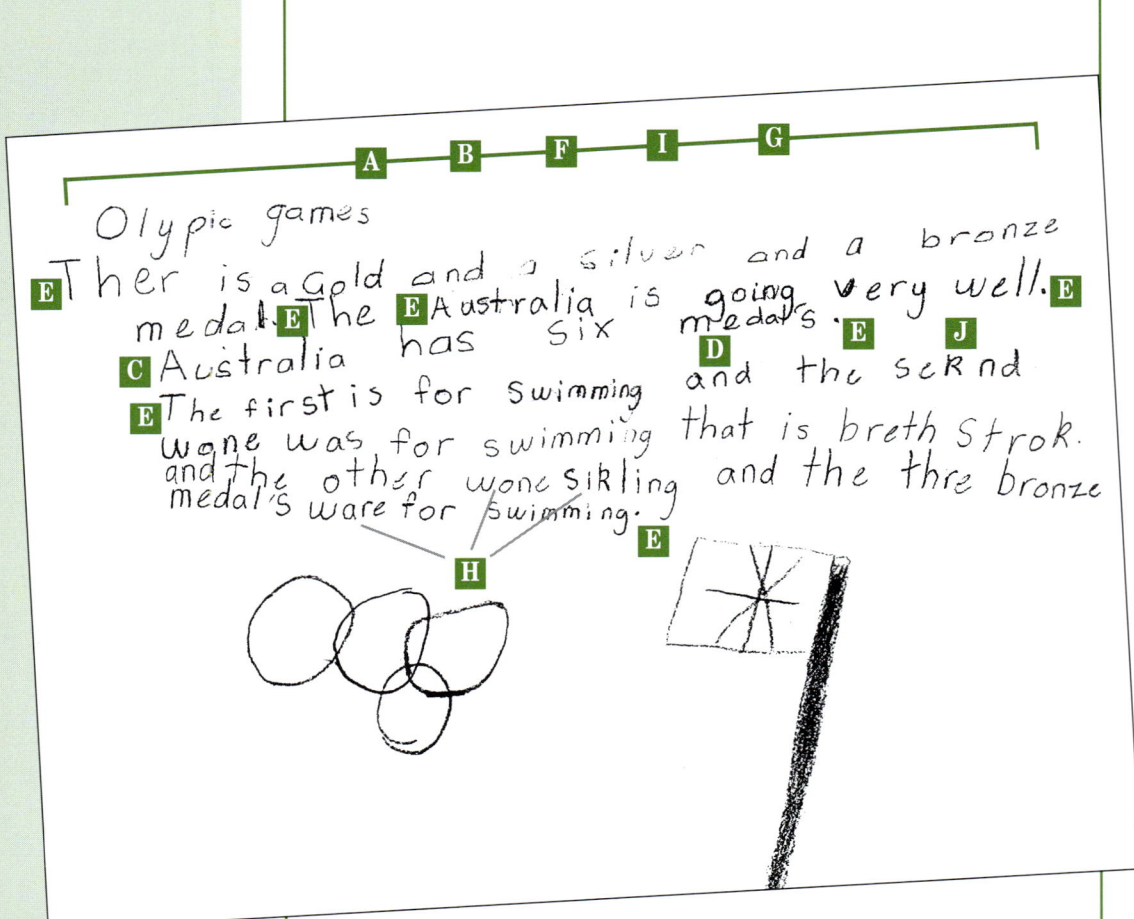

(2.9) Lists several items of related information about the topic; first sentence needs further explanation; inter-relationships between the ideas in each sentence are not clear (**A**).

(2.11) Writes from top to bottom, left to right, and uses spaces between words (**B**); uses basic sentence structure (**C**); links ideas using 'and' (**D**); uses capital letters to begin sentences and proper names and sometimes uses fullstops accurately (**E**); spells some common words such as 'going', 'very', 'well', 'first', 'for', 'is', 'and', 'the', 'that', 'other' accurately (**F**); forms letters of the alphabet correctly and attempts to write clearly in straight lines using letters of uniform size, shape, slope and spacing (**G**).

(2.12b) Attempts spelling by matching sounds within words with known phonic letter patterns, for example, 'wone' for one, 'sikling' for cycling, 'ware' for were (**H**); uses knowledge of familiar letter patterns when attempting to spell unknown words, for example, using suffixes such as -ed, -ing, -s (**I**); uses letters or letter combinations to represent most syllables in words, for instance, 'seknd' for second (**J**); uses spellings of words provided by the teacher (**K**).

Typed version of text
Olypic games
Ther is a Gold and a silver and a bronze medal. The Australia is going very well. Australia has six medals. The first is for swimming and the seknd wone was for swimming that is breth strok. and the other wone sikling and the thre bronze medal's ware for swimming.

Ghost story

Task

Students were required to write a story for their peers to read.

Relevant outcomes

2.9 Writes brief imaginative and factual texts which include some related ideas about familiar topics.

2.10 Recognises some of the purposes and advantages of writing.

2.11 Uses some basic linguistic structures and features of written language so that writing can be readily interpreted by others.

2.12a Uses talk to plan and review own writing.

2.12b Usually attempts to spell words by drawing on knowledge of sound-symbol relationships and of standard letter patterns.

Summary comment

The sample demonstrates sound achievement of level 2 outcomes. Beginning of experimentation with inter-relating ideas using story structure (a level 3 outcome) is evident. Although the student has drafted and rewritten the story, only spelling and punctuation have been reviewed here.

(2.9) Imaginary story sets scene in first sentence and presents ideas and events related to it. A beginning sense of story structure is evident (**A**).

(2.10) Teacher's notes indicate that the student appreciated the purpose of written language and was keen to have her text 'published' and read by others. She was aware that the purpose of this type of text was to entertain others and that others could readily read it if it was 'published' (**B**).

(2.11) Writes from top to bottom, left to right and uses spaces between words (**C**); demonstrates a sense of basic sentence structure; links ideas in writing by using pronouns to refer to preceding nouns: 'it' and 'he' to refer back to the ghost (**D**); links ideas using 'and' (**F**); indicates relationships between events and ideas using 'but' (**G**); sometimes uses fullstops and capital letters accurately (**H**); experiments with quotation marks [assisted by the teacher in this sample] (**I**); spells some high frequency words such as 'one', 'day', 'in', 'to', 'my', 'room', 'went' accurately in own writing (**J**); forms letters of the alphabet correctly (**K**); attempts to write clearly in straight lines using letters of uniform size, shape, slope and spacing (**L**); uses

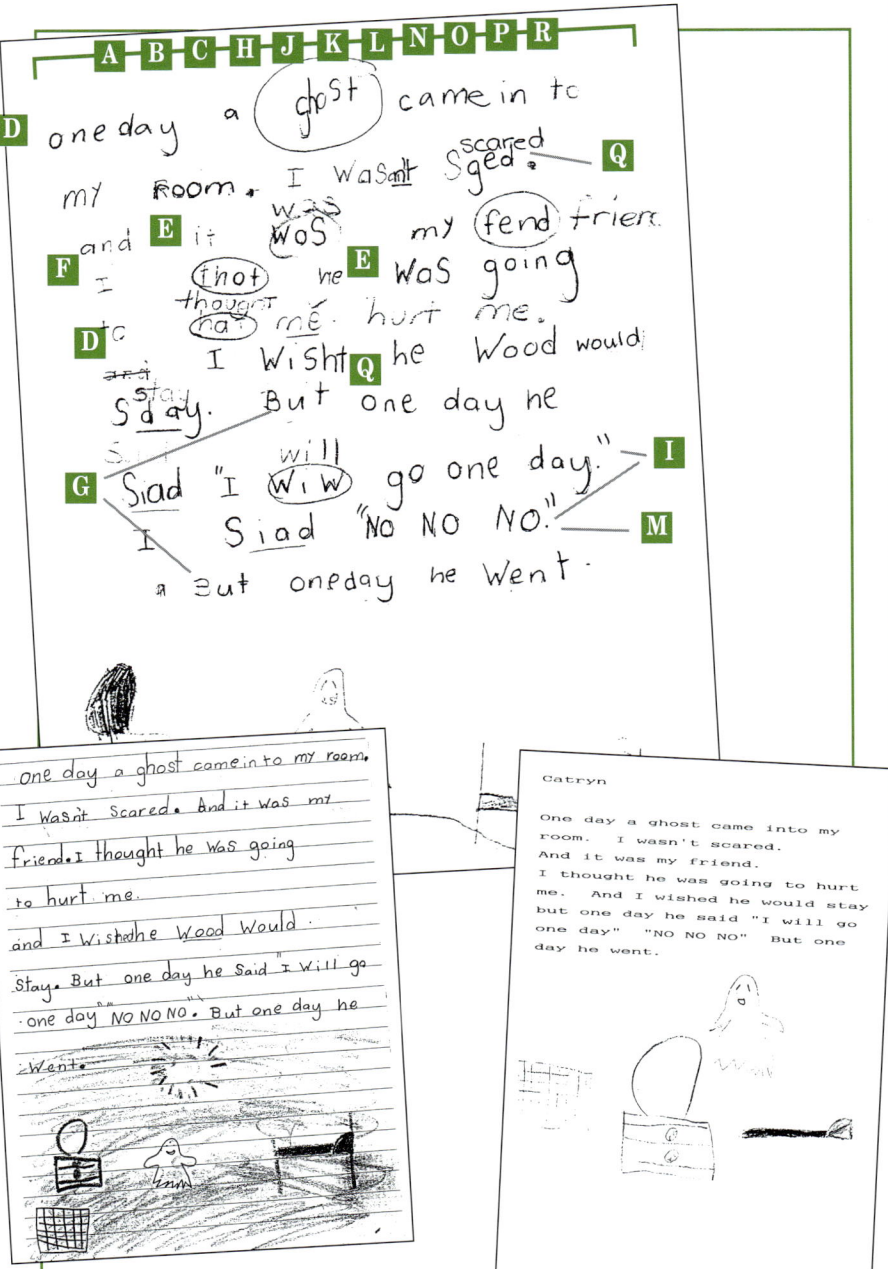

Typed version of text

One day a ghost came into my room. I wasn't scared. and it was my friend. I thought he was going to hurt me. and I wished he would stay but one day he said "I will go one day" "NO NO NO" But one day he went.

capitals to emphasise meaning, as in 'NO NO NO' (**M**).

(2.12a) Teacher noted that the student stated purpose and topic before writing; told key ideas or events to peers before writing; voiced thoughts while writing; read writing aloud during writing and revising to clarify meaning (**N**).

(2.12b) Attempts spelling by matching sounds within words with known phonic letter patterns, for example, 'wood' for would, 'wos' for was, 'gost' for ghost (**O**); uses knowledge of familiar letter patterns when attempting to spell unknown words, for example, using suffixes such as -ed, -ing, -s (used 'ed' at the end of scared although it was mispelled 'sged') (**P**); uses letters or letter combinations to represent most syllables in words, such as 't' for '-ed' (**Q**); identifies possible spelling errors by circling doubtful words (**R**).

Recipe for jelly

Task

A recipe for jelly.

Background

This is the same task as was presented for the level 1 sample but the student's work is at a higher level.

Relevant outcomes

2.9 Writes brief imaginative and factual texts which include some related ideas about familiar topics.

2.10 Recognises some of the purposes and advantages of using writing.

2.11 Uses some basic linguistic structures and features of written language so that writing can be readily interpreted by others.

2.12a Uses talk to plan and review own writing.

2.12b Usually attempts to spell words by drawing on knowledge of sound-symbol relationships and of standard letter patterns.

Summary comment

The sample provides a simple, intelligible set of directions for making jelly. Some details are left implicit in the procedure, which helps to distinguish it from level 3 work.

(2.9) Writes simple directions or instructions for a known procedure with a few steps (**A**).

(2.10) Teacher's notes indicate that during the preceding activities and preparation for writing the recipe, the student's discussions of the following pointed to achievement of this outcome: advantages of using writing to record and communicate procedures for doing an activity, how writing enables people to communicate with others over time and distance, how writing enables information to be distributed to many people, some purposes for which familiar people used written procedures, for example, people cooking at home (**B**); shows awareness of reader needs by using conventional layout and numbers to order steps in the recipe (**C**); adopts many distinguishing features of the text type demonstrated by the teacher and found by looking at text models (**D**).

(2.11) Always writes from top to bottom, left to right, and uses spaces between words (**E**); uses appropriate sentence structure for the text type, such as point form demonstrated by the teacher (**F**); links ideas in writing by using pronouns to refer to preceding nouns, for

example, 'Stir it' in point 4 refers to the jelly and hot water mixture in previous points (**G**); adopts grammatical patterns demonstrated by the teacher, such as the imperative form for procedural writing (**H**); uses capital letters to begin most sentences, full stops at the end of the each point (**I**); spells some common words accurately, for example, hot, cold, water, jug, in, again, stir (**J**); forms most letters of the alphabet correctly (**K**); attempts to write clearly, although only draft quality required (**L**); uses recipe format demonstrated by the teacher, leaving out title and a sub-heading (**M**).

(2.12a) The student took part in the class and group preparatory and planning activities. No revisions as only first draft was required by the teacher (**N**).

(2.12b) Attempts spelling by matching sounds within words with known phonic letter patterns, as in 'mesering' (**O**); uses knowledge of familiar letter patterns when attempting to spell unknown words, for example, using suffixes such as -ed, -ing, -s, as in 'mesering' (**P**); uses letters or letter combinations to represent most syllables when spelling unknown words (**Q**).

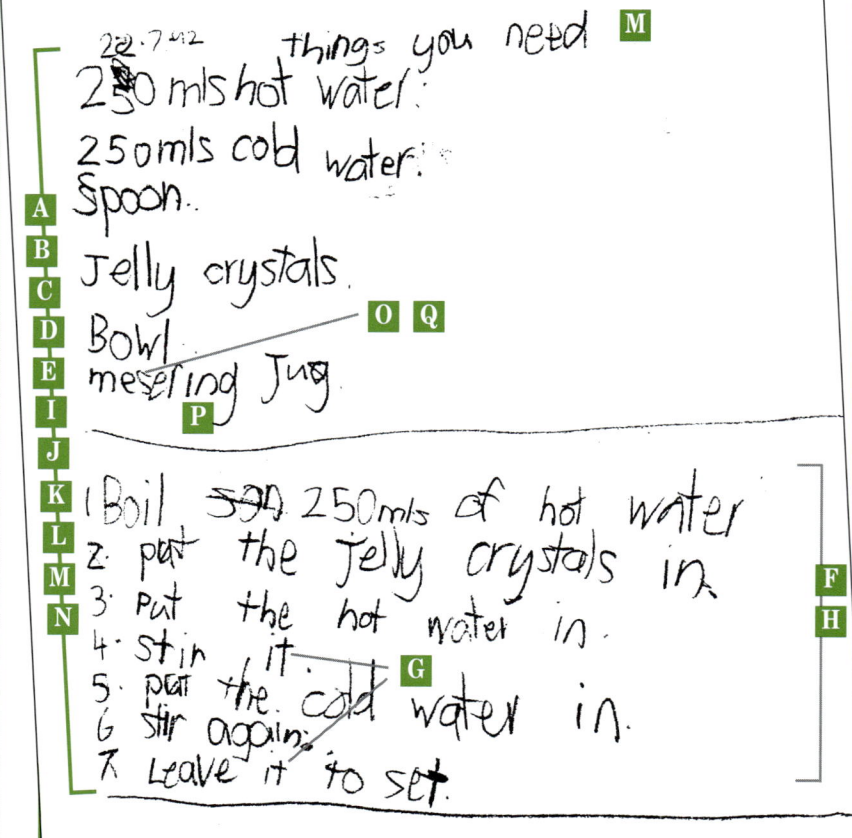

Typed version of text

things you need
250 mls hot water
250 mls cold water
spoon
Jelly crystals
Bowl
mesering Jug

1. Boil 250 mls of hot water
2. put the Jelly crystals in.
3. Put the hot water in.
4. stir it.
5. Put the cold water in.
6. stir again.
7. Leave it to set.

Fish story

Task

Students were required to write a story, choosing a text type and topic.

Background

Students in this class write every day, choosing from a variety of topics, including personal experiences, excursion reports, imaginative writing. Before this writing session, possible topics were discussed. The student spent 20 minutes writing, then read the text to the teacher, who suggested some alterations. At the end of the activity, the student read the text to the class.

Relevant outcomes

2.9 Writes brief imaginative and factual texts which include some related ideas about familiar topics.

(2.9) Imaginary story features two or more events: the character is introduced and a problem or complication follows (**A**).

(2.10) Student shows some awareness of the entertainment purposes of stories and of writing for a particular purpose, here a story for personal and others' entertainment (**B**).

(2.11) Always writes from top to bottom, left to right, and uses spaces between words (**C**); uses basic sentence structure and often marks accurately with full stops (**D**); links ideas by using pronouns to refer to preceding nouns, for example, use of 'his' and 'they' (**E**); uses capital letters to begin sentences and proper names ('Kim') (**F**); spells some common words accurately in own writing, such as 'once upon a time', 'there', 'was', 'fish', 'one', 'day', 'fell', 'on', 'said', 'to', 'they' (**G**); forms most letters of the alphabet correctly (**H**); attempts to write clearly in straight lines using letters of uniform size, shape, slope and spacing (**I**); adopts language patterns of stories (**J**).

(2.12b) Attempts spelling by matching sounds within words with known phonic letter patterns, for example, 'lef' as second attempt for leaf (**K**); uses letters or letter combinations to represent most syllables in an unknown word, as in 'tgev' for together (**L**).

2.10 Recognises some of the purposes and advantages of writing.

2.11 Uses some basic linguistic structures and features of written language so that writing can be readily interpreted by others.

2.12b Usually attempts to spell words by drawing on knowledge of sound-symbol relationships and of standard letter patterns.

Summary comment

The sample is typical of early efforts at story writing. It uses some distinguishing features of stories, such as use of 'once upon a time' to introduce the character and setting, a complication or problem, and the past tense. The storyline is not developed, which serves to distinguish it from level 3 work.

Typed version of text

Once upon a time there was a fish. his name was Kim. one day a lff fell on him. he said a lef fell on me the fish said to his friend his friend was a fish his name was just fish. they played together.

LEVEL THREE

LEVEL 3 Statement

Students who have achieved level three interpret and communicate familiar ideas and information for particular purposes and known audiences. They explore the features of different types of spoken, written and visual texts and experiment with ways of shaping their ideas to suit topics, purposes and audiences.

Students can use a range of types of spoken texts for different purposes in the classroom and school. They usually use language that others understand and are capable of adapting their language to suit their purposes.

Students can read texts produced for young readers. They recognise and discuss some relationships between ideas, information and events in these texts and in some visual texts. They have a grasp of simple symbolic meanings and stereotypes and of the purposes and characteristics of different types of texts. They can find ways of understanding written and visual texts and use methods demonstrated by the teacher for finding information sources and using them.

Students write longer texts, using ideas and information about familiar topics. They recognise and can use many of the linguistic structures and features of a small range of text types. Students experiment with ways of planning, reviewing and proofreading their writing demonstrated by the teacher and make attempts at spelling new words.

LEVEL 3
Table of outcomes

	Texts	Contextual understanding	Linguistic structures & features	Strategies
SPEAKING AND LISTENING	3.1 Interacts for specific purposes with people in the classroom and school community using a small range of text types.	3.2 Recognises that certain types of spoken texts are associated with particular contexts and purposes.	3.3 Usually uses linguistic structures and features of spoken language appropriately for expressing and interpreting ideas and information.	3.4 Reflects on own approach to communication and the ways in which others interact.
	See page 56	See page 56	See page 57	See page 57
READING AND VIEWING	3.5 Interprets and discusses some relationships between ideas, information and events in: – written texts with familiar content and a small range of unfamiliar words and linguistic structures and features – visual texts designed for general viewing.	3.6 Identifies simple symbolic meanings and stereotypes in texts and discusses their purpose and meaning.	3.7 Identifies and uses the linguistic structures and features characteristic of a range of text types to construct meaning.	3.8 a Integrates a variety of strategies for interpreting printed and visual texts. 3.8 b With teacher guidance, uses several strategies for identifying resources and finding information in texts.
	See page 58	See page 58	See page 59	See page 59
WRITING	3.9 Experiments with inter-relating ideas and information when writing about familiar topics within a small range of text types.	3.10 Recognises that certain text types and features are associated with particular purposes and audiences.	3.11 Controls most basic features of written language and experiments with some organisational and linguistic features of different text types.	3.12 a Experiments with strategies for planning, reviewing and proofreading own writing. 3.12 b Consistently makes informed attempts at spelling.
	See page 60	See page 60	See page 61	See page 61

LEVEL 3 Speaking and Listening

Level 2 outcomes:

2.1 Interacts in more confident and extended ways in structured and spontaneous school situations.

2.2 Considers how own speaking and listening is adjusted in different situations.

2.3 Experiments with different linguistic structures and features for expressing and interpreting ideas and information.

2.4 Speaks and listens in ways that assist communication with others.

Texts

At level 3, a student:

3.1 Interacts for specific purposes with people in the classroom and school community using a small range of text types.

Evident when students, for example:

- Create jokes, rhymes, funny stories and word play to entertain themselves and others.

- Retell and offer opinions about scenes from films, drama or stories heard read aloud, with attention to character, setting and plot detail.

- Deliver a prepared short talk to peers on a topic of mutual interest, giving mostly relevant, organised information.

- Exchange perceptions and feelings with peers about similar experiences (compare events in texts with incidents when they have felt jealous, angry, frustrated, excited, awed; recount an event, highlighting significant aspects).

- Listen and respond to peers in problem-solving groups, showing attention to the task (speculate on explanations and solutions, extend others' suggestions, generate plans for completing a task).

- Report briefly to the class on a group discussion or activity (present a list of ideas generated by the group).

- Attempt to persuade others in the class to a point of view or action, presenting a few reasons (why a classroom rule should be changed).

- Listen to and obtain specific information from spoken texts and retell this to others (details from a coach about joining a sports team; information about a character in a short story read aloud by the teacher; information about a familiar topic from a radio broadcast).

- Conduct brief interviews with children and adults to obtain information about an issue or topic (their preferences for the canteen menu).

Contextual understanding

At level 3, a student:

3.2 Recognises that certain types of spoken texts are associated with particular contexts and purposes.

Evident when students, for example:

- With teacher guidance, roleplay or view on video different types of spoken language texts—oral or signed reports, story telling, an interview—in order to discuss their purposes and some of their distinguishing features (how parts or stages of a text function in achieving its purpose).

- With teacher guidance, compare the features of different spoken texts and talk about how these are related to purpose or context (consider how the setting in story telling and the beginning of an interview serve an introductory function for listeners; compare the explicitness of telephone conversations with face-to-face discussions).

- Usually select, from a small known range, an appropriate text type for a speaking purpose and explain the choice.

- Keep a record of the purposes and audiences for which they have spoken and the text types they used.

- Compare the features of informal, personal speaking with those of more formal and public purposes and audiences.

Linguistic structures & features

At level 3, a student:

3.3 Usually uses linguistic structures and features of spoken language appropriately for expressing and interpreting ideas and information.

Evident when students, for example:

- Recognise the main organisational elements of group discussions; brainstorming activities, recounts, reports, instructions, and often use these to construct spoken texts.

- Use accurately common grammatical structures such as subject/verb agreement, noun/pronoun agreement, and consistency of tense.

- Express logical relations in speech through the use of linking words such as 'although', 'instead of', 'so that'.

- Interpret and try to use metaphorical language in spoken texts ('That car is a petrol-guzzling monster.').

- Use specialised language on a variety of topics and select words carefully to achieve precise meanings.

- Emphasise their own spoken language by using pauses and repetition effectively.

Strategies

At level 3, a student:

3.4 Reflects on own approach to communication and the ways in which others interact.

Evident when students, for example:

- Correct their own speech for meaning and accuracy.

- Select and organise ideas before giving a short prepared talk (list main ideas on cue cards).

- Rehearse and modify a talk before presenting it to peers or the class (re-order presentation of ideas, change concluding statement).

- Listen actively to a speaker by attempting to identify the topic and focus, and asking relevant questions.

- Initiate discussion of ideas and issues with the teacher and peers.

- Reflect on and attempt to adopt strategies for effectively taking part in structured small group activities (taking into account other opinions; expanding on others' ideas; asking for and giving explanations and reasons; being tolerant of and responsive to others' contributions; asking peers for more detail on a shared topic; asking questions to gain more information; attempting to solve problems with the group).

- Discuss with peers and the teacher strategies for assisting communication with others in different situations.

Level 4 outcomes:

4.1   Interacts confidently with others in a variety of situations to develop and present familiar ideas, events and information.

4.2   Considers aspects of context, purpose and audience when speaking and listening in familiar situations.

4.3   Controls most linguistic structures and features of spoken language for interpreting meaning and developing and presenting ideas and information in familiar situations.

4.4   Assists and monitors the communication patterns of self and others.

LEVEL 3 Reading and Viewing

Level 2 outcomes:

2.5 Constructs and retells meanings from:

– short written texts with familiar topics and vocabulary, predictable text structures and frequent illus-trations, and

– visual texts with predictable narrative structures.

2.6 Understands that texts are constructed by people and represent real and imaginary experience.

2.7 Recognises and interprets basic linguistic structures and features of texts.

2.8a Uses basic strategies for interpreting written and visual texts and maintains continuity in understanding when meaning is disrupted.

2.8b With teacher guidance, selects own reading material, and gathers and sorts information on a topic from a variety of sources.

Texts

At level 3, a student:

3.5 Interprets and discusses some relationships between ideas, information and events in:

- **written texts with familiar content and a small range of unfamiliar words and linguistic structures and features**
- **visual texts designed for general viewing.**

Evident when students, for example:

- Read, for personal enjoyment and interest, poetry, short stories, autobiographies and novels produced for younger readers, junior non-fiction and simple instructional texts.

- Re-tell and discuss interpretation of texts read or viewed, with attention to main ideas and supporting details in informational texts or to elements such as key events, main characters and setting in narratives.

- Make some inferences about ideas implicit in a text (infer the motives of characters in stories from their actions).

- Interpret and follow short printed instructions or directions such as those in recipes, maps, games, safety guidelines.

- Use junior informational texts to find information on a research topic, commenting on how texts present information (recognise grouping of information according to various aspects of a topic).

- Make generalisations based on interpretation of texts viewed or read (confirm, extend or correct own knowledge through reading or viewing).

- Discuss possible reasons for the choice of visual images in different advertisements for similar products.

Contextual understanding

At level 3, a student:

3.6 Identifies simple symbolic meanings and stereotypes in texts and discusses their purpose and meaning.

Evident when students, for example:

- Recognise that the use of symbols in texts depends on shared cultural understandings (stop signs need to be interpreted in the same way).

- Identify the symbolic significance of colour, music, gesture and expression in texts, recognising that these are socially constructed representations (that red may represent emotion, anger or excitement; smiling happiness; loudness anger, engagement or excitement).

- Discuss the ways in which people are stereotyped in texts, recognising that people could have been represented differently (comment on whether only clever people wear glasses, mothers only work at home, fathers never look after babies, scientists wear white coats and are male).

- Recognise the symbolic link between a product name or a trade logo and a product.

- Recognise recurring character types and their traits (describe the stereotypical characteristics of 'goodies' and 'baddies' in books and film and television stories).

- Discuss how people from different socio-cultural or minority groups or people in particular roles are represented in texts and whether these representations are accurate or fair.

Linguistic structures & features

At level 3, a student:

3.7 Identifies and uses the linguistic structures and features characteristic of a range of text types to construct meaning.

Evident when students, for example:

- Recognise the characteristic features of particular text types (in stories, identify main elements of structure such as setting, problem, episodes, resolution, and aspects of language such as description or dialogue).

- Identify and explain the role of organisational features such as paragraphs and chapters in written texts.

- Construct timelines, story maps or flow charts to represent event sequences or the organisation of information in printed and visual texts (view a feature film in segments, contribute to a class summary of each segment and construct a story map to demonstrate understanding of the plot).

- Identify how language is used to signal logical relationships in texts (problem-solution, cause-effect relationships).

- Make general statements about the similar characteristics of visual texts (identify similarities between a western movie and a cartoon set in the west such as Deputy Dawg).

- Recognise and adopt the conventions of a variety of stereotypes (construct an original superhero using drawing and labels; imitate stereotypical behaviours of different characters based upon television or film characters).

- Identify symbolic use of music, sound effects and voice style (tension is heightened in films by dramatic music, sound effects such as a heartbeat or a squeaking chair, and the use of a deep voice).

Strategies

At level 3, a student:

3.8a Integrates a variety of strategies for interpreting written and visual texts.

Evident when students, for example:

- Predict and attempt to work out the meaning of unknown words in written texts through using strategies such as considering context, sounding out using knowledge of common letter combinations or initial letters, drawing on knowledge of grammar, sentence structure and text organisation.

- Clarify or correct meaning by pausing, re-reading or reading on.

- Adjust reading strategies for different texts and different purposes (scan information books for selected topics, look for keys or symbols when reading a diagram, examine both pictures and text when reading picture books).

- Draw on experience of objects, clothing, sound effects, dialogue to establish when and where the action is occurring in a visual text.

- Integrate symbols to construct meaning (infer from a poster showing a smiling, well-groomed police officer holding the hand of a happy child that an image of police as trustworthy and reliable is being presented).

3.8b With teacher guidance, uses several strategies for identifying resources and finding information in texts.

Evident when students, for example:

- Participate in class brainstorming activities to identify and narrow a research topic, to cluster and categorise ideas, and to develop focus questions to guide search for information.

- Predict and list a range of resources for answering focus questions (print and non-print, fiction and non-fiction, films, photographs, charts, people).

- Find information in junior reference material using the table of contents, index, page numbers, headings and captions, key words.

- Make brief notes of information relevant to the topic, recording resources used.

- Make some comparisons between information from different formats and sources.

Level 4 outcomes:

4.5 Justifies own interpretation of ideas, information and events in texts containing some unfamiliar concepts and topics and which introduce relatively complex linguistic structures and features.

4.6 Explains possible reasons for people's varying interpretations of a text.

4.7 With teacher guidance, identifies and discusses how linguistic structures and features work to shape readers' and viewers' understanding of texts.

4.8a Selects, uses and reflects on strategies appropriate for different texts and reading or viewing purposes.

4.8b With peers, identifies information needs and finds resources for specific purposes.

LEVEL 3 Writing

Level 2 outcomes:

2.9   Writes brief imaginative and factual texts which include some related ideas about familiar topics.

2.10   Recognises some of the purposes and advantages of writing.

2.11   Uses some basic linguistic structures and features of written language so that writing can be readily interpreted by others.

2.12a   Uses talk to plan and review own writing.

2.12b   Usually attempts to spell words by drawing on knowledge of sound-symbol relationships and of standard letter patterns.

Texts

At level 3, a student:

3.9 Experiments with interrelating ideas and information when writing about familiar topics within a small range of text types.

Evident when students, for example:

- Recount in sequence several aspects of a personal experience or an event, commenting on their significance (list events and conclude with an overall comment on them).

- Write a report which includes information on several aspects of the topic.

- Construct riddles and jokes in which the second part depends on the first.

- Write an imaginative story with a distinguishable storyline in which some events are clearly related to the resolution of a problem.

- Devise a simple recipe or a set of instructions for a game with some attention to detail and logical sequence (refer to equipment or materials and include essential steps).

- Give a few related reasons that support a position (why the school canteen should sell a particular kind of food).

- Write a broad description of a familiar item or person with attention to several distinguishing characteristics (a wanted poster or character portrait).

- Write an advertisement which includes most relevant details for a class or school event.

Contextual understanding

At level 3, a student:

3.10 Recognises that certain text types and features are associated with particular purposes and audiences.

Evident when students, for example:

- With teacher guidance, examine models of a text type (a poster, a recipe, a report or a story) discussing its purpose and some of its distinguishing features (why informational reports usually do not include personal views and opinions, the function of different parts or stages of a text).

- Compare, with teacher guidance, the features of two different text types and talk about how these differences are related to purpose (compare the function of a setting in a story with the list of ingredients in a recipe).

- Select, from a small known range, an appropriate text type for a particular writing purpose and explain why they have chosen it.

- Keep a record of the purposes and audiences for which they have written and the text types used.

- Compare the features of personal writing with those of texts written for more formal and public purposes and audiences (attention to presentation, accuracy of conventions).

- Consider, with teacher guidance, some needs of readers before writing (predict what a particular reader may need to know, or the topics for a story likely to appeal to a specified audience).

Linguistic structures & features

At level 3, a student:

3.11 Controls most basic features of written language and experiments with some organisational and linguistic features of different text types.

Evident when students, for example:

- Control basic sentence structure and attempt to vary sentence beginnings and clause structure.

- Relate ideas in writing, using a variety of conjunctions suited to the purpose.

- Select language that enhances meaning (use known technical terms or precise descriptive words).

- Spell many common words correctly in own writing.

- Write legibly on most occasions, using consistent shape, size and slope and cursive script (when rewriting a draft for presentation to an audience, when making a sign for display).

- Use some conventions of layout to assist the reader (group related ideas or information under sub-headings), and experiment with various ways of presenting written work to appeal to the reader (by using different headings, layout, colours and illustrations).

- Use time order to organise writing of recounts and stories.

- Use correct tense for selected text type (simple present tense when reporting information).

- Write with clearly discernible beginnings, middles and ends.

- With teacher guidance, use text organisation to develop ideas and information (a recipe including a list of ingredients and directions; a story with setting, problem, episodes and resolution; an information report with a general classification and elaborating details).

Strategies

At level 3, a student:

3.12a Experiments with strategies for planning, reviewing and proofreading own writing.

Evident when students, for example:

- Attempt some revising during writing (delete or add words to clarify meaning; add information; re-read work to clarify meaning before continuing with writing).

- Use other texts as models for aspects of writing such as expression, text organisation, grouping of information under headings, or kind of language.

- Add information to their texts following suggestions from teacher or peers (include an extra sentence describing a character or add a missing step to instructions).

- Use a proofreading guide provided by the teacher to identify and correct such things as spelling errors, incomplete sentences or missing punctuation in own writing.

- Set and monitor realistic short-term goals for development as a writer (to write for different purposes using different text types, to correctly spell particular words, or to use full stops consistently).

3.12b Consistently makes informed attempts at spelling.

Evident when students, for example:

- Use new words in writing even though unsure of exact spelling.

- Use visual strategies, such as knowledge of letter patterns and critical features of words, to attempt to spell words.

- Draw on some spelling generalisations to spell unknown words (use some double letters correctly).

- Recognise most misspelt words in own writing and use a variety of resources for correction.

- Discuss strategies used for spelling difficult words (try a number of ways of spelling a word before deciding which version looks or sounds correct).

Level 4 outcomes:

4.9 Uses writing to develop familiar ideas, events and information.

4.10 Adjusts writing to take account of aspects of context, purpose and audience.

4.11 Controls most distinguishing linguistic structures and features of basic text types such as stories, procedures, reports and arguments.

4.12a When prompted, uses a range of strategies for planning, reviewing and proofreading own writing.

4.12b Uses a multi-strategy approach to spelling.

Spoken tasks

Task

The work sample covers three spoken tasks by one student:

- a prepared five-minute 'news talk' to the class on two items chosen from a television news broadcast
- a prepared speech advertising a fundraising Lunch Day, which was then presented to other classes in the school
- a prepared commentary for a short video segment on an aspect of the school produced by the whole class for class penfriends in a country town.

Background

News talk

For the three talks in class each morning, volunteers choose a news talk, a book review or a free talk. Although not required to write out their talks, students often do. After their talks, they respond to three comments or questions from the class. News can be gathered from television, radio or newspapers. The student here wrote out her talk.

Lunch Day advertisement

A visiting speaker promoting a banking scheme for young people prompted the teacher to examine aspects of advertising with the class. As a follow-up, the class prepared advertising material for their Lunch Day—a written notice to parents and a speech for other classes. After class discussion of the information needed in both and ways the two would differ, each student drafted a notice and a speech, rehearsing the speech with a partner, who was expected to provide comment on content and clarity. The speeches were then presented to the class, using a

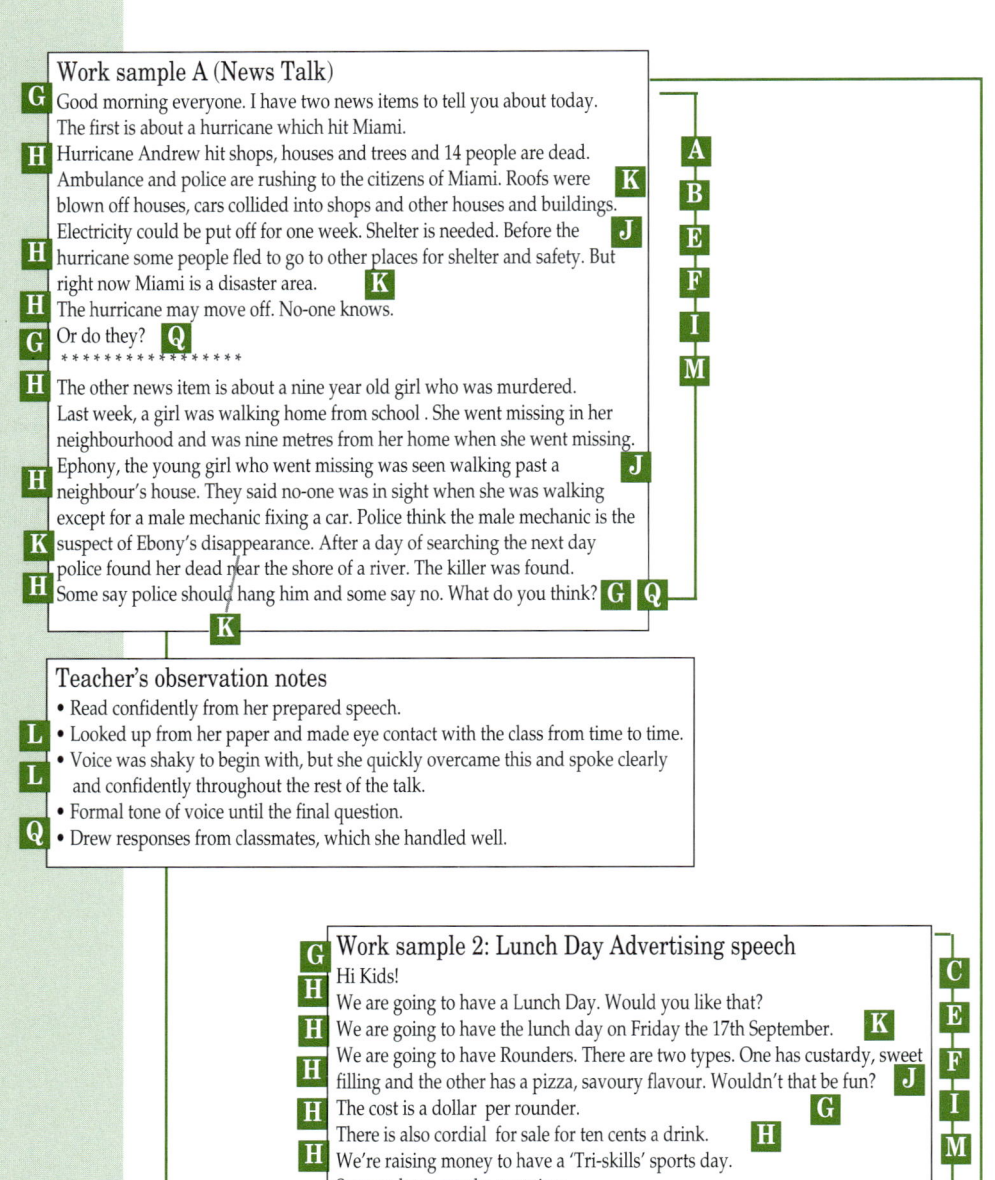

Work sample A (News Talk)

G Good morning everyone. I have two news items to tell you about today. The first is about a hurricane which hit Miami.

H Hurricane Andrew hit shops, houses and trees and 14 people are dead. Ambulance and police are rushing to the citizens of Miami. Roofs were **K** blown off houses, cars collided into shops and other houses and buildings. Electricity could be put off for one week. Shelter is needed. Before the **J**
H hurricane some people fled to go to other places for shelter and safety. But right now Miami is a disaster area. **K**
H The hurricane may move off. No-one knows.
G Or do they? **Q**
****
H The other news item is about a nine year old girl who was murdered. Last week, a girl was walking home from school . She went missing in her neighbourhood and was nine metres from her home when she went missing.
Ephony, the young girl who went missing was seen walking past a **J**
H neighbour's house. They said no-one was in sight when she was walking except for a male mechanic fixing a car. Police think the male mechanic is the **K** suspect of Ebony's disappearance. After a day of searching the next day police found her dead near the shore of a river. The killer was found.
H Some say police should hang him and some say no. What do you think? **G** **Q**
K

Teacher's observation notes
- Read confidently from her prepared speech.
L - Looked up from her paper and made eye contact with the class from time to time.
L - Voice was shaky to begin with, but she quickly overcame this and spoke clearly and confidently throughout the rest of the talk.
- Formal tone of voice until the final question.
Q - Drew responses from classmates, which she handled well.

A
B
E
F
I
M

Work sample 2: Lunch Day Advertising speech
G Hi Kids!
H We are going to have a Lunch Day. Would you like that?
H We are going to have the lunch day on Friday the 17th September. **K**
H We are going to have Rounders. There are two types. One has custardy, sweet filling and the other has a pizza, savoury flavour. Wouldn't that be fun? **J**
H The cost is a dollar per rounder. **G**
There is also cordial for sale for ten cents a drink. **H**
H We're raising money to have a 'Tri-skills' sports day.
See you later, maybe next time.
H Thank you.

C
E
F
I
M
R

Teacher's observation notes
- Delivered talk to younger class.
L - Bright and bubbly style, smiling all the while.
- Emphasised words italicised above by increasing volume and pitch and slowing pace.

(3.1) Prepares and delivers a short news talk to peers on a topic of interest that includes mostly relevant, organised information (**A**); listens to obtain specific information from television news and retells this to others (**B**); prepares and presents a brief spoken advertisement that includes key information and attempts to entice listeners (**C**); prepares and presents a video commentary that provides spoken information about what is seen (**D**).

(3.2) With teacher guidance, prepares and presents three different types of spoken language texts, showing awareness of their purposes and some of their distinguishing features (**E**); with teacher guidance, considers the features of the different spoken texts and how these relate to purpose and context (**F**); adapts style and tone of spoken language to the demands of purpose and audience: informal greeting for video commentary and introduction to advertisement, formal greeting for news talk; seeks to engage listeners at stages in each presentation; varies language in emotive quality and expression (**G**).

(3.3) Recognises and uses the main elements of the three text types.

News talk: Introduction; Items of information; Conclusion/Invitation to comment.

Advertisement: Introduction; What; When; What are we

simple cue card, and taped. The students then presented their speech to another class.

Video commentary

Students worked in small groups and as a class to prepare a video to introduce themselves and their school to their penfriends in a country town. Each student chose a topic or location to speak about on the video, drafted, discussed and revised their commentary and shot plans and listed key words on cue cards. After rehearsing their commentaries in front of small groups of peers and discussing their ideas for videotaping their segments, the video was made.

Relevant outcomes

3.1 Interacts for specific purposes with people in the classroom and school community using a small range of text types.

3.2 Recognises that certain types of spoken texts are associated with particular contexts and purposes.

3.3 Usually uses linguistic structures and features of spoken language appropriately for expressing and interpreting ideas and information.

3.4 Reflects on own approach to communication and the ways in which others interact.

Summary comment

Considered together, the three work samples provide consistent evidence of achievement of all level 3 outcomes for speaking and listening. They provide evidence of readiness to move on to the more complex topics and ideas characteristic of level 4 outcomes.

---

eating; How much; Why; Conclusion.

Video commentary: Greeting; Description and explanation of shots 1, 2 and 3 (**H**).

Usually correctly uses common grammatical structures such as subject/verb agreement, noun/pronoun agreement and consistency of tense (**I**); incorporates some complex sentence structures into speech (**J**); chooses words to achieve precise meaning ('custardy, sweet filling', 'pizza savoury flavour', 'original building', 'cars collided', 'suspect', 'disappearance') (**K**); varies delivery by using pauses, repetition, changes in tone, modulation, stress and expression (**L**); sustains consistent style and tone in each text (**M**).

(3.4) Selects and organises ideas for a short prepared talk: lists main ideas on cue cards, writes scripts (**N**); rehearses and modifies texts before presenting talks (reorders ideas, adds information) (**O**); listens actively to television speaker, attempting to identify topic and focus (**P**); initiates discussion of ideas and issues with teacher and peers after news talk (**Q**); discusses with peers and teacher useful strategies for assisting communication in different situations when rehearsing advertisement and video commentary (**R**).

Work sample 3: Video commentary

Shot between demac and our building.

G 1. Far off
2. Close up for speech
Hi. I'm Sophia. Hi Steph.
This is the building where our classroom is (gestures towards building). It was original and was from the 1930s. **K**
G As you can see it is two storeys (points). There are two ways you could go upstairs. We have two types of stairs. **H**
Shot of outside fire escape.
1. Close up for speech
2. Far off
G As you can see here, (pointing) this is the stairs we use for sports and excursions. It's VERY useful. It's the fire escape. **H**
Shot of inside stairs.
1. Close up.
2. Far off (speech)
Over here (gestures towards stairs) are the inside stairs. We go down them normally for Italian lessons, recess and lunch.

(side annotations: D E F I M R H)

Teacher's observation notes

- Used cue cards and shot plans to present her commentary on videotape. **L**
- Used gesture appropriately, pointing to the items she was describing. **L**
- Paced her talk well. **L**
- Spoke clearly.

18-8-92

What, is it? Lunch day
When? Friday — Sept
What are we eating? Rounders savoury
Sweet filling pluscordial
How much? $1.00 & 10¢
Why? Raising money for our Tri-skills sports days

Hi kids! we are going to have a lunch day would you like that? We are going to have the lunch day on a Friday 11 Sept. We are going to have rounders. they are soft & has a pizza flavour & the other one has & a sweet custard flavour. wouldn't that be fun? The cost is $1.00 per rounders. We are having raising money to have a Tri-skills sports day. see ya later
maybe next time
Thankyou

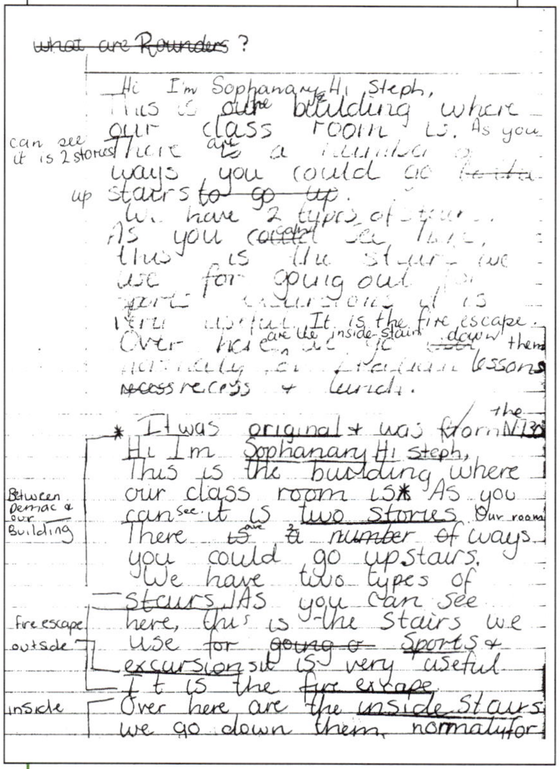

---

what are Rounders?

Hi I'm Sophanary Hi Steph,
this is our building where our class room is. As you can see it is 2 stories. There are a number of ways you could go up stairs to go up.
we have 2 types of...
As you could see, this is the stairs we use for going out... sports excursions it is very useful. It is the inside stair... Over here are the inside stairs down them normally for Italian lessons recess recess & lunch.

It was original & was from the 1930...
Hi I'm Sophanary Hi steph, this is the building where our class room is. As you can see it is two stories. Our room There is a number of ways you could go upstairs. We have two types of stairs. As you can see here, this is the stairs we use for going & sports & excursions it is very useful It is the fire escape. Over here are the inside stairs we go down them, normally for...

(margin notes: can see it is 2 stories / Between demac & our Building / Fire escape outside / inside)

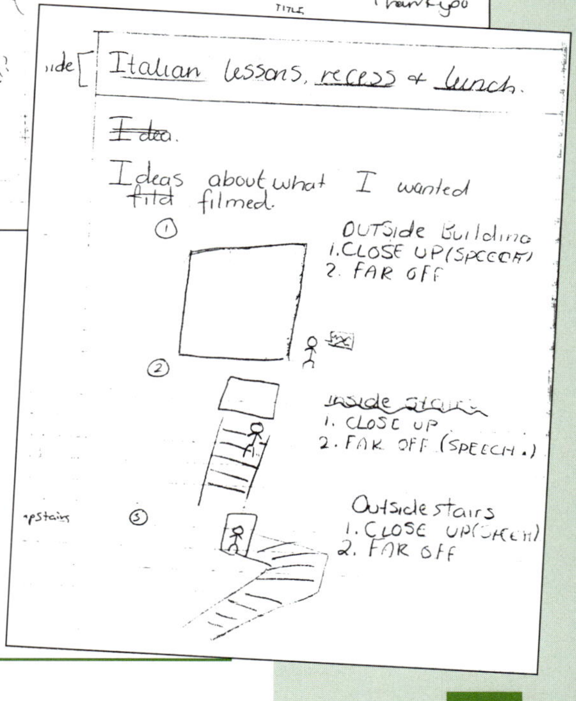

Italian lessons, recess & lunch.

Idea.

Ideas about what I wanted filmed.

① OUTSIDE Building
1. CLOSE UP (SPEECH)
2. FAR OFF

② INSIDE STAIRS
1. CLOSE UP
2. FAR OFF (SPEECH.)

Outside stairs
1. CLOSE UP (SPEECH)
2. FAR OFF

(margin note: upstairs ⑤)

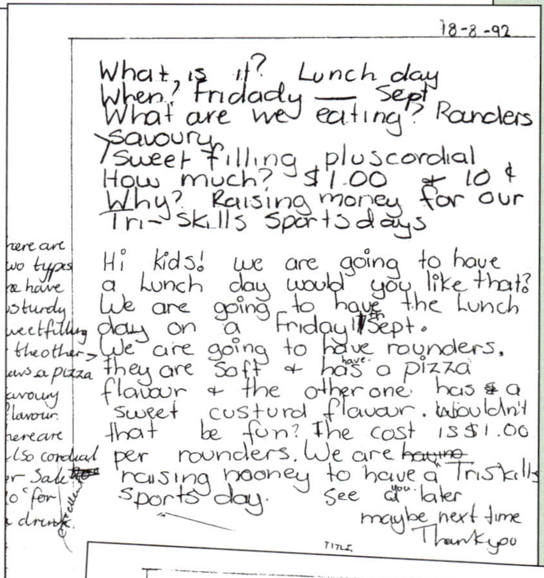

Hansel and Gretel drawings

Task

The students were required to draw illustrations for a text and discuss them.

Background

The students listened to the teacher read the story *Hansel and Gretel: The Brothers Grimm,* illustrated by Anthony Browne. They were not shown the illustrations.

After hearing the story, the teacher asked the students to draw separate pictures of the stepmother and father as they thought Anthony Browne would draw them, showing their faces and clothes, and using speech bubbles to show what they said.

The class then discussed the way each student had represented the characters' traits before looking at the book's illustrations.

Background

The teacher's aim in this activity was to challenge students to consider the stereotypical representation of the characters in the book and to recognise and discuss the illustrator's symbols for female wickedness and male weakness.

Relevant outcomes

3.6   Identifies simple symbolic meanings and stereotypes in texts and discusses their purpose and meaning.

Summary comment

Work sample A's recognition of simple symbols and stereotypical representations indicates progress towards level 3 outcomes. Work sample B shows a more complex understanding of the power of symbolism in the visual and verbal representation of stereotypes in texts and indicates the achievement of a level 3 outcome.

Work sample A

Work sample B

Work sample A
(3.6) Identifies the symbolic significance of colour (black) and clothing (pointed hat) in the representation of stereotypes (**A**); explains understanding of how writers and illustrators use these symbols (**B**); recognises a recurring character type and their traits by drawing some simple, stereotypical features of a 'baddie' (**C**).

Work sample B
(3.6) Identifies the symbolic significance of: colour (green, exotically made-up face and purple hair of the woman in contrast to blonde hair and rugged features of the man), clothing (well-dressed woman, raggedly dressed man), behaviour (calm woman, crying man), objects (the sack of coins representing the woman's greed) (**D**); recognises the stereotypical representation of good and evil by contrasting the two characters (**E**); indicates evil by showing contradiction between the woman's words (in speech bubble) and her thoughts (in speech cloud) (**F**); attributes a simple, heartfelt statement to the father (**G**); contrasts father's statement with woman's relatively long rationalisation (**H**).

Task

Students were required to keep a written logbook of responses to their reading of texts of their own choice.

Background

The teacher and students' parents read and sometimes respond in writing to the students' written comments about their reading.

Relevant outcomes

3.5 Interprets and discusses some relationships between ideas, information and events in:

– written texts with familiar content and a small range of unfamiliar words and linguistic structures and features…

Summary comment

The logbook extracts show reading of a range of narrative texts typical of this level in their linguistic and conceptual complexity. The written responses indicate the achievement of a level 3 outcome by their interpretation of meaning, engagement with the stories and attention to key ideas and relationships.

4-8-92
Hooray for pig! I loved it becouse pig lernt to swim becouse Otter tort him. finshed
4-8-92

5-8-92
Rabbit on Bear Mountain
I liked how woodchuck and skunk and Raccoon thourgt that Rabbit can't get up to the top of bear mountain but he Could the bet the rest.

Magic Bear - it had 3 storiys in side of it I liked Bears Magic Best.
10-8-92
Sara and the Pinch?
I liked how the class allways blamnd Sara for all the things she did So Mr Zamatsky's wood help her out of the truble.

6.8.92
Possum magic I m goyd it. It was and very nice and it was written by Mem Fox. finished 6-8-92
6-8-92
The Useless Donkeys
I thought it was bourying all thear was to it was the to Useless Donkeys.

12-8-92
Desperate for a Dog
I liked how the kids allways Were asking for a Dog then One day there neighbour had to go into hospital and she had a Dog and So the kids had to look after it then one day when they come home from school they saw Dad playing waith Toby. then One day they got a dog.
12-8-92 nfinshd

18-8-92
Nina's Machines.
I think it was ex becouse Nina kept on manking machines like her cat got all the mice and then she maid a dusting machine and lots more <u>see you now</u>

Reskusdownunder.
I think it was perficttit.

24-8-92
Jessy Runs away.
Jessy semes to allways run away but I dont no wig. One time she sees a buttfly drees so she gous of and looks at when she come back she cant see her sister or her mum or Dad

19-8-92
The Velveteen Rabbit
I think it was ok.
Because the boy loved the Rabbit so much that he was real.
24-8-92
Jacko. Jacko was relly good because Jacko tolld lots of storys but they wernt troow but they seemd troow.

(3.5) Reads for personal enjoyment and interest short stories and novels written for younger readers (**A**); explains opinions about texts read, giving attention to main ideas and supporting details and elements such as key events, main characters and setting (**B**).

Reading response proformas

Task

Students were required to complete response to reading proformas before, during and after reading texts.

Background

Proforma 1 was developed to assist the student to reflect on a short novel, *Who's George?* by Helen Gibson, thought by the teacher likely to cause difficulties. The student was asked to choose three events from the text and a) summarise the content (what happened?), b) reflect on the action (what I think about what happened), c) consider personal responses to the fictional circumstances (what I would have done instead), d) reflect on cultural differences (is it different to the Nunga way?). Point d) is particularly relevant to this class because all students are of Aboriginal background. The

(3.5) Reads for personal enjoyment and information novels and stories written for younger readers (**A**); retells and discusses interpretation of narrative texts read, giving attention to key events, main characters and setting (**B**); reads and compares stories told long ago, identifying different aspects of each (**C**); considers own possible reaction to a fictional situation (**D**); considers events in a text in relation to own cultural experience (**E**).

(3.6) Identifies the symbolic and cultural significance of Dreaming stories (**F**); considers how people from different social and cultural groups are represented in texts and compares these representations with own experience (**G**).

(3.7) Recognises and identifies the main features of Dreaming stories (**H**); compares similarities between two texts of the same type, such as Dreaming stories (**I**); identifies distinct events within a story (**J**).

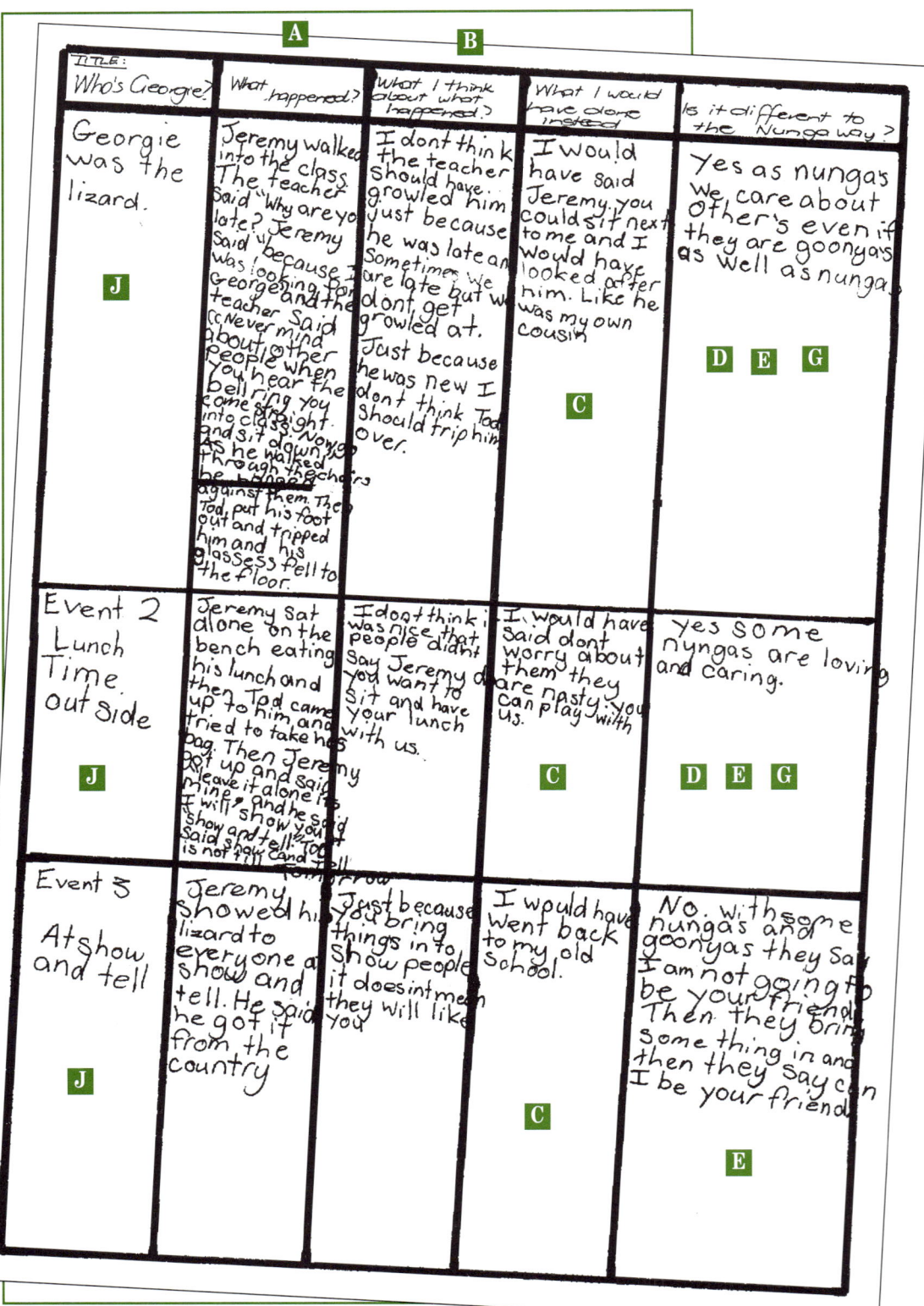

teacher encourages students to first consider texts from the perspective of their own cultural experiences as they often have difficulty responding to texts unless given the chance to compare the two cultures they live in. ('Nunga' means Aboriginal person. 'Goonya' means white person.)

Proforma 2 was developed to assist the students' understanding of Dreaming stories. (Definitions: Narrunga–the people of Yorke Peninsula area, Ngarrindjeri–people of south-eastern South Australia, pondi–a large fish, Ngurunderi–an important person in Ngarrindjeri history.)

Relevant outcomes

3.5 Interprets and discusses some relationships between ideas, information and events in:

– written texts with familiar content and a small range of unfamiliar words and linguistic structures and features...

3.6 Identifies simple symbolic meanings and stereotypes in texts and discusses their purpose and meaning.

3.7 Identifies and uses the linguistic structures and features characteristic of a range of text types to construct meaning.

Summary comment

The work samples involve texts of linguistic and conceptual complexity typical of level 3 and provide evidence of ability to reflect on key ideas, information and events in them. The work samples also indicate awareness of how the cultural orientation of the reader can affect interpretation of a text, which shows growth towards achievement of the level 4 outcome 4.6.

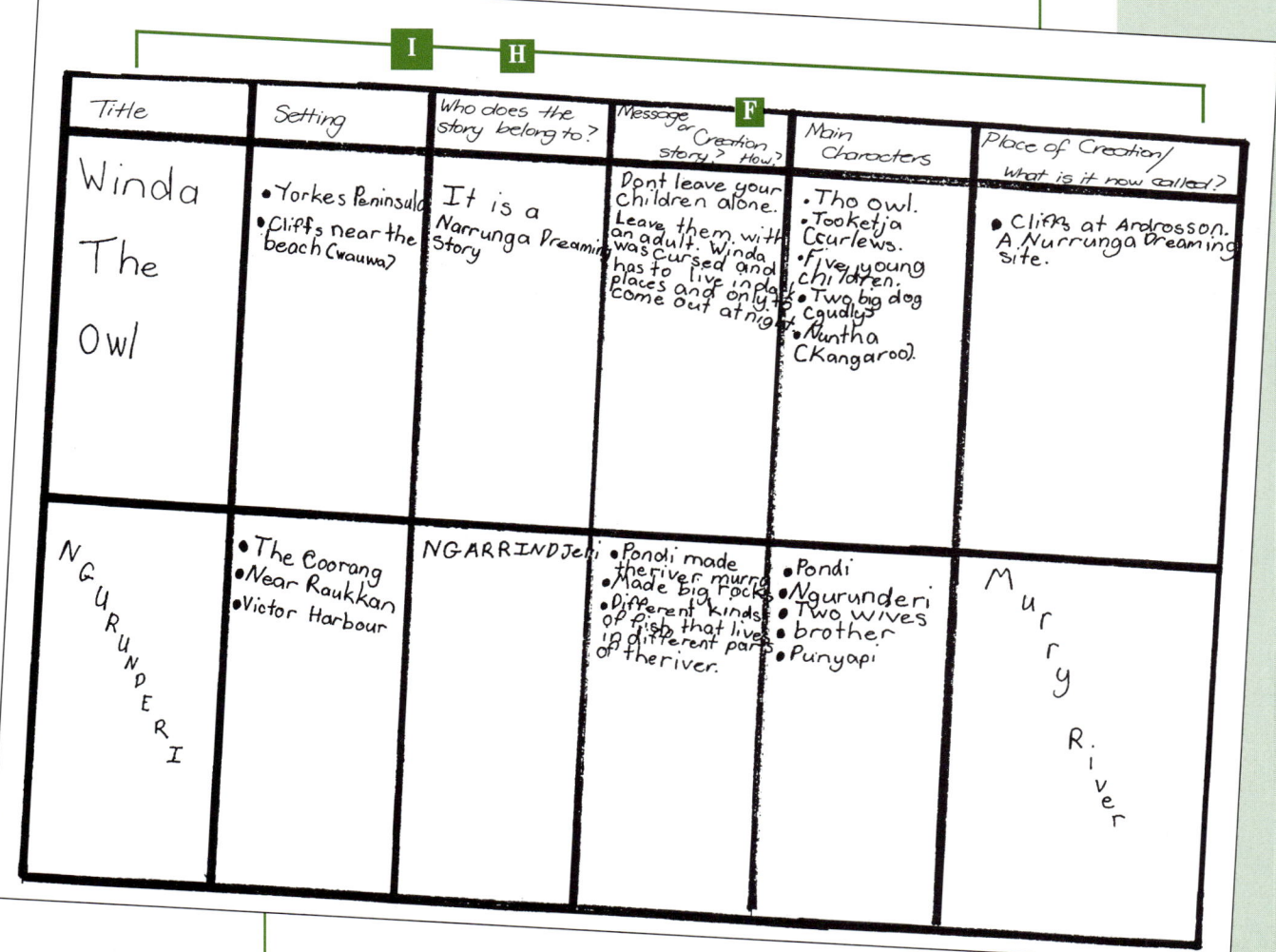

Title	Setting	Who does the story belong to?	Message or Creation story > How?	Main Characters	Place of Creation/ what is it now called?
Winda The Owl	• Yorkes Peninsula • Cliffs near the beach (waauwa)	It is a Narrunga Dreaming Story	Dont leave your children alone. Leave them with an adult. Winda was Cursed and has to live in dark places and only to come out at night	• Tho owl. • Tooketja Ccurlews. • Five young children. • Two big dog Cqudlys • Nuntha (Kangaroo).	• Cliffs at Ardrosson. A Nurrunga Dreaming site.
Ngurunderi	• The Coorang • Near Raukkan • Victor Harbour	NGARRINDJeri	• Pondi made the river murray • Made big rocks • Different kinds of fish that lives in different parts of the river.	• Pondi • Ngurunderi • Two wives • brother • Punyapi	Murry River

Oral reading, retelling, reading log and journal

Task

The student was required to discuss with the teacher a book recently read, *Callie's Castle*, by Ruth Park, read aloud to the teacher an extract from the text, and make entries in a reading journal and reading record.

Background

As part of the classroom reading program, students choose texts from the school and classroom library to read both in and out of school. They keep a record of texts read, using these headings: date started, kind of text, name of text, author or section, choice, source (F friend, S school library, C class library), interest rating 1 to 5, readability rating 1 to 5, date finished. Students sometimes record their impressions of texts in a reading journal.

Relevant outcomes:

Speaking and listening

3.1 Interacts for specific purposes with people in the classroom and school community using a small range of text types.

3.3 Usually uses linguistic structures and features of spoken language appropriately for expressing and interpreting ideas and information.

Reading and viewing

3.5 Interprets and discusses some relationships between ideas, information and events in:

– written texts with familiar content and a small range of unfamiliar words and linguistic structures and features...

3.8a Integrates a variety of strategies for interpreting printed and visual texts.

Summary comment

The transcript provides evidence of ability to interpret a challenging text for this level and the ability to consider relationships between key events in the text. (Level 4 achievement would require a summary of the plot or an attempt to comment on the overall themes and issues raised.) The record of reading indicates use of strategic reading behaviours and, even if not always successful, sound efforts to identify unknown words. These show that having achieved outcome 3.4a, the student is now working within outcome 4.4a.

The transcript records a worthwhile discussion with the teacher, distinguished from level 2 achievement by the extended nature of the responses. Level 4 achievement would require less prompting by the teacher's questions.

(3.5) Reads for personal enjoyment and interest novels produced for independent readers (**A**); retells and discusses interpretation of the text with attention to key events, main characters and setting (**B**); makes some inferences about information and ideas implicit (not literally stated) in a text (**C**); puts self in place of the main character (**D**); relates events and people in texts to own experiences (**E**).

A

I

Date Started	Kind of text	Name of text	Section - if newspaper; Author - if book etc.	Choice	Source	Interest Rating	Readability Rating	Date Finished
10-2-93	cartoon	Peter Pan	Eric Kincaid	Because Because I like peter Pan	F Chapter book	5	3	1-3-93
2-3-93	cartoon	speedy	Colin Thiele	Becous I red it becr	S chapter book	5	2	20-3-93
19-3-93	cartoon	Blinky bill	Yoram gross	hes cute	S capter book	5	2	2-3-93 28 m
27th	Story	Silver brumbies of the south	Elyne J Mitchell	Because it about horses	S chapter book	1	2	3 m
29th	Story	karen's school trip.	Ann M. Mar'en	Becaus it is interesting	S chapter book	5	4	10h
4th	Story	Callies Castle	Ruth Lack	Becaus I didnt hav e a book	C chapter book	5	3	
20th may	Story	Sally & Rebecca	Mary Brigus White	Because the cover looked interesting	F chapter book			
21 may	Story	Sky maze	Gillan Rubinstein	Becaues it Sounded interesting when I Read it.	S Chapter Book			

I

Record of oral reading.

As Callie came out of the school gate, she almost turned left along the way she used to walk to her old home. But when she heard Frances calling her, she ran off quickly in the right direction.

Until a week ago, Frances and she had been best friends. What had they quarrelled about? It had been something so small, so silly, that Callie couldn't remember it. She didn't want to, either, for the fight had ended with her blurting out such cruel things that now her face scorched at the thought of them.

To say such things to Frances! Callie nearly groaned aloud. And yet, as Frances came pounding along behind her, she turned in silence, putting on a hostile face.

"Oh, it's all right!" bristled Frances. "I don't want to talk to you. Mrs Wheeler said you were to give this to your mother."

Callie looked at the envelope, on which was written, *Mrs Beck, per courtesy of Carol.*

"Take it yourself!" she said.

Frances glowered. "No, I won't, you pig." She threw the letter on the ground and walked away.

Callie waited until Frances had disappeared around the corner. Then she picked up the letter and dawdled down the hill. She was worried. What was Mrs Wheeler writing to her mother about?

On the way home Callie had a day-dream about pushing that letter down a stormwater drain and saying nothing about it. But Mrs Wheeler would be sure to ask about it. All right then, stand up and say boldly, "My mother says you're a nutsy old lady. Teachers ought to stick to teaching and not write letters home about their pupils, my mother says."

Callie could just see Mrs Wheeler's face going red as everyone roared. That would fix her.

"It means child takes it."

"It means students"

(3.8a) Predicts and attempts to identify the meaning of unknown words through using strategies such as considering context, sounding out using knowledge of common letter combinations or initial letters, drawing on knowledge of grammar, sentence structure and text organisation (**F**); clarifies or corrects meaning where necessary by pausing, re-reading or reading on (**G**); adopts appropriate reading behaviours for the type of text and purpose for reading: ignores miscues which do not disrupt meaning, makes meaningful substitutions (**H**); shows awareness of the text's level of difficulty (**I**).

(3.1) Retells and offers opinions about scenes from the novel, with attention to character, setting and plot detail (**J**); expresses perceptions and feelings about experiences similar to those of characters in the novel (**K**).

(3.3) Usually accurately uses common grammatical structures such as subject/verb agreement, noun/pronoun agreement and consistency of tense (**L**); expresses logical relations in speech through the use of linking words such as 'although' 'instead of', 'so that' (**M**); uses appropriate expression when reading aloud from the text (**N**).

Continues next page

[F] "Fix her for what?" thought Callie deso- *dos, dos*
lately. *later*

Only *Just* last term she had loved Mrs Wheeler
generously, delighted when she was asked to
do something special, *or* proud when her mother

and stepfather had laughed at those jokes and

sayings of Mrs Wheeler's that she had retold.
Then, all of a sudden, (like) everything else,
Mrs Wheeler had turned sour.

Well, perhaps she could put the letter
[H] between the *two* pages of her social studies book
and forget about it.

[F] Callie stopped outside the hibiscus hedge [G] *hibiscus* *sc edge*
of their new house and opened *R* her school-
case. Just as she took the letter from her
pocket, her brother Dan wandered out of the
[H] gate. He was (as) thin and pale *stand* as a whitebait,
with frail silvery hair blowing over his brainy
skull.

Callies castle 26-5-92

[A] I am engoying the book so far. I like the
bit were Callie's brothers and sisters
go though all her personall pesesons. If
I was in that posititon I would
[E] get some were etsx else to put them, and.
put a padlock on it and put the key in
a safe place where little kids can't
get it.

Extracts of *Callie's Castle* by Ruth Park reprinted with
permission of the publisher, Angus & Robertson.

Transcript of teacher - student discussion about "Callie's castle" by Ruth Park

(Teacher's questions and responses in italics.)

B **J** It was about a girl who had brothers and sisters and she came home from school one day and her brothers and sisters had been in her room and they went through all her possessions... right through her diary and all her jewellery and, um, all this other stuff that she had kept from her father, cos her mother and father had split up and she had it in her diary and they had paints and glue all over it and all that and she was really mad and upset so she went to her mum... And her mum came and she said, her mum said, "Sorry" and she, she came, walked out of the room and her mum found this piece of diary and it said um "To dad, I wish you were here".

Had they been split up long or just a short time?

C It didn't really say but I think it was a fairly long time cause she saw him when she was about four so...

How old did you think Callie was now?

About 12 or 11

What made you think she was about 11 or 12?

C Well, the way that, um, how the story said that she had her grandpa and her brothers and sisters age.

What happened after her mum found that bit from the diary?

B **J** She came in and she goes, "You're not allowed to look at my diary" but she found it and she said "I'm really sorry". Then she went out and and, um, she ran away to her, um... grandpas and she, um, got some directions from someone else and ....

Did her grandfather live a long way away?

B **J** Um, yeah, well not very long.... she went by bus and and she um, and she went to her grandpa and her grandpa made her ....(?) and they do gardens and that sort of thing and they had a talk and you know she went back she goes"Oh, I'm really going to be in trouble because I ran away and her grandfather goes, "Well I'll talk to your mum".

That was nice of him. Is he like other granddads - what you would imagine other granddads would do?

E No, not like my granddad (laughter)

Don't you think all granddads would be as understanding as that one?

No

I notice a castle is in the title. Does it mention something about the castle in the story?

B Oh, she has, um, she has this dream house I think, um, I can't remember, um she has this dream house thing that she always goes to ... and she sort of pretends it's her bedroom but she calls it Carrie's castle.

Is it a real place or an imaginary place?

B It's an imaginary place in her bedroom.

Does eventually she ever get a real place of her own?

B Um, I think they get a new bedroom or something...

Has she got lots of brothers and sisters has she?

B Oh yeah she has and her mum babysits and she's got little kids that she babysits. ... and she's got this older brother who's about six.

What kind of person do you think Callie was ? What kind of girl was she?

B Um, understanding, like she doesn't like get all aggressive and start punching or anything. Like she can understand really well and she can sort of work things out.

Does she ever get cross do you think?

Oh like she would get a bit sad and cross but she wouldn't go punching and kicking anyone or anything like that I don't think ...

What was the most important part of the story to you? Or what was your favourite part?

B When, when she went to her grandfather's and had a talk to her grandfather.

......

The teacher went on to ask further probing questions about the student's interpretation of the text but received very short responses

Do you think it's important that people can have somewhere where they can go that they can call their own?

E Yes

Do you have a spot like that

E Yes, (describes her favourite place)

Do you think the character changed much at all through the story?

B She stayed the same

Do you think her mother came to understand her more after reading the diary?

B Yeah, I think she understands why she was. why she got mad cause her mum was reading the diary,

Rainbow bee eater report

Task

Students were required to write a structured research report.

Background

This task was one of a series of activities designed to develop students' research skills.
Students were asked to do the following:

1. Select a text on a topic they were researching.
2. Read it carefully to decide on the seven most important facts it contained.
3. List one fact on each of seven strips of paper (without referring back to the text).
4. Decide which fact to use first, order remainder or group similar facts.
5. Discuss information and organisation with others.
6. Write an expository piece summarising the information collected.

Relevant outcomes:
Reading and viewing

3.5 Interprets and discusses some relationships between ideas, information and events in:
– written texts with familiar content and a small range of unfamiliar words and linguistic structures and features, and
– visual texts designed for general viewing.

3.8b With teacher guidance, uses several strategies for identifying resources and finding information in texts.

Writing

3.9 Experiments with inter-relating ideas and information when writing about familiar topics within a small range of text types.

3.10 Recognises that certain text types and features are associated with particular purposes and audiences.

3.11 Controls most basic features of written language and experiments with some organisational and linguistic features of different text types.

3.12a Experiments with strategies for planning, reviewing and proofreading own writing.

3.12b Consistently makes informed attempts at spelling.

Summary comment

The sample features a sound response to the structured task. Many organisational and linguistic features of report writing are evident in the text, and the student uses the guidance provided by the task to plan, review and revise. The writing also demonstrates level 3 outcomes for reading. The fact strips indicate that the student is able to read and select relevant items from an informational text and discuss them in writing.

Typed version of text (final draft)
Rainbow Bee Eater

(3.9) Writes report that includes relevant information on several aspects of the topic, 'The Rainbow Bee Eater' (**A**).

(3.10) Readily adopts appropriate text type for this task, a factual report (**B**).

(3.11) Controls basic sentence structure (**C**); varies sentence beginnings and clause structure (**D**); inter-relate ideas in writing using 'because' (**E**); uses appropriate and varied vocabulary, such as 'immune', 'raided' (**F**); spells many common words accurately (**G**); writes legibly in the draft (**H**); presents final draft using consistent shape, size and slope (**I**); includes illustration to assist reader, but omits title in final draft (**J**); uses simple present tense to report information (**K**); sequences information logically, but omits the expected general classification (**L**).

(3.12a) Uses fact strips recorded from reading to organise ideas and information before writing (**M**);

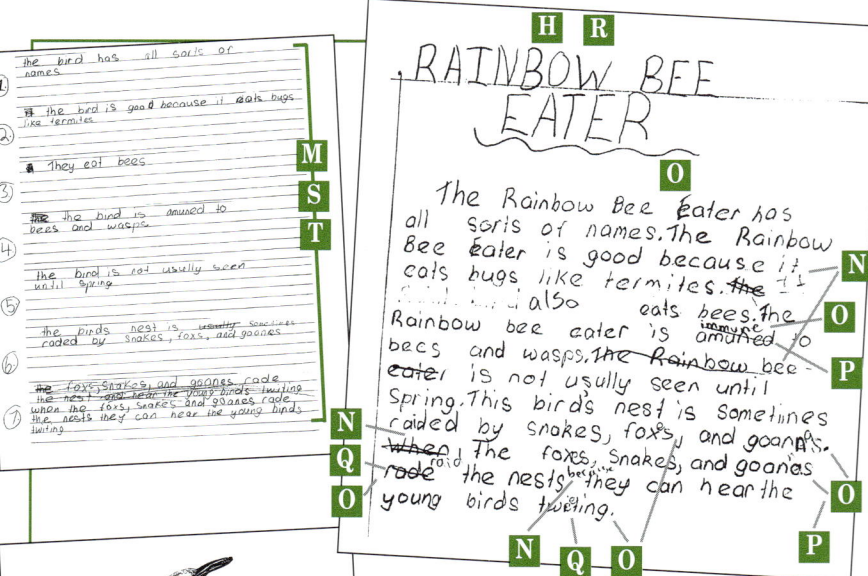

(3.12a) continued
attempts some revision during and after writing, for example, deletes and inserts words and phrases to clarify meaning and cohesion, substitutes 'it' to refer to name of the bird (**N**); proofreads to identify and correct spelling errors, incomplete sentences and missing punctuation (**O**).

(3.12b) Uses visual strategies, such as knowledge of letter patterns and critical features of words, to attempt to spell words, as in 'amuned', 'twiting', 'goanas' (**P**); draws on knowledge of some spelling generalisations to spell unknown words, as in 'rade' for raid, corrects 'foxs' and 'twieting' (**Q**); recognises most misspelt words in own writing and attempts correction (**R**).

(3.5) Uses an informational text to select material relevant to a research topic and summarises it in writing (**S**).

(3.8b) Carries out guided reading and uses fact strips to note items of information relevant to the topic (**T**).

The Rainbow Bee Eater has all sorts of names. The Rainbow Bee Eater is good because it eats bugs like termites. It also eats bees. The Rainbow Bee Eater is immune to bees and wasps. It is not usually seen until spring. This bird's nest is sometimes raided by snakes, foxes, and goannas. The foxes, snakes, and goannas raid the nests because they can hear the young birds twieting tweeting.

Why the kangaroo jumps: story

Task

Students were required to write a story modelled on Aboriginal Dreaming stories.

Background

As part of becoming familiar with the narrative text types, this class was read a number of examples of Aboriginal Dreaming stories and heard a guest speaker on the nature of these stories. Many books containing Dreaming stories were available in the classroom. The class had several discussions about the themes of Aboriginal Dreaming stories and their distinguishing linguistic structures and features. The whole class also wrote Dreaming stories, with the teacher acting as a scribe.

For this task, the students were given a short time to discuss their topics with a peer before writing their own stories.

The work featured here was reviewed alone by the writer, who did not request a discussion with the teacher before completing the final version.

Relevant outcomes

3.9 Experiments with interrelating ideas and information when writing about familiar topics within a small range of text types.

3.10 Recognises that certain text types and features are associated with particular purposes and audiences.

3.11 Controls most basic features of written language and experiments with some organisational and linguistic features of different text types.

3.12a Experiments with strategies for planning, reviewing and proofreading own writing.

3.12b Consistently makes informed attempts at spelling.

Summary Comment

The work sample provides evidence that the student appreciates the purpose of the text type, has grasped its essential features and can use these to write an effective text.

(3.9) Selects appropriate subject matter and writes an imaginative story modelled on Aboriginal Dreaming stories with a distinguishable storyline in which events are in clear sequence and interrelated (**A**).

(3.10) With teacher guidance examines models of the text type, discussing its purpose and distinguishing features (**B**); selects and uses an appropriate text type for the required task (**C**); uses language characteristic of Dreaming stories (**D**).

(3.11) Controls basic sentence structure (needs to work on this; placement of fullstops) (**E**); attempts to vary sentence beginnings and clause structure, ('Long, long ago...', 'All of the animals') (**F**); interrelates ideas in writing using 'and', 'but', 'so' (**G**); selects appropriate and varied vocabulary to enhance meaning, for example, 'evacuate', 'leapt' (**H**); spells many common words accurately in own writing (**I**); writes legibly in first draft (**J**); writes the final copy using consistent shape, size and slope and cursive script (**K**);

Typed version of text
Why the Kangaroo Jumps
Long Long ago in the dream time their was a bush fire. All of the animals had to evacuate but the kangaroo was to slow. And he was surrounded by a ring of fire the kangaroo new that he soon would die. So he leped over the fire and went on jumping for years and year and the kangaroos realised that it was much much easier to jump than to walk.

includes illustration to assist reader, but omits title in final draft (**L**); uses time order to sequence and organise writing of the story (**M**); uses past tense (**N**); writes in third person (**O**); structures writing with a clear setting and complication (**1**), middle/events (**2**), resolution/end(**3**), explanation (**4**) (**P**); sequences events in time order and attempts to show cause and effect (**Q**).

(3.12a) Circles spelling of 'evacuate' in first draft, corrects spelling and that of 'relised', 'srounded'and 'eaisar' in final draft (**R**).

(3.12b) Uses new words in own writing even though unsure of exact spelling, as in 'evacuwat' for evacuate, 'leped' for leapt (**S**); uses visual strategies, such as knowledge of letter patterns and critical features of words, to attempt to spell words, as in 'relised', 'srounded', 'eaisar' (**T**); sometimes combines different strategies (phonetic, visual and meaning-based) when attempting to spell words, as in 'srounded' (**U**).

LEVEL FOUR

LEVEL 4 Statement

Students who have achieved level four have a sound basic knowledge of how to use English. This enables them to experiment with their speaking, listening, reading, viewing and writing on different topics, and for different purposes, audiences and text types.

Students speak and listen for a variety of purposes. They are aware of the ways in which the considered use of speech can entertain, inform and influence others. They plan, rehearse and think about the way they listen and speak.

Students try to understand texts containing unfamiliar concepts and topics and which use language in relatively complex ways. They justify their own interpretations by referring to the text and to their own knowledge and experience. They are finding ways of dealing with difficult texts and working with peers on research tasks.

Students use familiar ideas and information in their writing, showing control over the way some basic text types are written. They try to adjust their writing to meet readers' needs and, prompted by the teacher, plan, review and proofread their prose.

LEVEL 4
Table of outcomes

	Texts	Contextual understanding	Linguistic structures & features	Strategies
SPEAKING AND LISTENING	4.1 Interacts confidently with others in a variety of situations to develop and present familiar ideas, events and information.	4.2 Considers aspects of context, purpose and audience when speaking and listening in familiar situations.	4.3 Controls most linguistic structures and features of spoken language for interpreting meaning and developing and presenting ideas and information in familiar situations.	4.4 Assists and monitors the communication patterns of self and others.
	See page 78	See page 78	See page 79	See page 79
READING AND VIEWING	4.5 Justifies own interpretation of ideas, information and events in texts containing some unfamiliar concepts and topics and which introduce relatively complex linguistic structures and features.	4.6 Explains possible reasons for people's varying interpretations of a text.	4.7 With teacher guidance, identifies and discusses how linguistic structures and features work to shape readers' and viewers' understanding of texts.	4.8 a Selects, uses and reflects on strategies appropriate for different texts and reading or viewing purposes. 4.8 b With peers, identifies information needs and finds resources for specific purposes.
	See page 80	See page 80	See page 81	See page 81
WRITING	4.9 Uses writing to develop familiar ideas, events and information.	4.10 Adjusts writing to take account of aspects of context, purpose and audience.	4.11 Controls most distinguishing linguistic structures and features of basic text types such as stories, procedures, reports and arguments.	4.12 a When prompted, uses a range of strategies for planning, reviewing and proofreading own writing. 4.12 b Uses a multi-strategy approach to spelling.
	See page 82	See page 82	See page 83	See page 83

LEVEL 4 Speaking and Listening

Level 3 outcomes:

3.1 Interacts for specific purposes with people in the classroom and school community using a small range of text types.

3.2 Recognises that certain types of spoken texts are associated with particular contexts and purposes.

3.3 Usually uses linguistic structures and features of spoken language appropriately for expressing and interpreting ideas and information.

3.4 Reflects on own approach to communication and the ways in which others interact.

Texts

At level 4, a student:

4.1 Interacts confidently with others in a variety of situations to develop and present familiar ideas, events and information.

Evident when students, for example:

- Present a strong point of view to friends in a group, offering some considered reasons or arguments.

- Listen attentively and respond constructively to other points of view in group and class discussions.

- Rehearse and tell a story to peers or younger children, using approaches that attempt to engage listeners.

- Prepare and present to the class a detailed account on a known topic, showing attention to quality of content, organisation and method of presentation.

- Prepare and present accurate summaries of decisions reached in group activities (the decisions the group was in favour of and the reasons for them).

- Prepare a short set of questions for an interview seeking information about an issue or topic.

- Offer explanations or lodge complaints which include one or two reasoned arguments.

- Listen and respond to short presentations or arguments that offer alternative viewpoints on a familiar issue (challenge or comment on a point made).

- Identify the main idea and supporting details of a spoken report and summarise it for others (presentations by peers or guest speakers on environmental issues, a current affairs report).

Contextual understanding

At level 4, a student:

4.2 Considers aspects of context, purpose and audience when speaking and listening in familiar situations.

Evident when students, for example:

- Select a suitable text type according to purpose for speaking.

- Recognise and discuss ways that physical conventions are used and understood differently in different socio-cultural contexts (that acceptable distance from others varies according to cultural factors, that eye contact may be regarded as aggressive, insolent or desirable according to context).

- Discuss situations where slang and colloquial language might be considered suitable or unsuitable (at a formal school event or in the news on radio or television).

- Consider when an audience is most likely to expect standard Australian English and discuss reasons.

- Recognise and discuss some indicators of socio-cultural bias or prejudice in spoken texts (a speaker's use of discriminatory language).

- Consider the needs of a familiar audience when preparing a spoken presentation (predict likely questions and prepare answers).

Linguistic structures & features

At level 4, a student:

4.3 Controls most linguistic structures and features of spoken language for interpreting meaning and developing and presenting ideas and information in familiar situations.

Evident when students, for example:

- Select, order and organise subject matter clearly for prepared spoken presentations (a report to the class, oral instructions to a group).

- Use conjunctions to interpret and express causal and temporal relationships between ideas in texts.

- Use pace, volume, pronunciation, enunciation and stress to enhance meaning (in a rehearsed reading of a story with dialogue).

- Use body movement, facial expression and gestures to enhance meaning (in a role in a play, telling a story).

- Recognise introductory phrases which indicate that an opinion is being offered ('I believe that…', 'I feel that …', 'In my opinion…').

- Adopt the grammatical patterns of standard Australian English where suitable (role-playing a television newsreader, making a formal presentation at a school assembly, introducing a guest speaker).

Strategies

At level 4, a student:

4.4 Assists and monitors the communication patterns of self and others.

Evident when students, for example:

- Tailor information or tone of voice to a listener's reaction (pause to think what to say next, summarise ideas, answer questions).

- Use strategies to assist small-group discussions (invite other group members to contribute; ask questions to help clarify others' viewpoints; negotiate — 'So, will we say…?' — to ensure that ideas are clearly understood and developed; justify feelings and opinions; volunteer relevant ideas and information; and elaborate and explain own point of view).

- Identify patterns in people's approaches to communicating (parody or roleplay distinctive communication styles).

- Listen and respond constructively to alternative ideas or viewpoints and express ideas and opinions without dominating discussions.

- Detect strategies speakers use to influence an audience (emotive language, one-sided presentation of information, exaggerated claims).

- Check own interpretation during a discussion by paraphrasing or summarising ('Are you saying…?' 'Do you mean…?').

- Make brief notes or tape record interviews for later review of information.

Level 5 outcomes

5.1   Interacts with peers in structured situations, using a variety of text types to discuss familiar or accessible subjects involving challenging ideas and issues.

5.2   Identifies the effect of context, audience and purpose on spoken texts.

5.3   Discusses and experiments with some linguistic structures and features that enable speakers to influence audiences.

5.4   Listens strategically and systematically records spoken information.

LEVEL 4 Reading and Viewing

Level 3 outcomes:

3.5 Interprets and discusses some relationships between ideas, information and events in:

– written texts with familiar content and a small range of unfamiliar words and linguistic structures and features

– visual texts designed for general viewing.

3.6 Identifies simple symbolic meanings and stereotypes in texts and discusses their purpose and meaning.

3.7 Identifies and uses the linguistic structures and features characteristic of a range of text types to construct meaning.

3.8a Integrates a variety of strategies for interpreting printed and visual texts.

3.8b With teacher guidance, uses several strategies for identifying resources and finding information in texts.

Texts

At level 4, a student:

4.5 Justifies own interpretation of ideas, information and events in texts containing some unfamiliar concepts and topics and which introduce relatively complex linguistic structures and features.

Evident when students, for example:

- Read for their own pleasure and interest novels and books of a series such as C.S. Lewis' *Narnia* stories and construct considered responses to them, justifying opinions with references to the text.

- Find information on an unfamiliar topic in reference sources such as encyclopedias and reference books, recognising the breadth of information in complex texts.

- Explore and discuss humour in stories, novels, film and television, showing an awareness of how humour is constructed (bizarre or unusual situations, events, people, dialogue as in Randolph Stow's *Midnite* or Lewis Carroll's *Jabberwocky*).

- With teacher guidance, identify another level of meaning in a text (allegory in a picture book such as Mem Fox's *Feathers and Fools* or a story such as Lilith Norman's *Dream of Seas*).

- Consider events in texts from characters' points of view (roleplay or write in the role of a character, being consistent with the original character).

- Discuss the treatment of information in articles from a magazine or tabloid newspaper and television news broadcasts on a local issue or newsworthy event (a large fire, a visit by a pop star).

- View a documentary film made for a general audience and extract information from the text using a set of key questions provided by the teacher (a documentary film on the life cycle of a crocodile).

- Justify interpretation of rock video clips, plays or print advertisements that use some abstract or symbolic images.

Contextual understanding

At level 4, a student:

4.6 Explains possible reasons for people's varying interpretations of a text.

Evident when students, for example:

- Recognise that interpretations of some texts are more readily agreed upon than others (compare agreement on the meaning of a stop sign with agreement on the motivation of a character from a novel such as Libby Hathorn's *Thunderwith*).

- Consider how their different interpretations of or reactions to a text can be explained (by differing purpose or circumstances when reading or viewing).

- Report on different interpretations of a text after a group discussion or interviewing people (what different people considered to be the reasons for a character's actions; whether they thought the resolution to a story was appropriate).

- Discuss and justify their own preferences for a particular interpretation of a text, referring to text details and their own knowledge and experience.

- Recognise that an interpretation of a text will be more readily accepted by others if evidence from the text supporting that interpretation is cited.

- Consider how changes to aspects of a text can alter people's interpretation of meaning such as reversing the roles of males and females in a novel, poem or play (consider the effects of making Judy a boy in Ethel Turner's *Seven Little Australians* or change the point of view from which Alfred Noyes' poem *The Highwayman* is narrated).

Linguistic structures & features

At level 4, a student:

4.7 With teacher guidance, identifies and discusses how linguistic structures and features work to shape readers' and viewers' understanding of texts.

Evident when students, for example:

- Justify inferences about information and ideas implicit in texts by referring to text features such as vocabulary and text structure.

- Discuss the effect of language forms such as figurative language, jargon and technical words in texts and the possible impact of these on different readers (ambiguity or conflicting messages).

- Recognise and discuss the purpose of important organisational elements of different types of text (main elements of story in narratives; main argument, supporting points and conclusion in persuasive texts; general statement and descriptive details in reports; acts and scenes in plays).

- Identify text features which may help readers to distinguish fact from opinion (use of 'I think…', 'It has been reported that…', citing of sources).

- Consider how logical relationships (time, cause and effect, comparison and addition) are signalled by linking words in texts (because, then, soon, first of all, after that, however, like, different from, otherwise, on the other hand).

- Identify the viewer position in visual texts and how this affects meaning (an over the shoulder shot from the point of view of one character looking at another).

- Recognise a variety of film and television genres from features of the setting and characters' dress (westerns, outback dramas).

- Discuss some techniques used to establish mood in films (sombre lighting to imply mystery or fear, music and sound effects to convey a variety of emotions).

Strategies

At level 4, a student:

4.8a Selects, uses and reflects on strategies appropriate for different texts and reading or viewing purposes.

Evident when students, for example:

- Use a range of automatic monitoring and self-correcting methods when reading (re-reading, reading on, slowing down, sub-vocalising).

- Use word identification strategies (apply knowledge of words and their parts such as root words, morphographs, prefixes).

- Select information important to the purpose for reading (scan a novel for sections that support a particular interpretation of a text).

- Attempt several strategies when reading more difficult texts such as Tolkien's *The Hobbit* or Kenneth Grahame's *Wind in the Willows* (talking to others about the ideas and information; keeping a reading log to reflect on interpretation; re-reading or re-viewing parts of the text; making notes about key features; consulting the index, contents page, diagrams; searching for links with personal experience).

- Make predictions about plot in film and television based on setting (underground car parks are often the scene of violent action).

4.8b With peers, identifies information needs and finds resources and information for specific purposes.

Evident when students, for example:

- Discuss with peers key characters and events in texts read and viewed to select information and ideas needed for particular tasks (writing a description of a character, describing conflict and its resolution).

- Work with peers to identify and narrow a research topic (brainstorm and cluster ideas, develop focus questions).

- Predict possible resources, considering a wide range of possibilities, and devise a search plan.

- Identify and locate resources by using a range of strategies (subject/key word/author/ title searches; consulting encyclopedias, atlases, yearbooks, data bases [PressCom and Nexus], CD-ROMs in the reference section of resource centres; considering and sometimes using information sources such as government departments, local people and organisations, magazines, pamphlets and newspapers).

- Make notes on focus questions and record details of research sources.

Level 5 outcomes:

5.5 Discusses themes and issues in accessible texts with challenging structures and ideas, and constructs responses interpreting these.

5.6 Recognises that texts are constructed for particular purposes and to appeal to certain groups.

5.7 Draws on knowledge of linguistic structures and features to explain how texts are constructed.

5.8a Uses knowledge of principal conventions of narrative texts to construct meaning from a range of text types.

5.8b Systematically finds and records information.

English profile

81

LEVEL 4 Writing

Level 3 outcomes:

3.9 Experiments with interrelating ideas and information when writing about familiar topics within a small range of text types.

3.10 Recognises that certain text types and features are associated with particular purposes and audiences.

3.11 Controls most basic features of written language and experiments with some organisational and linguistic features of different text types.

3.12a Experiments with strategies for planning, reviewing and proofreading own writing.

3.12b Consistently makes informed attempts at spelling.

Texts

At level 4, a student:

4.9 Uses writing to develop familiar ideas, events and information.

Evident when students, for example:

- Construct stories in which ideas, details and events are developed and relevant to the storyline.

- Argue in writing a position or point of view, raising a few related points in support of a thesis.

- Discuss in writing some pros and cons of a topical issue, attempting to relate these to one another.

- Construct an information report that elaborates on and classifies details on a number of aspects of the topic.

- Write a detailed description of a person, place or object, selecting details that develop an overall image of what is being described.

- Write a short play for a performance by peers in which characterisation is developed through events and dialogue.

- Create poetry in varying forms, attempting to use language economically to develop ideas or images.

- Incorporate some detailed description and reflection into a written account of a personal experience.

- Devise a set of explicit instructions that involve related steps (how to ride a bicycle).

- Experiment with humorous adaptations of standard text types to amuse or entertain readers.

Contextual understanding

At level 4, a student:

4.10 Adjusts writing to take account of aspects of context, purpose and audience.

Evident when students, for example:

- Consider and attempt to incorporate alternative viewpoints on an issue when writing to persuade others to a point of view.

- Recognise the importance of being well-informed on a topic when writing, doing extra research if necessary, especially if the purpose is to persuade others or to describe situations and events in a plausible way.

- Consider an audience's likely knowledge of a topic and provide helpful explanations or definitions.

- Explore options for influencing readers in writing (appeals to authority or emotions; use of humour).

- Recognise occasions where slang and colloquial language might be inappropriate and adjust writing style (letter to the editor, writing for formal, unknown audiences).

- Consider whether their own writing takes into account the interests and needs of potential readers (in a report, choose illustrative examples familiar to both girls and boys; avoid sexist or racist terms; consider how different readers will respond to characters' qualities and actions).

- Discuss influences on their own choice of topics for writing (film and television, reading preferences).

Linguistic structures & features

At level 4, a student:

4.11 Controls most distinguishing linguistic structures and features of basic text types such as stories, procedures, reports and arguments.

Evident when students, for example:

- Adopt organisational conventions when given a structured format for writing a particular type of text (write a story with a setting, problem, events and a resolution; a play with a setting, characters and dialogue; a report with a general introductory statement and information grouped under relevant headings; an explanation with a general statement, followed by a series of logical steps).

- Discuss with the teacher and peers how particular aspects of grammar are characteristic of particular text types and attempt to adopt these consistently in own writing (use of simple present tense in reports and procedures, use of imperative in instructions, use of particular kinds of conjunctions).

- Recognise meaningful divisions between sections of text and set these out as paragraphs.

- Use a range of conjunctions to indicate relationships between ideas in writing.

- Consistently use most common punctuation marks and discuss the purpose of less familiar punctuation in text models (dashes, colons and semi-colons).

- Select vocabulary for precise meaning and discuss the effect of vocabulary choices in their own writing and text models.

- Use a legible handwriting style and cursive script as required by audience and purpose for writing.

- Use a variety of print and script styles to emphasise or highlight parts of the text (bold or underlined headings, italics, capitals).

Strategies

At level 4, a student:

4.12a When prompted, uses a range of strategies for planning, reviewing and proofreading own writing.

Evident when students, for example:

- Plan writing through discussion with others and by making notes, lists or drawing diagrams.

- Record information from a variety of sources before writing.

- Decide when help is needed with writing and know where to get it (go to friend for an idea, or to a thesaurus or dictionary for the best word or spelling).

- Attempt to rearrange sections of text to improve organisation of ideas.

- Use a variety of drafting techniques (crossing out, cutting and pasting, using carets or arrows to show insertions).

- Use a checklist to guide proofreading of their own and others' completed texts.

- Respond to others' writing with specific and constructive comment ('Where you've written... I think you should... because...').

- Monitor their own progress as writer (keep dated records of discussions about writing with teacher and peers, noting points to be acted upon).

4.12b Uses a multi-strategy approach to spelling.

Evident when students, for example:

- Recognise most misspelt words and attempt corrections through an understanding of word usage, including visual and phonic patterns, word derivations and meanings.

- Use letters to represent all vowel and consonant sounds in a word.

- Use visual strategies, such as recognition of common letter patterns and critical features of words (silent letters).

- Use knowledge of word parts (prefixes, suffixes, compound words, sign – signature).

Level 5 outcomes:

5.9   Uses a variety of text types for writing about familiar or accessible subjects and exploring challenging ideas and issues.

5.10   Identifies the specific effect of context, audience and purpose on written texts.

5.11   Controls the linguistic structures and features necessary to communicate ideas and information clearly in written texts of some length and complexity.

5.12   Draws on planning and review strategies that assist in effectively completing particular tasks.

The day the dinosaur egg hatched

Task

Students were required to write a narrative to entertain peers.

Background

Students were asked to write a narrative based on a title selected from a list suggested by the teacher and students. The student chose 'The day the dinosaur egg hatched' and spoke to a small group about a plan for the story.

A draft and the final version were completed in a week during three class writing sessions. The student showed the text to other students as it progressed but did not seek teacher assistance before writing the final version.

Relevant outcomes

4.9   Uses writing to develop familiar ideas, events and information.

4.10   Adjusts writing to take account of aspects of context, purpose and audience.

4.11   Controls most distinguishing linguistic structures and features of basic text types such as stories, procedures, reports and arguments.

4.12a When prompted, uses a range of strategies for planning, reviewing and proofreading own writing.

4.12b Uses a multi-strategy approach to spelling.

Summary comment

The sample is typical of level 4 work because it shows control of basic story structure and draws on everyday subject matter. Language use and story are somewhat stilted to an experienced reader but reflect a good grasp of the choices writers can make when constructing stories to suit particular audiences.

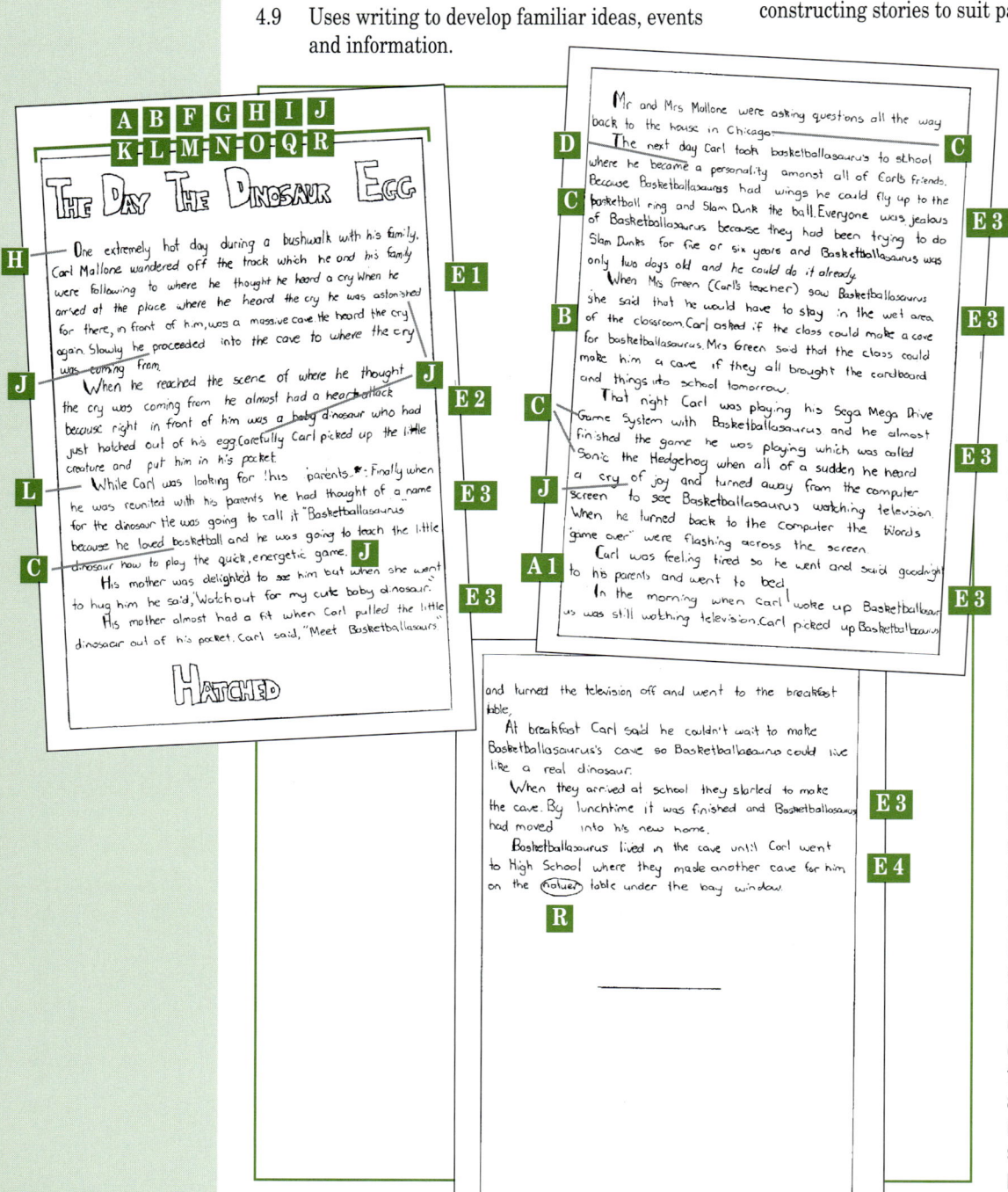

(4.9) Constructs an imaginative story in which ideas, details and events are developed and relevant to the overall storyline, although some extraneous details are included such as going to bed (**A**); selects familiar subject matter on which to base the events of the story (**B**).

(4.10) Selects events and subject matter such as basketball, video games, setting in an American city that will appeal to an audience of peers (**C**); attributes characteristics to main character (ability to 'slam dunk', popularity with others) likely to appeal to intended readers (**D**).

(4.11) Writes a story with a clear organising structure, that is, a setting (1), problem (2), series of related events (3) and a resolution (4) (**E**); uses paragraphs to signal meaningful divisions between sections of the text (**F**); uses a range of conjunctions (because, but, if, so, while, and, until) to show relationships between ideas (**G**); uses a variety of complex sentences, for example, first sentence (**H**); consistently uses most common punctuation marks: fullstops, commas, apostrophes, quotation marks, capital letters (**I**); selects words and phrases for precise meaning, as in

The Day The Dinosaur Egg Hatched

One extremely hot day during a bushwalk with his family, Carl Mallone wandered off the track which he and his family were following to where he thought he heard a cry. When he arrived at the place where he heard the cry he was astonished, for there, in front of him, was a massive cave. He heard the cry again. Slowly he proceeded into the cave to where the cry was coming from.

When he reached the scene of where he thought the cry was coming from he almost had a heart-attack because right in front of him was a baby dinosaur who had just hatched out of his egg. Carefully Carl picked up the little creature and put him in his pocket.

While Carl was looking for his parents he was thinking of a name for the little dinosaur. Finally when he was reunited with his parents he had thought of a name for the dinosaur. He was going to call it "Basketballasaurus" because he loved basketball and he was going to teach the cute little dinosaur how to play the quick energetic game.

His mother was delighted to see him but when she went to hug him he said, "Watch out for my cute baby dinosaur."

His mother almost had a fit when Carl pulled the little dinosaur out of his pocket. Carl said, "Meet Basketballasaurus."

Mr and Mrs Mallone were asking questions all the way back to the house in Chicago.

The next day Carl took Basketballasaurus to school where he became a personality amongst all of Carl's friends. Because Basketballasaurus had wings he could fly up to the basketball ring and slam Dunk the ball. Everyone was jealous of Basketballasaurus because they had been trying to do slam dunks for five or six years and Basketballasaurus was only two days old and he could do it already.

When Mrs Green (Carl's teacher) saw Basketballasaurus she said that he would have to stay in the wet area of the classroom. Carl asked if the Class could make him a Cave. Mrs Green said that the children could make a cave for Basketballasaurus if they all brought the cardboard and things in to school tomorrow.

That night Carl was playing his Sega MegaDrive Game system with Basketballasaurus and he almost finished the game he was playing which was called Sonic the Hedgehog when all of a sudden he heard a cry of joy and turned away from the computer screen to see Basketball-asaurus watching television. When he turned back to the computer the words "Game Over" were flashing across the screen.

Carl was feeling tired so he went and said goodnight to his parents and went to bed.

In the morning when Carl woke up Basketballasaurus was still watching television. Carl picked up Basketballasaurus and turned the television off and went to the breakfast table.

At breakfast Carl said he couldn't wait to make Basketballasaurus's cave so Basketballasaurus could live like a real dinosaur should.

When they arrived at school they started to make the cave. By lunchtime it was finished and Basketballasaurus had moved into his new home.

Basketballasaurus lived in the cave until Carl went to High School where they made another cave for him on the nature table under the bay window.

'extremely hot', 'astonished', 'proceeded', 'carefully', 'quick, energetic game' (**J**); uses a legible handwriting style in both drafts (**K**); uses a special script style for first letter of each paragraph to enhance presentation of final version (**L**); maintains use of past tense and third person throughout (**M**); spells the majority of words in the draft correctly (**N**).

(4.12a) Teacher's notes indicate that the student discussed ideas with others, re-read text while writing to maintain meaning, used dictionary to check spelling (**O**); reviews text during and after writing first draft by changing and inserting words and phrases to enhance clarity of meaning, for example, 'it' became 'the quick, energetic game', added 'cute' and 'little' to describe the dinosaur (**P**); proofreads first draft effectively for spelling, punctuation and grammar (**Q**).

(4.12b) Recognises most misspelt words and corrects them independently (**R**); uses visual strategies, such as recognition of common letter patterns and critical features of words, for example, changes 'herd' to heard (**S**).

Church visit

Task

Students were required to write a formal letter of request.

Background

The students were asked to write a letter asking Mr B if the class could visit the local church and graveyard. As a group, they discussed why they wanted to go, when, and revised the setting out of formal letters. The class worked on their letters for four 30-minute writing sessions over the week.

Relevant outcomes

4.9 Uses writing to develop familiar ideas, events and information.

4.10 Adjusts writing to take account of aspects of context, purpose and audience.

4.11 Controls most distinguishing linguistic structures and features of basic text types such as stories, procedures, reports and arguments.

4.12a When prompted, uses a range of strategies for planning, reviewing and proofreading own writing.

4.12b Uses a multi-strategy approach to spelling.

Summary comment

The sample indicates control over the basic text type used. A number of strategies for convincing the reader to accede to the request are attempted, providing a good grounding in writing persuasively about more complex issues (a feature of level 5).

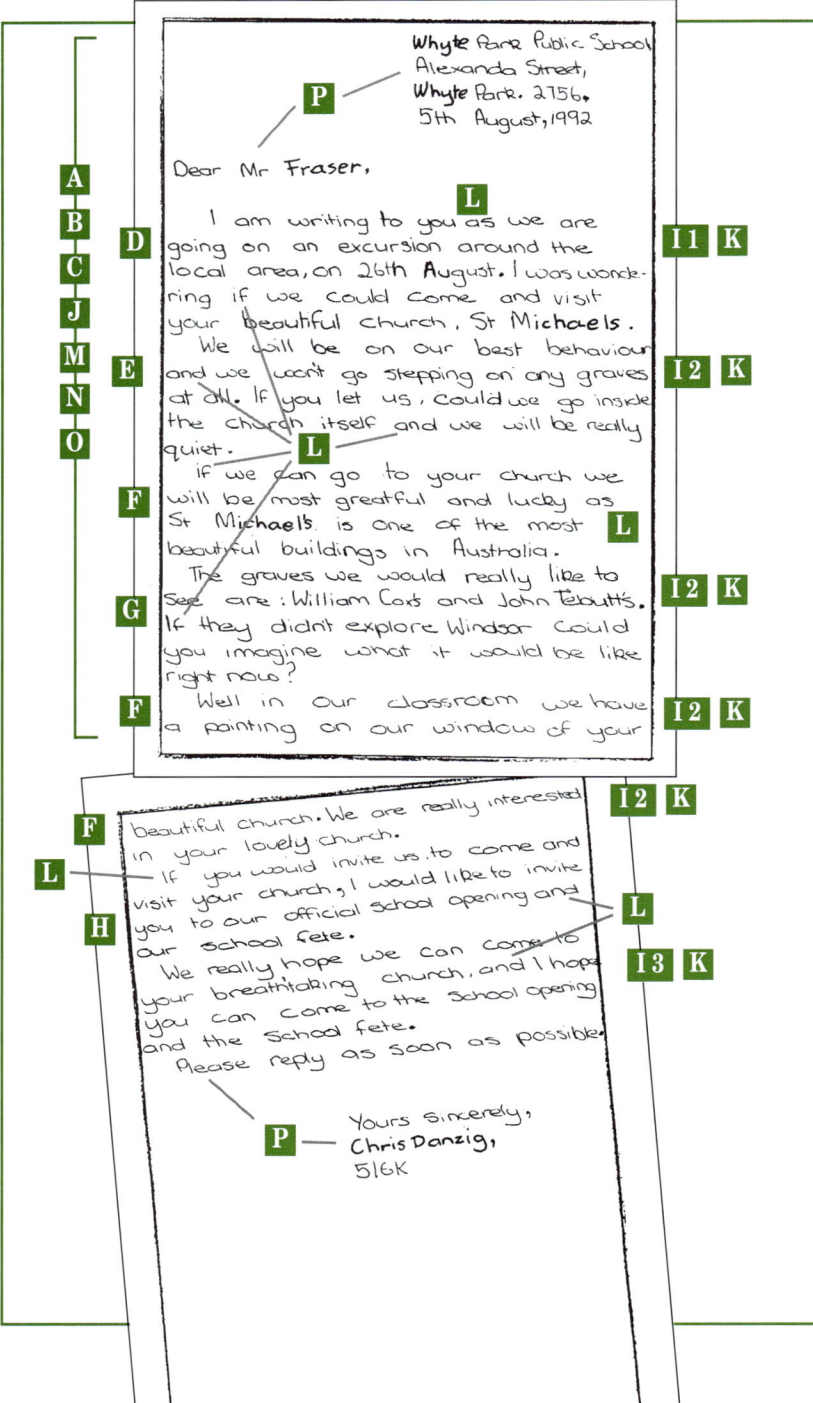

(4.9) Letter requesting permission raises several related points in support of the request (**A**); selects appropriate subject matter: draws on knowledge of the church's significance and history to attempt to convince reader of the importance of visit (**B**).

(4.10) Adjusts writing style to purpose: uses a formal, almost pleading tone to influence the reader (**C**); provides information about the request: date of proposed visit (**D**); considers reasons why the reader may refuse the request and addresses them, for example, behaviour, not stepping on graves, being quiet (**E**); attempts to influence the reader by making positive remarks about the church's features, (its 'breathtaking beauty') and the students' interest in seeing it and their appreciation if allowed to (**F**); tries to convince the reader of the importance of the request: rhetorical question emphasises significance of the explorers whose graves are in the graveyard (**G**); offers something in return for the request being granted: invitation to the official opening of the school fete (**H**).

(4.11) Organises ideas and information clearly and sequences reasons logically: introduction (1), reasons (2) and conclusion (3) (**I**); uses first person and present and future tense correctly (**J**); recognises meaningful divisions between sections of text and set these out as paragraphs — one each for the introduction and conclusion and one for each argument (**K**); uses conjunctions (as, if, and) to indicate inter-relationships between ideas in writing (**L**); consistently uses most common punctuation marks (**M**); selects words and phrases with attention to precise and effective meaning: 'really quiet', 'best behaviour', 'really interested', 'beautiful church', 'lovely church', 'breathtaking church', 'most grateful and lucky', 'could you imagine' (**N**); uses a legible handwriting style in both draft and final copy (**O**); uses conventional letter format accurately, as in address, salutation, ending (**P**).

(4.12a) Discusses ideas with others before writing (see task background) (**Q**); considers knowledge relevant to the writing task: has seen church before, knowledge of explorers buried in the church graveyard (**R**); re-reads work during writing to maintain sequence and meaning, change words and phrases or check for errors (indicated by crossing out) (**S**); amends text during and after writing the first draft by changing and inserting words and phrases to enhance clarity of meaning: inserts descriptive words, chooses a word of more precise meaning, provides more detail (**T**); proofreads draft effectively: corrects spelling, punctuation and grammar (**U**).

4.12b Recognises most misspelt words and attempts correction, reflecting an understanding of word usage, including visual and phonic patterns, word derivations and meaning (**V**); recognises common letter patterns and critical features of words as in 'sincearly', 'greatful', 'possable' (**W**).

Q R S T U V W

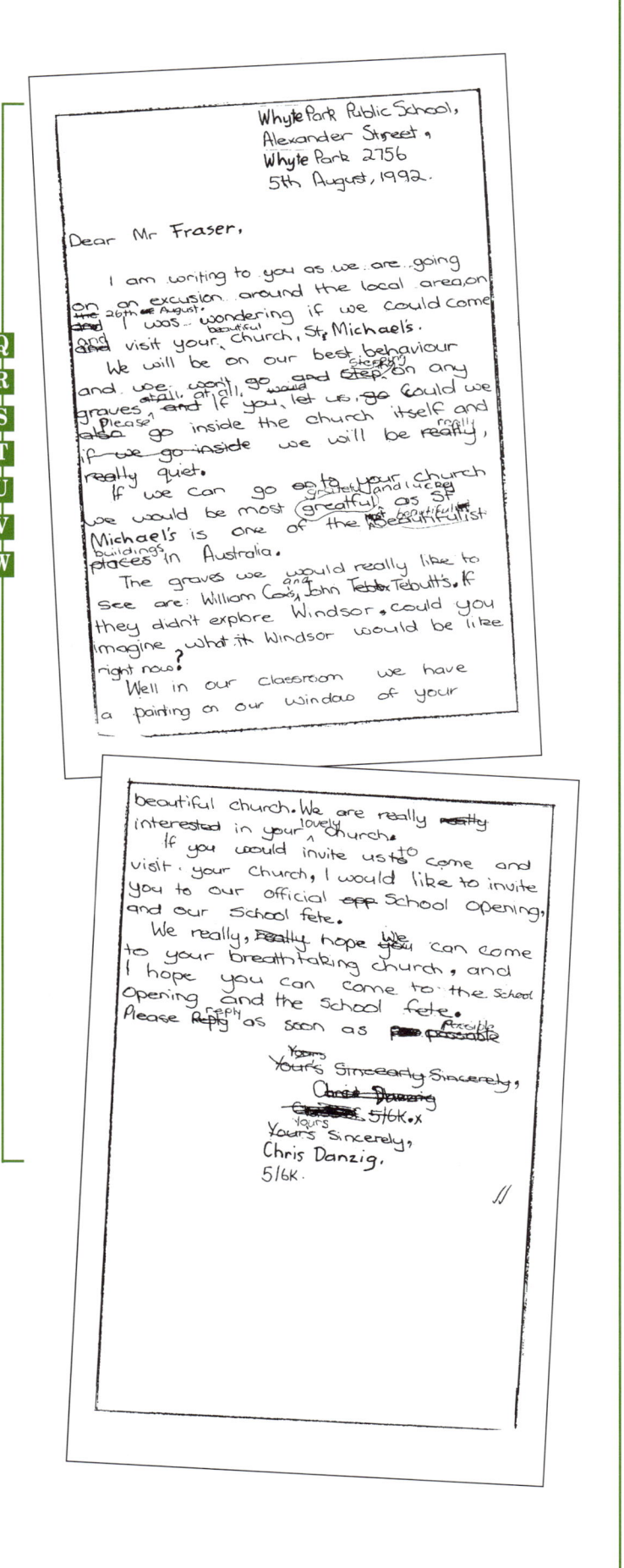

How to teach year 7s

Task

Students were required to write a set of amusing instructions.

Background

Students had three sessions on how to write instructions before this task. They were given a range of examples of instructions and encouraged to find others. Common features and purposes of the text type were identified in a model provided before students wrote joint efforts and their own instructions. The students chose their own topics, purposes, and audiences for writing their own humorous instructions, using the model as a guide. The teacher provided a simple guide for planning their writing, and students were allowed about two hours to draft, review and discuss their writing with peers and to proofread before 'publishing' their completed texts.

Relevant outcomes

4.9   Uses writing to develop familiar ideas, events and information.

4.10 Adjusts writing to take account of aspects of context, purpose and audience.

4.11 Controls most distinguishing linguistic structures and features of basic text types such as stories, procedures, reports and arguments.

4.12a When prompted, uses a range of strategies for planning, reviewing and proofreading own writing.

4.12b Uses a multi-strategy approach to spelling.

Summary comment

The sample provides evidence of achievement of all the level 4 outcomes. The parody shows control over the linguistic structures and features of the text type and an awareness of the need to adjust writing to suit context, purpose and audience. These features help distinguish it from level 3 work.

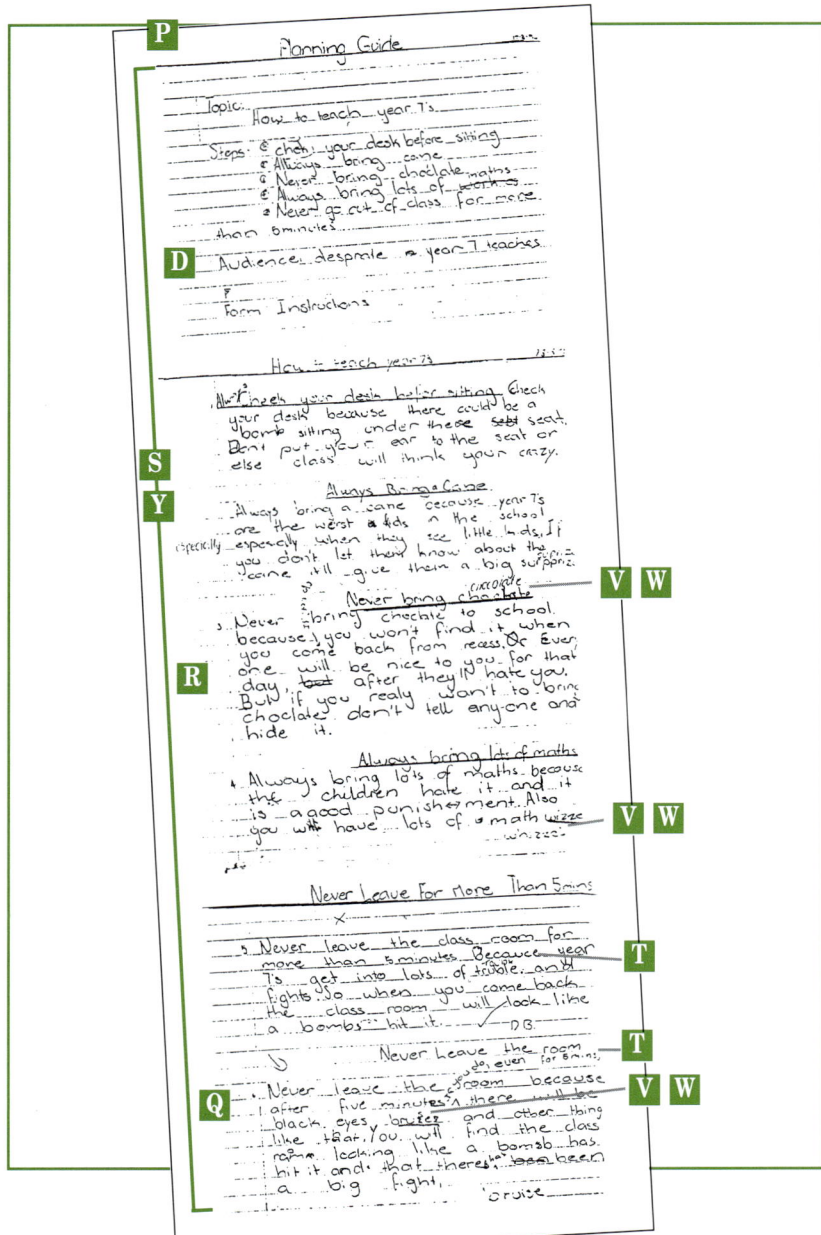

(4.9) Experiments with a humorous adaptation of standard instructional writing to amuse or entertain readers by parodying instructions for teaching year 7s (**A**); selects familiar ideas about the characteristics of students and how they might behave. Develops them by incorporating explicit explanations for each instruction (**B**); achieves a humorous effect through content selection (**C**).

(4.10) Content indicates that the student has considered the characteristics of the imaginary audience, as in 'desperate year 7 teachers' and items likely to appeal to the readers (peers) (**D**); achieves humorous effect by providing explicit explanations or warnings for each instruction (**E**); adjusts writing style to purpose and audience by adopting the tone of formal instructions and a colloquial style to appeal to peer readers — see H, I, M (**F**).

(4.11) Adopts organisational conventions (instruction-explanation sequence, groups these under sub-headings) based on the model provided (**G**); uses imperative form and timeless present tense to achieve correct tone (**H**); uses colloquial vocabulary ('crazy', 'kids') to achieve appropriate style (**I**); sets out each instruction as a separate paragraph with a sub-heading (**J**); uses a range of conjunctions (if, because, but, or) to indicate inter-relationships between ideas in each section (**K**); consistently uses most common punctuation marks correctly (**L**); selects words ('always', 'never',) with attention to precise meaning (**M**); uses a legible handwriting style in draft and presents work effectively with titles, borders and diagrams (**N**); uses a variety of devices (block and underlined headings, all capitals, layout decisions) to emphasise or highlight parts of the text (**O**).

(4.12a) Plans writing by making notes using teacher's guide and through discussion with others: decides on five instructions before attempting to write explanations (**P**); rewrites unsatisfactory sections of text: instruction 5 completely rewritten (**Q**); uses a variety of drafting techniques such as crossing out, cutting and pasting, and using carets or arrows to show insertions (**R**); proofreads own text thoroughly (**S**); re-reads work during writing to maintain sequence and meaning, change words and phrases or check for errors, as shown by changes on the draft (**T**); uses peers as resources for developing and improving the draft (according to teacher, made changes to the text following discussions) (**U**).

(4.12b) Recognises most misspelt words in the draft and corrects them (**V**); misspellings indicate understanding of visual and phonic patterns, as in 'brusez' for bruises and 'wizzes' for whizzes (**W**); uses letters to represent all vowel and consonant sounds and syllables in an attempted spelling (**X**); recognises

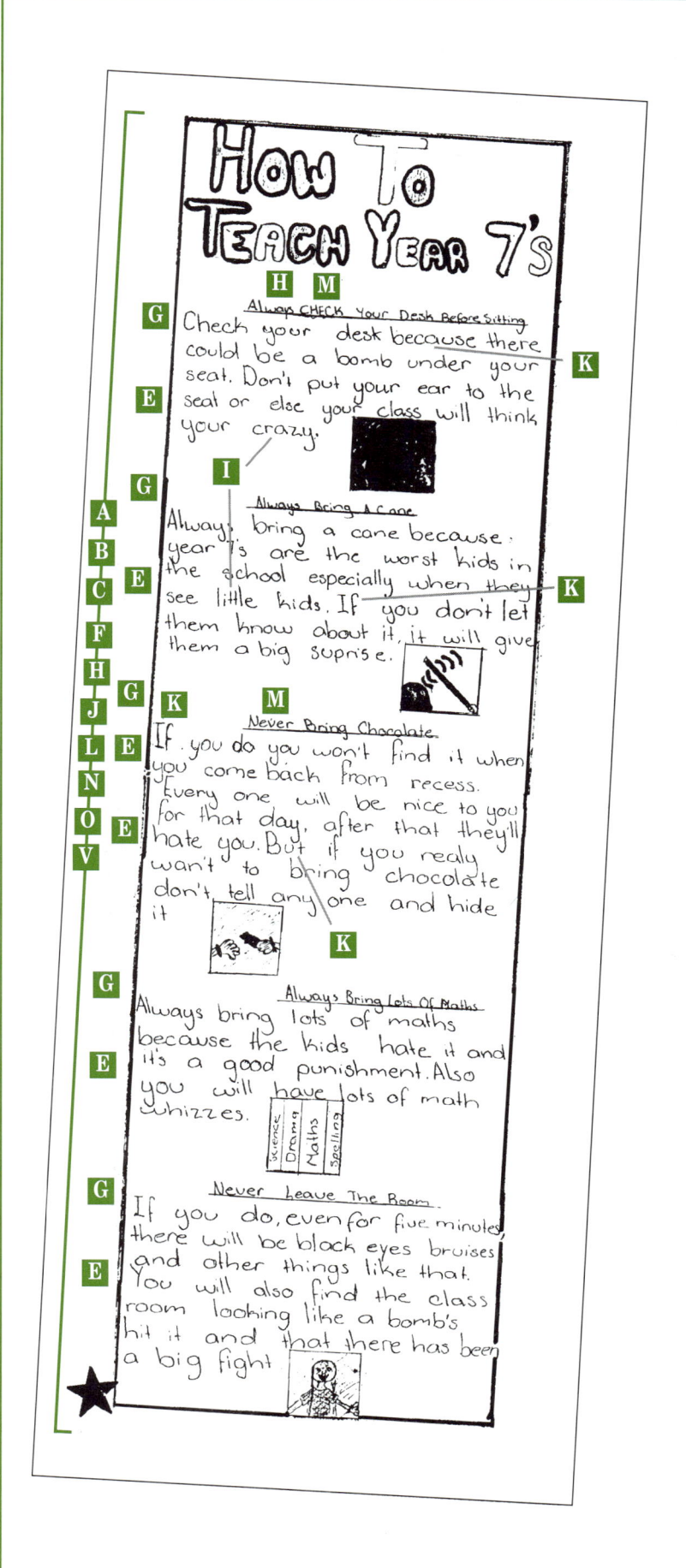

Compare and contrast two novels

Task

Students were required to compare and contrast elements of two books. They chose *Crumbs* by Emily Rodda and *George Speaks* by Dick King-Smith.

Background

Students choose their own reading material from the school library. Reading follow-up activities are selected in consultation with the teacher. This was one of several available. The student had read these books independently during the school year . (The framework for the activity comes from Macon, J.M., *Responses to Literature Grades K-8*, International Reading Association.)

Relevant outcomes

4.5 Justifies own interpretation of ideas, information and events in texts containing some unfamiliar concepts and topics and which introduce relatively complex linguistic structures and features.

Summary comment

The student uses the compare and contrast framework provided by the teacher to reflect on, analyse and justify interpretation of the text. The teacher's notes suggest that the student referred more explicitly to examples from both texts when speaking on the work to the class. Level 5 achievement would require consideration of the themes and issues underlying the texts.

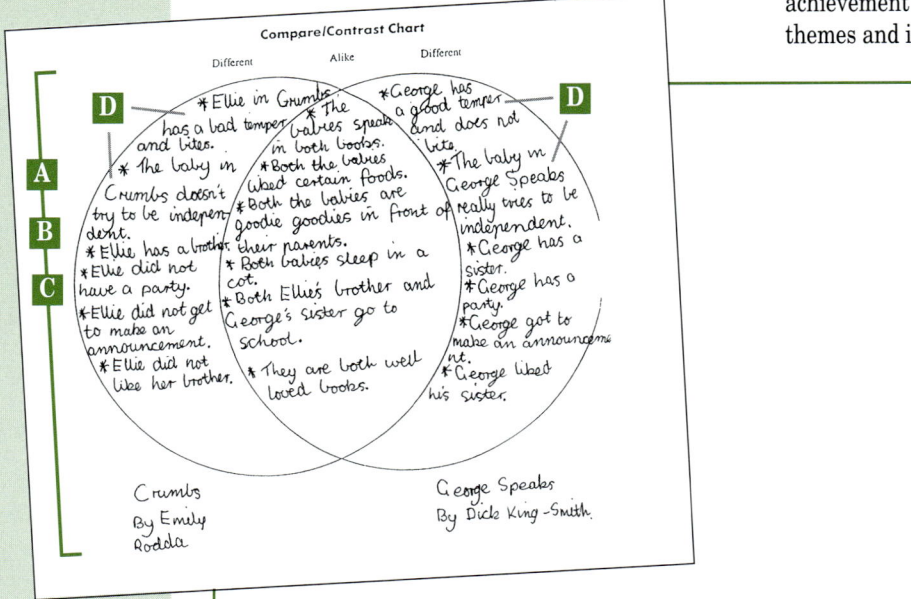

(4.5) Reads extended novels for own pleasure and interest and makes considered responses to these, justifying opinions by referring to the text (**A**); refers to incidents from the texts to make comparisons and contrasts (**B**); categorises similarities and differences between characters (**C**); evaluates characters' behaviour and makes generalisations based on own interpretation (**D**); expresses opinions about the texts (**E**); gives examples to explain similarities and difference between the texts (**F**).

Task

Students were required to fill in a feelings chart after reading *The Shell* by Colin Theile.

Background

Students were asked to list the feelings they experienced while reading the story and then to identify the words in the text that produced these feelings. Students compared and discussed their charts with one another in small groups.

Relevant outcomes

4.5 Justifies own interpretation of ideas, information and events in texts containing some unfamiliar concepts and topics and which introduce relatively complex linguistic structures and features.

4.6 Explains possible reasons for people's varying interpretations of a text.

4.7 With teacher guidance, identifies and discusses how linguistic structures and features work to shape readers' and viewers' understanding of texts.

Summary comment

The work sample indicates explicit awareness of the ways in which the author's use of imagery through selection of vocabulary and sentence structure influence personal interpretation of the text.

(4.5) Identifies a range of personal feelings generated by reading of the text (**A**); refers to the text to justify own interpretation of it (**B**).

(4.6) The teacher's notes indicate that, in group discussion, the student realised that other students experienced similar and different emotions in response to the text, and that the ways in which others interpret the words of a text can vary (**C**); finds and quotes sections of a text to explain own interpretations and feelings (**D**).

(4.7) Recognises that vocabulary, content and sentence structure can be manipulated to influence readers in particular ways: identifies metaphors ('The green sea swept into the shallows and seethed there like slaking quicklime.'); identifies similes ('the seas — like a cat rubbing its back against his legs'); identifies simple literal sentences that create feelings and atmosphere (**E**).

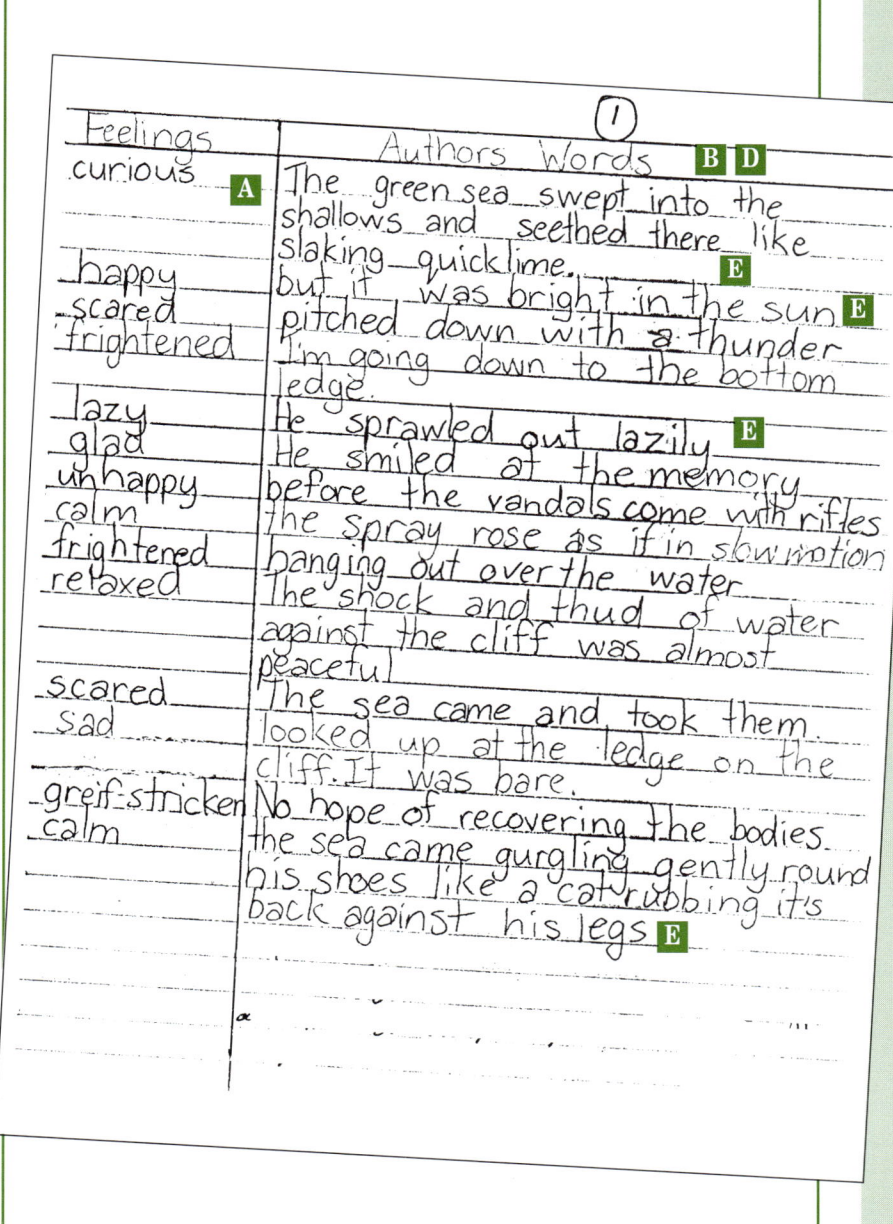

Newspaper story

Task

Students were required to read and discuss a short newspaper article headlined 'Dog victim out of hospital' and to complete three tasks: 1, retell the story from as many points of view as possible; 2, complete a fact–opinion chart listing key phrases under each heading; 3, rewrite the article in various text types — fantasy, a factual report, science fiction, historical fiction and and fable. Key words were underlined and written down before each task.

Background

Students had read and discussed controversial newspaper articles throughout the year. They had done oral retellings from different points of view. The 'indicator words' which suggest opinion had been introduced and searched for in other articles. The class was familiar with phrases such as, 'it is claimed', 'it was alleged', 'it appears', 'it has been suggested' and others as indicators that the writer is expressing an opinion. Most text types had been discussed and read to the class. They had also written a variety of text types and were familiar with their features. This task was completed over two one-hour sessions.

Relevant outcomes:
Reading and viewing

4.5 Justifies own interpretation of ideas, information and events in texts containing some unfamiliar concepts and topics and which introduce relatively complex linguistic structures and features.

4.6 Explains possible reasons for people's varying interpretations of a text.

4.7 With teacher guidance, identifies and discusses how linguistic structures and features work to shape readers' and viewers' understanding of texts.

4.8a Selects, uses and reflects on strategies appropriate for different texts and reading or viewing purposes.

Writing

4.9 Uses writing to develop familiar ideas, events and information.

4.10 Adjusts writing to take account of aspects of context, purpose and audience.

4.11 Controls most distinguishing linguistic structures and features of basic text types such as stories, procedures, reports and arguments.

Summary comment

The work sample indicates achievement of level 4 outcomes for both reading and writing. While the newspaper text is not particularly complex, the work shows careful analysis and interpretation of the ways in which the English language can be manipulated to influence readers' interpretation of texts. This, together with the obvious control over a variety of basic written text types, marks the sample as level 4 work.

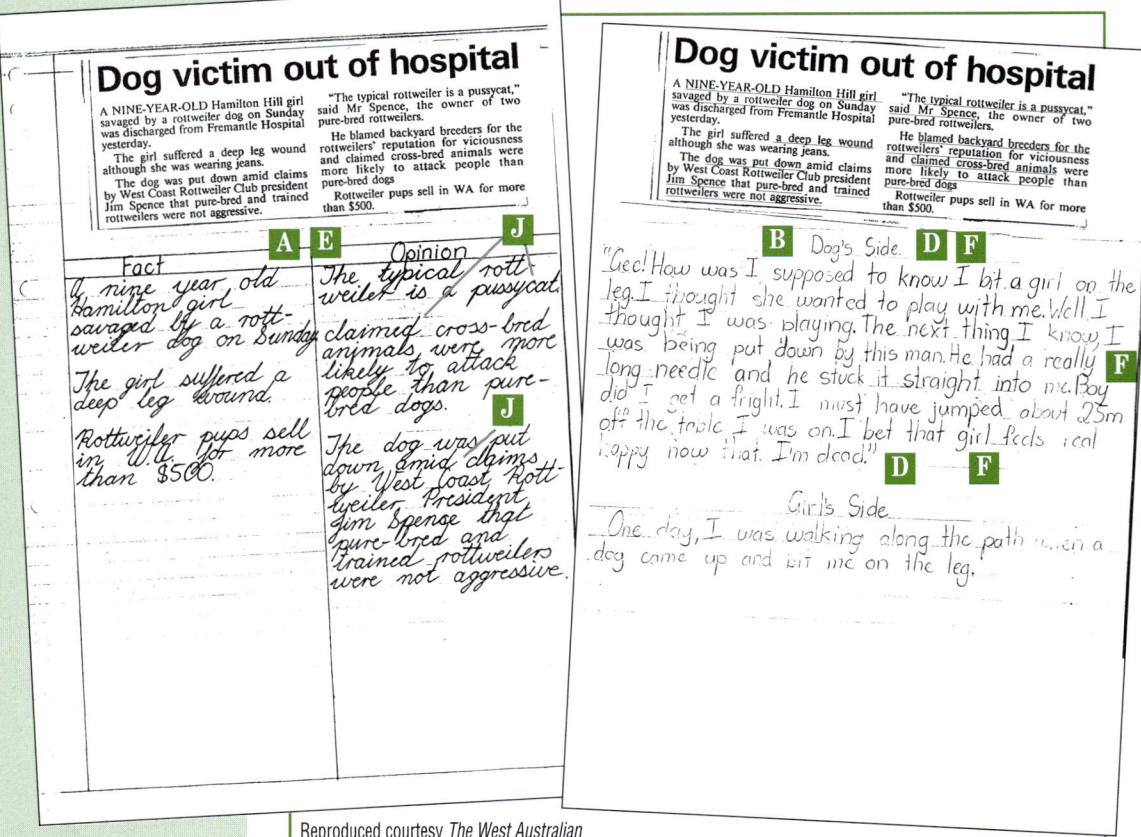

Reproduced courtesy *The West Australian*

(4.9) Considers the treatment of information in the article: whether it is fact or opinion (**A**); rewrites the text from a different point of view, showing insight into selection and omission of information (**B**); analyses and produces various interpretations of the information in the newspaper article (**C**).

(4.6) Recognises that the writer's point of view influences construction of texts and the ways they are interpreted by readers: writes from a different point of view (**D**); considers how the presentation of fact and opinion in the text can influence readers' interpretation of the news story (**E**); changes aspects of the text to influence people's interpretation of meaning: reports factual information from a different point of view with differing opinions expressed; presents facts in different settings; rewrites in different text types; selects and omits information according to purpose — includes information about the way the dog was put down and omits details about the severity of the girl's wound (**F**).

(4.7 and 4.11) Selects content and vocabulary to suit different purposes for writing and with attention to precise meaning (**G**); constructs appropriate settings for each type of story (**H**); recognises and uses the key organisational stages of different types of text: narrative structure for historical fiction, science fiction, fantasy; news report structure; fable structure (**I**); identifies and uses linguistic features that distinguish fact from opinion (**J**); interprets and uses a range of conjunctions for indicating logical relationships between ideas in writing (time, cause-and-effect, comparison and addition) (**K**); uses aspects of grammar characteristic of particular text types in own writing: past tense in narratives (**L**); recognises meaningful divisions between text sections and sets these out as paragraphs (**M**); consistently uses most common punctuation marks within an acceptable range of style options and discusses the purpose of less familiar punctuation in text models (**N**); uses a legible handwriting style, cursive script and clear layout with headings (**O**).

(4.8a) Identifies key words in the newspaper story to guide content decisions for the various writing tasks (**P**); ignores information irrelevant to each writing purpose (**Q**); adopts different reader and writer roles to explore alternative interpretations and constructions of a text (**R**).

Research activity

Task

Students were required to complete independently a guided research and report writing activity.

Background

The teacher gave the students the framework for a small independent research task on the topic 'Dragonflies'. She asked them to devise focus questions about the topic, read and extract key information from several texts, construct a concept map organising this information, and finally to write an organised, concise scientific report on their research. Students were given a headings framework for the report. All aspects of the activity were familiar to the students from tasks undertaken with teacher assistance earlier in the year. The teacher revised these before this activity.

Relevant outcomes: Reading and viewing

4.5 Justifies own interpretation of ideas, information and events in texts containing some unfamiliar concepts and topics and which introduce relatively complex linguistic structures and features.

4.8a Selects, uses and reflects on strategies appropriate for different texts and reading or viewing purposes.

4.8b With peers, identifies information needs and finds resources for specific purposes.

Writing

4.9 Uses writing to develop familiar ideas, events and information.

4.11 Controls most distinguishing linguistic structures and features of basic text types such as stories, procedures, reports and arguments.

Summary comment

The work samples show ability to carry out the reading and writing aspects of the research task guided by the teacher's frameworks. The work is typical of level 4 in that it deals with a straightforward topic and develops research and reporting skills.

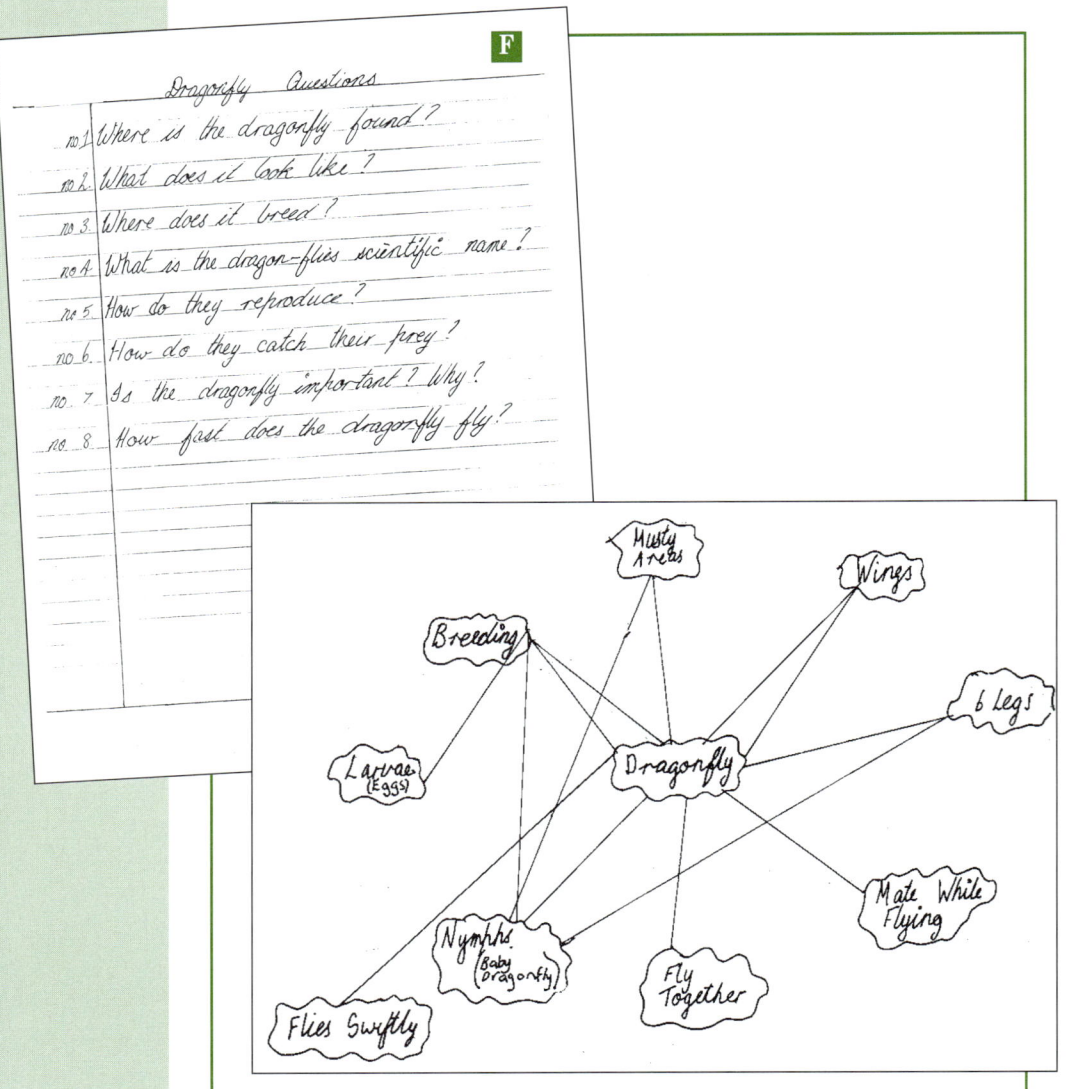

F

Dragonfly Questions

no 1 Where is the dragonfly found?
no 2 What does it look like?
no 3 Where does it breed?
no 4 What is the dragon-flies scientific name?
no 5 How do they reproduce?
no 6 How do they catch their prey?
no 7 Is the dragonfly important? Why?
no 8 How fast does the dragonfly fly?

(4.5) Finds information on an unfamiliar topic in reference material such as encyclopedias and reference books (**A**); draws together and reports on relevant information from more than one source: bibliography (**B**); presents accurate information drawn from reading (**C**).

(4.8a) Selects key information relevant from reading and ignores irrelevant information (**D**); skims and scans texts to find relevant information (**E**).

(4.8b) Develops and records focus questions before reading (**F**); constructs a concept map as a strategy for organising information gathered from texts, using colour coding as an aid (**G**); devises extra sub-headings based on focus questions for inclusion in the written report: Eating habits, Flying, and Reproduction (**H**); skims and scans texts to find relevant information (**I**); records details of sources for notes (**J**); identifies key information and supporting detail in appropriate texts (**K**).

N O P Q R S

DRAGONFLIES

M Classification - There are 5,000 different species of dragonfly. Its scientific name is Australopetalia patricia.

M **T** Description - The dragonfly has 4 large wings which are fragile. The body is red, green or blue. The markings are white, yellow or black. The dragonfly has large compound eyes covering most of the head and 6 legs covered in spines.
Baby dragonflies are called Nymphs. They have thick bodies, big heads and mouths and no wings when they are first hatched. Nymphs have a folding lower lip called a mask which is half as long as their body. The lip has a hook to catch its prey.

M Location - Dragonflies are found in many different habitats. Some of these places are:
Australia
Europe
North America and
Deserts of Nevada

M **H** Dynamics - Eating Habits - The dragonfly catches its prey with its legs or jaw. It can eat its prey while flying. Nymphs feed on small fish and other small water animals.
Flying - It can fly upto 80-97 Km an hour. The dragonfly flies so swiftly it can escape from most of its prey.
Reproduction - The male and female dragonfly usually fly together, occasionally the male while in flight. The female deposits her eggs in water or inside the stem of a plant. The nymph hatches within 1-2 weeks. The nymph remains in water 1-5 years. It sheds its skin about 12 times. On the last molt the nymph climbs onto a rock or reed and sheds its skin for the last time. It finally emerges as an adult and can soon fly.

M Summary - Dragonflies are a common insect and are not in any danger of becoming extinct. They are found in several parts of the world.

A B J

Bibliography

Encyclopedia of the Animal World.
Published by Bay Books PTY LTD
Sydney 1977

The World book Encyclopedia

The World book Encyclopedia

(4.9) Produces an information report that elaborates on and classifies details relevant to a number of aspects of the topic (**L**).

(4.11) Adopts suitable organisational conventions using the teacher's format for report writing: a general introductory statement, information grouped under relevant headings, summary comment (**M**); uses grammatical features typical of reports, such as simple present tense (**N**); recognises text sections and sets these out as paragraphs (**O**); uses a range of conjunctions to indicate relationships between ideas (**P**); consistently uses most common punctuation marks within an acceptable range (**Q**); uses a legible handwriting style and cursive script appropriate to purpose (**R**); lays out written text effectively (**S**); uses a variety of print and script styles to emphasise or highlight parts of the text: bold or underlined headings, italics, all capitals (**T**).

Bullants lecture

Task

Students were required to present to the class a short lecture based on a factual report they had researched and written as project work.

Background

The teacher modelled a short lecture and discussed elements such as voice projection and using palm cards as prompts. Homework and a small amount of class time were allocated for preparation of the lecture.

Relevant outcomes

4.1 Interacts confidently with others in a variety of situations in order to develop and present familiar ideas, events and information.

4.2 Considers aspects of context, purpose and audience when speaking and listening in familiar situations.

4.3 Controls most linguistic structures and features of spoken language for interpreting meaning and developing and presenting ideas and information in familiar situations.

4.4 Assists and monitors the communication patterns of self and others.

Summary comment

The work sample shows thorough treatment of straightforward information in a formal presentation for peers. It is distinguished from level 3 work in that there is no extraneous information and most points are well-developed and illustrated. The relaxed but formal presentation shows some evidence that the student is beginning to work within level 5 of the contextual understandings outcome.

---

a. Palm (cue) cards used by student to guide spoken presentation.

1.
Bull Ant
Insect
Hymenoptera
All insects that follow
this order have
wings in one
stage of their
life.

A
E

2.
Bull ant
LARGE HORN
Shaped JAS. CATCH-
ING INSECTS
JAWS Also HOLDING +
CARRYING FOOD,
LARVAE + EGGS (Picture) **D**
GROWS 40mm. HAIRS +
LONG Antennae Sensors
LARGE EYES see very
well. Long strong legs,
Move quickly
Poisonous stinger, Abdomen
ward off Predators.

3.
Bull-ants live in underground
nests, Norm' Rainforests in
North East Aus. Bull-ants foud
Many Towns + Cities, Rainforests
may have once been.
3 stages, Larvae Pupae + Adult.
population. 5-6 hundred B'-ants.
Queen lays spe' eggs. larger, worker
or Soldier, ← Queens + Males.
Wings, fly from nest, Mate.
Male dies Queen Digs sm nest
lays eggs in it. Worker + Soldier
ants. This cycle repeats itself
continually.

4. Bull -ant talks, antennae or
behaviour.
4 types bull ants nest Queen
Male, Worker + Soldier B'- ants
S' bigger, larger heads + jaws.
Tougher skin than Worker ants
Queen+ young larvae, fed
infertile eggs, laid by workers.
Older larvae eat have fed insects
workers caught. ¿ Soldier + Worker
ants eat nectar or honey Dew from
other insects.
D Book, Head, Abdomen, thorax,
Picture of Bull ant.

(4.1) Prepares and presents a detailed spoken account on a known topic to the class, showing attention to quality and organisation of content and presentation (**A**).

(4.2) Selects a suitable text type for the purpose (factual report) (**B**); considers occasions when an audience is likely to expect standard Australian English (**C**); considers need to illustrate information with visual aids (**D**); considers the needs of a familiar audience (classmates) when preparing a spoken presentation: predicts questions and prepares answers, uses palm cards to plan and prompt (**E**).

(4.3) Selects, sequences and organises subject matter clearly; assists listeners by giving a general introduction and grouping information:

b. Transcript of 'lecturette'

[F] Bullants are insects which follow the order hymenopetra.
(Prompting from children to say good morning.)
Oh! My project is on Bullants. All insects follow this order at least one stage in their life.
Bullants have large horn-shaped jaws used for catching other insects. (Looks at chart of
[D] bullants.) The jaws are also used for holding and carrying, um, prey as I've already said, **[H]**
and um, eggs. (Looks at chart and points.) The jaws are here. **[D] [K] [L]**
[F] The bullant isn't actually that long, it's only about four centimetres long. **[Q]**
They have antennae which they use as sensors which are here. (Points to chart.) It's a bit
hard to see (refers to poster, points). They also use for sensors their hairs on their bodies, **[B]**
which are here (points to chart). They have long, strong legs which enable them to move
very quickly. There's also a stinger on the end of their body (points). They use this to
ward off enemies. **[D] [K] [L]**
[F] Bullants live in underground nests in North East Australia, normally in rainforests. **[C]**
[F] Bullants are found in many towns and cities where rainforests have once been.
[F] There are three stages in a bullant's life — larva, pupae, adult.
[F] Once the population reaches about 500 or 600 the queen ant lays special ants which are
larger than regular or soldier ants. These are young queens and males. Shortly after ... **[G]**
when they are grown, they fly from the nest and mate. After this the male dies ... (uses
hands) and, um, the queen flies down and drops its wings and digs a nest and lays eggs
and these are the worker and soldier ants to start the new nest. This cycle repeats itself
continually. (Refers to palm cards, pause.) **[H]**
[F] Bullants can talk to one another by using their antennae or by their behaviour.
There are four types of bullant in the nest. Queen, male, soldier and worker ants. Soldier **[I]**
[F] ants are bigger and stronger than worker ants. They have large heads (points to his head)
[D] and (looking at chart) larger jaws than worker ants. The queens and young larvae are fed **[K]**
[F] on infertile eggs laid by males. Old larvae are fed by insects that workers have caught. **[Q]**
[H] The soldier and worker ants eat honeydew and nectar. Honeydew comes form other
insects, some caterpillars and some beetles. The ants (softly) treat this honeydew ... and **[M]**
protect (hands) the insects that feed it to them from other insects, like the praying-mantis.
[D] This is a bullants' nest. (Shows project.) That shows, this shows the head, thorax,
abdomen, stinger and the... (Puts project back on display stand.)
[F] That's all I have today. Does anyone have any questions? ...Yes? **[H]**
A: Do the workers and soldiers have any eggs?
Student: No, they don't have eggs. **[P]**
B: What ant...What bullant lives the longest, like, does the queen live the
        longest?
[P] Student: Yes. The queen ant can live up to 25 years.
B: In what part of Australia are they found?
Student: Um... North East Australia. Mainly around our area.
C: How long do the soldiers live for?
Student: I don't know but I'll try to find out.
D: How big is the stinger? **[K] [L]**
Matthew: Only very small, so you can't see it. (Points to ant on poster.)
        Any more questions?

c. Teacher's observation notes.

[A] Delivers speech confidently and in an unhurried manner.
Obviously well-rehearsed.
Knows exactly what he wants to show and explain in the accompanying pictures.
[J] Voice projected well — at times husky because of his cold.
[K] Looks at all of his audience.
Answers to classmates' questions thoughtfully given.
[R] Looks directly at classmates when answering questions.

physical attributes of bullants, where they live, how they live and reproduce, communication, types, food, concluding illustration (**F**); uses mostly conjunctions to report information in sequence (**G**); uses specialised vocabulary suited to topic (**H**); uses both simple and complex sentence constructions fluently (**I**); uses pace, volume, pronunciation, enunciation and stress effectively to enhance meaning (**J**); uses body movement and gestures to enhance meaning (**K**); uses visual props and aids to enhance presentation and meaning (**L**); uses standard Australian English in a formal situation (**M**).

(4.4) Pauses to think about what to say next (**N**); prepares and uses palm cue cards to ensure organised flow of information (**O**); invites and responds to questions (**P**); acknowledges and attempts to clarify possible problems for listeners: notes difficulty in seeing a diagram, gestures to indicate an action and where listeners should look (**Q**); makes eye contact with audience (**R**).

The rules for a game: teacher notes

Task

Students were required to work in small groups to devise the rules for a game to be played by most of the children in the school on Olympic Games Day.

Background

Students formed groups, made up of both girls and boys, according to the game they wanted to work on. The work sample consists of the teacher's notes on one student's part in a group discussion.

Relevant outcomes

4.1 Interacts confidently with others in a variety of situations to develop and present familiar ideas, events and information.

4.2 Considers aspects of context, purpose and audience when speaking and listening in familiar situations.

4.3 Controls most linguistic structures and features of spoken language for interpreting meaning and developing and presenting ideas and information in familiar situations.

4.4 Assists and monitors the communication patterns of self and others.

Summary comment

The teacher's notes show that the student can operate effectively in a group discussion with peers on familiar subject matter, using well-developed strategies for cooperating with others on a task.

(4.1) Takes an effective part in a small group discussion with peers, cooperatively developing and extending familiar ideas (**A**); presents a point of view strongly on an issue in a group of friends, offering some considered reasons or arguments (**B**).

(4.2) Shows understanding of the nature of group discussion work and own role in it by taking on an active and collaborative role (**C**); appreciates the purpose of the task and the need for others to have their say (**D**); uses group discussion to clarify own ideas ('basically, one person can only touch the ball, no, perhaps more', 'You have to serve overarm — well no, it's optional...') (**E**); adopts an informal tone and style of language suitable to the setting ('Big deal, we can mark it out') (**F**).

(4.3) Makes clear, concise contributions to the discussion (**G**); frames questions and statements succinctly to address specific issues (**H**); uses tone of voice, volume and stress effectively when speaking (**I**); uses conjunctions to express causal and contrasting relationships between ideas ('But older kids have to…') (**J**); signals intention to summarise ('Basically…')

or review ('Now let's see', 'Now what have we got down?') (**K**); follows patterns of question, comment, response, challenge, clarification (**L**).

(4.4) Summarises ideas, responds directly to questions or issues raised by others (**M**); encourages contributions by others ('Yes, That's good…') (**N**); invites other group members to contribute ('Will it work?') (**O**); asks questions that help to clarify others' viewpoints ('That's a bit technical isn't it?') (**P**); challenges the group to ensure that propositions are clearly understood, worded and developed ('Now what have we got down?') (**Q**); listens and responds constructively to alternative ideas or problems raised by others (**R**); maintains group focus on the task ('Now, number 3...', 'Now let's see, what else do we need?') (**S**); volunteers relevant ideas and information, continually bringing up new points (**T**); expresses ideas and opinions without dominating the discussion (examines other ideas, willingly accepting some) (**U**); checks own interpretation of discussion by paraphrasing or summarising 'Basically, one person can only touch the ball...') (**V**).

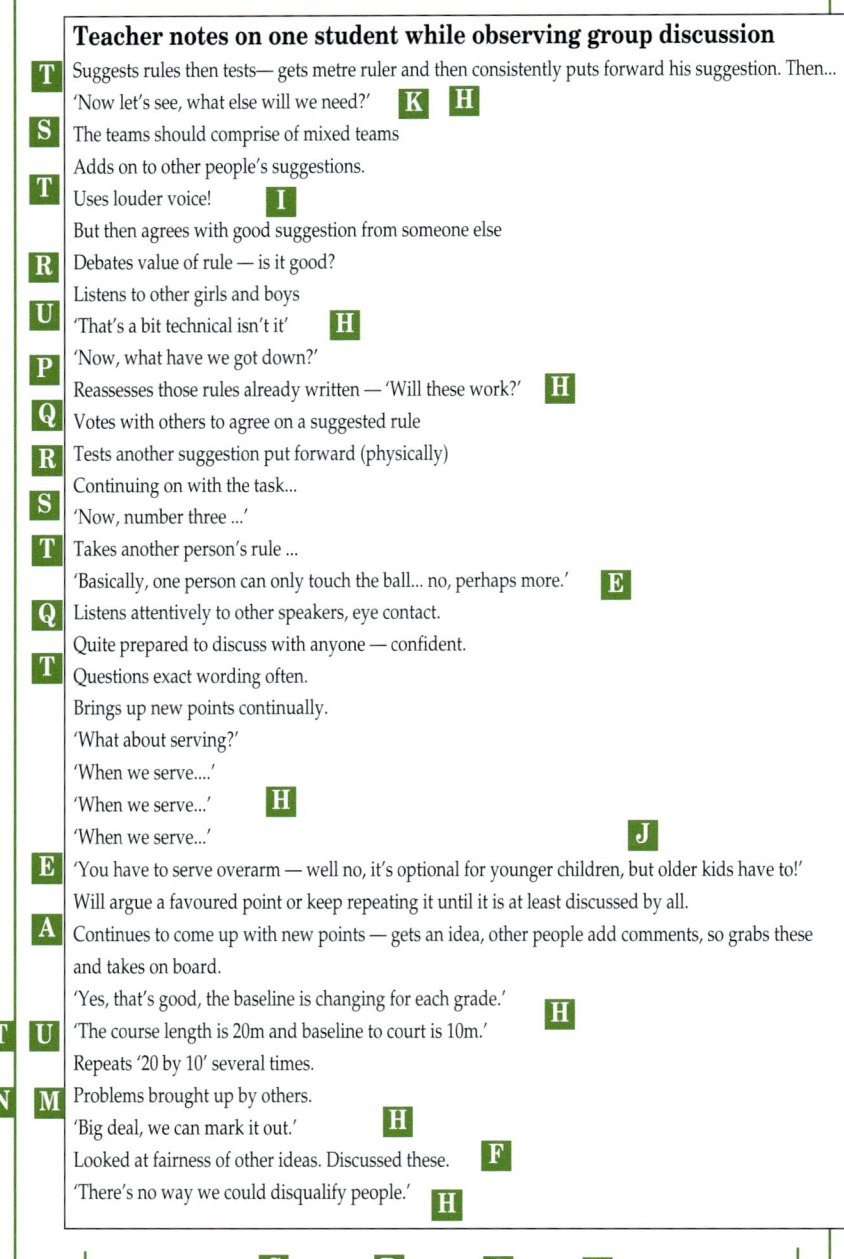

Teacher notes on one student while observing group discussion

T Suggests rules then tests— gets metre ruler and then consistently puts forward his suggestion. Then...

'Now let's see, what else will we need?' **K** **H**

S The teams should comprise of mixed teams

Adds on to other people's suggestions.

T Uses louder voice! **I**

But then agrees with good suggestion from someone else

R Debates value of rule — is it good?

Listens to other girls and boys

U 'That's a bit technical isn't it' **H**

'Now, what have we got down?'

P Reassesses those rules already written — 'Will these work?' **H**

Q Votes with others to agree on a suggested rule

R Tests another suggestion put forward (physically)

Continuing on with the task...

S 'Now, number three ...'

T Takes another person's rule ...

'Basically, one person can only touch the ball... no, perhaps more.' **E**

Q Listens attentively to other speakers, eye contact.

Quite prepared to discuss with anyone — confident.

T Questions exact wording often.

Brings up new points continually.

'What about serving?'

'When we serve....'

'When we serve...' **H**

'When we serve...' **J**

E 'You have to serve overarm — well no, it's optional for younger children, but older kids have to!'

Will argue a favoured point or keep repeating it until it is at least discussed by all.

A Continues to come up with new points — gets an idea, other people add comments, so grabs these and takes on board.

'Yes, that's good, the baseline is changing for each grade.'

'The course length is 20m and baseline to court is 10m.' **H**

Repeats '20 by 10' several times.

T **U** Problems brought up by others.

N **M** 'Big deal, we can mark it out.' **H**

Looked at fairness of other ideas. Discussed these. **F**

'There's no way we could disqualify people.' **H**

C   **D**   **G**   **L**

LEVEL FIVE

LEVEL 5 Statement

Students who have achieved level five have command of a range of standard text types and features and experiment with writing longer texts that discuss challenging aspects of subjects and present justified views on them. They understand important elements of how texts are constructed and experiment with these elements in their own writing.

Students work well in formal groups where they take on roles, responsibilities and tasks, and they show progress in planning and delivering formal spoken presentations to their peers. They systematically listen to and record spoken information.

Students can give detailed accounts of texts in speech and writing, justifying them by referring to the text. They compare texts to examine their structures and ideas more closely, and show a sound understanding of the conventions of narrative texts.

Students use a variety of text types to write at length and with some sense of complexity. In writing longer pieces, they ensure clarity by checking layout, cause-and-effect sequences and grammar. They show a sense of the requirements of readers and experiment with manipulating prose for effect.

LEVEL 5
Table of outcomes

	Texts	Contextual understanding	Linguistic structures & features	Strategies
SPEAKING AND LISTENING	5.1 Interacts with peers in structured situations, using a variety of text types to discuss familiar or accessible subjects involving challenging ideas and issues.	5.2 Identifies the effect of context, audience and purpose on spoken texts.	5.3 Discusses and experiments with some linguistic structures and features that enable speakers to influence audiences.	5.4 Listens strategically and systematically records spoken information.
	See page 102	See page 102	See page 103	See page 103
READING AND VIEWING	5.5 Discusses themes and issues in accessible texts with challenging structures and ideas, and constructs responses interpreting these.	5.6 Recognises that texts are constructed for particular purposes and to appeal to certain groups.	5.7 Draws on knowledge of linguistic structures and features to explain how texts are constructed.	5.8a Uses knowledge of principal conventions of narrative texts to construct meaning from a range of text types. 5.8b Systematically finds and records information.
	See page 104	See page 104	See page 105	See page 105
WRITING	5.9 Uses a variety of text types for writing about familiar or accessible subjects and exploring challenging ideas and issues.	5.10 Identifies the specific effect of context, audience and purpose on written texts.	5.11 Controls the linguistic structures and features necessary to communicate ideas and information clearly in written texts of some length and complexity.	5.12 Draws on planning and review strategies that assist in effectively completing particular tasks.
	See page 106	See page 106	See page 107	See page 107

LEVEL 5 Speaking and Listening

Level 4 outcomes:

4.1 Interacts confidently with others in a variety of situations to develop and present familiar ideas, events and information.

4.2 Considers aspects of context, purpose and audience when speaking and listening in familiar situations.

4.3 Controls most linguistic structures and features of spoken language for interpreting meaning and developing and presenting ideas and information in familiar situations.

4.4 Assists and monitors the communication patterns of self and others.

Texts

At level 5, a student:

5.1 Interacts with peers in structured situations, using a variety of text types to discuss familiar or accessible subjects involving challenging ideas and issues.

Evident when students, for example:

- Explore ideas and topics in groups set up by teacher as well as with friends, giving considered reasons for opinions and ideas and listening to those of others.

- Give, to the whole class or a group, succinct accounts of important personal experiences or events and reflect on their significance.

- Give prepared talks to their class on familiar or accessible subjects, pointing out more complex aspects of the topic (world news related to the theme of a novel being studied in class).

- Take part in a range of team speaking situations (readers' theatre and debates), taking responsibility for aspects of the preparation and performing own part in the presentation.

- Listen to a range of sustained material, such as guest speakers, recordings and information videos, on challenging ideas and issues, noting key ideas and information in a systematic way.

- Describe a person or object in detail and with attention to order and sequence so that another student can guess who or what it is (describe a familiar but complicated object so that someone can draw it accurately).

Contextual understanding

At level 5, a student:

5.2 Identifies the effect of context, audience and purpose on spoken texts.

Evident when students, for example:

- Understand that speakers have to set the scene and compare the ways people do this in different situations (informal greetings like 'how are you?'; introductions and requests like 'Hullo, my name is... Can you tell me...?' when phoning a stranger; introductions like 'Today I'm going to talk about...' when speaking formally to the class).

- Compare the experience of working with groups of friends with working in teacher-selected groups (the need to overcome distractions such as chatting with friends; the difficulty of being frank with people you don't know or trust or like).

- Show some awareness of the difference between speaking to a small working group and speaking to the whole class (that speech would probably be more formal, less exploratory, and more organised when talking to a larger number of people).

- Show some awareness of the advantages of writing over speaking (comment on the degree of frankness possible in a letter compared to the embarrassment of confronting someone face to face).

- Show some awareness of the disadvantages of writing compared to speaking (a lack of clarity in vocabulary or expression may be compensated for by intonation, gestures, and response from the listener, whereas writing has to be more explicit).

Linguistic structures & features

At level 5, a student:

5.3 Discusses and experiments with some linguistic structures and features that enable speakers to influence audiences.

Evident when students, for example:

- Observe and discuss the way that voice and body language affect audiences and can be used to enhance meaning and influence interpretation (the way gestures, posture, facial expression, tone of voice, pace of speaking may engage the audience's interest).

- Note aspects of language use, such as vocabulary, rhythm, similes, which enhance particular spoken texts (by amusing the audience in order to persuade them of a point of view).

- Discuss and experiment with the effect of intonation on meaning (say the same word, phrase or sentence in different ways to convey regret, anger, annoyance, humour).

- Identify the way familiar text types are organised and explain why (logical sequence of events in a spoken account or report assists comprehension; clear conclusion helps listeners focus on the importance of what has been said).

- Recognise statements of attitude and opinion even when they are not clearly identified as opinions (recognise the implicit point of view conveyed by tone of voice and expression in a television interview; recognise that formulations like 'It is quite clear that' express a point of view).

- Discuss the function of colourful language and jargon in language situations such as sports commentaries (to involve listeners in a game's excitement, to give listeners the feeling of being insiders by using jargon and other specialised language).

Strategies

At level 5, a student:

5.4 Listens strategically and systematically records spoken information.

Evident when students, for example:

- Prepare for listening (take pen and notebook or laptop computer to the viewing of an information video or to a talk by a guest speaker).

- Note cues such as change of pace and particular words which indicate a new or important point is about to be made.

- Develop and use a personal abbreviation system to record information quickly.

- Select essential ideas and information in a text and note these in point form, one point per line.

- Jot down points in the order made so that information can be readily summarised or interpreted later.

Level 6 outcomes:

6.1 Conveys detailed information and explores different perspectives on complex issues through interacting with known social groups, principally peers, in structured and unstructured situations.

6.2 Identifies ways in which listeners' socio-cultural backgrounds, knowledge and opinions influence the meaning they obtain from spoken texts.

6.3 Experiments with knowledge of linguistic structures and features, and draws on this knowledge to explain how speakers influence audiences.

6.4 Critically evaluates others' spoken texts and uses this knowledge to reflect on and improve own.

LEVEL 5   Reading and Viewing

Level 4 outcomes:

4.5   Justifies own interpretation of ideas, information and events in texts containing some unfamiliar concepts and topics and which introduce relatively complex linguistic structures and features.

4.6   Explains possible reasons for people's varying interpretations of a text.

4.7   With teacher guidance, identifies and discusses how linguistic structures and features work to shape readers' and viewers' understanding of texts.

4.8a   Selects, uses and reflects on strategies appropriate for different texts and reading or viewing purposes.

4.8b   With peers, identifies information needs and finds resources for specific purposes.

Texts

At level 5, a student:

5.5 Discusses themes and issues in accessible texts with challenging structures and ideas, and constructs responses interpreting these.

Evident when students, for example:

- Discuss the motives and feelings of characters or people in fictional and non-fictional texts (such as Alan's desire for independence in Alan Marshall's *I Can Jump Puddles* or Jane's long-suffering obedience in Charlotte Brontë's *Jane Eyre*), as well as showing interest in action and events.

- Write personality profiles of characters and people in texts produced for young adults or in other accessible texts, paying attention to implied as well as stated meanings (interpret what a character's dialogue reveals about the person; compare characters from the same or different texts in terms of the way they react to the same or similar events and situations).

- Support a point of view about themes and issues in texts by distinguishing between plot and theme, identifying major points of conflict and significant turning-points in plots, and using an understanding of cause and effect.

- Identify similarities and differences between texts produced by different people on the same or similar themes, focusing on elements such as setting, family relationships, ways of resolving problems (compare Tim Winton's treatment of relationships in *Lockie Leonard, Human Torpedo*, with John Marsden's treatment of these issues in *So Much to Tell You*).

- Discuss topical items published in mass media such as magazines, local papers, and current affairs programs and relate these critically to their own experience (compare the ways that male and female sports are represented and discuss in relation to the prestige and popularity of particular sports in their own school).

Contextual understanding

At level 5, a student:

5.6 Recognises that texts are constructed for particular purposes and to appeal to certain groups.

Evident when students, for example:

- Understand that many texts and text types are constructed to meet the needs and expectations of audiences (adventure stories provide escapist pleasure by concentrating on action and suspense more than on relationships between characters).

- Use understanding of the orientation and purpose of particular texts and text types to hypothesise about them (predict that a romance will end either happily with marriage or with a vindication of the stand made by the heroine).

- Discuss the enjoyment most people get from narratives, such as stories in songs, novels and anecdotes, stories about disasters and achievements on television news programs, and note how this is used by writers who want to do more than tell a story (such as advertisers selling products, writers presenting a point of view).

- Recognise that people with special interests and expectations are the target audience for particular texts (surfing movies and movie magazines) and that design and advertising as well as content reflect this.

- Discuss techniques advertisements use to appeal to particular audiences (identify the emotive effect and cultural meaning of images and symbols such as those of young people doing exciting things and having fun in soft drink commercials).

- Show awareness that language reflects particular purposes, audiences and socio-cultural settings by investigating the ways written language changes over time and through the influence of different cultures.

Linguistic structures & features

At level 5, a student:

5.7 Draws on knowledge of linguistic structures and features to explain how texts are constructed.

Evident when students, for example:

- Examine aspects of structure such as chronology, plot and sub-plot in fictional texts such as novels and films (discuss the way supporting characters are used to move the action along, cause conflict).

- Use knowledge of text structure to work out possible themes (stories often have a moral in their conclusion; poetry often makes readers think about life in a different way by comparing things that aren't normally related; films juxtapose images to create specific meanings — fast car, alarmed face, blackout, accompanied by scream of brakes and thud imply a car crash).

- Identify the contribution to meaning of imagery such as simile and metaphor in narrative and other types of writing (consider choice, use and effectiveness of images in poems such as Coleridge's *The Rime of the Ancient Mariner* or compare D.H. Lawrence's use of images in his poem *Snake* and Judith Wright's in her poem *The Killer*).

- Recognise that shot types and camera angles are used with purpose in visual texts such as cartoons and films (close-ups may be used for highly dramatic moments or to focus the viewer's attention on a significant object; long-shots establish setting).

- Compare the connotations of words that mean similar things and discuss the way authors use particular words to convey precise or subtle meaning.

- Show understanding that paragraphs are used as structural devices (summarise information in expository texts paragraph by paragraph and talk about the sequence of ideas).

Strategies

At level 5, a student:

5.8a Uses knowledge of principal conventions of narrative texts to construct meaning from a range of text types.

Evident when students, for example:

- Explore the purposes and effects of the manipulation of chronological order in narrative (to create suspense in a mystery tale or to provide insights into characters as in, for example, Ruth Park's *Playing Beatie Bow* or Gillian Rubinstein's *Space Demons*).

- Understand that readers' or viewers' sympathies are directed to particular characters, and discuss examples of this in texts read and viewed.

- Apply experience of narrative conventions to a range of television genres such as news, soap opera and quiz shows (explain that the news presents the events of the day as stories with setting, character, conflict and resolution, and entertain as well as inform).

- Identify features of visual narrative texts used as short cuts to construct meaning in other kinds of texts (the use of the setting, characters, language of the western genre in a poster advertising jeans to create an instantly recognisable image for the product).

- Keep a reading journal as a way of formulating questions about narrative texts (try to work out why as readers they feel sympathetic to some characters and antagonistic toward others).

5.8b Systematically finds and records information.

Evident when students, for example:

- Compare different reference sources and assess each for a given purpose (magazines compared to encyclopedias, and one encyclopedia compared to another).

- Scan their own or class-constructed chapter summaries of novels or running sheets of films to find suitable evidence to support a point of view about a character or situation in a text.

- Select a note-making strategy suited to the task and the information source (if the task is to research the way published authors get their ideas, make notes under individual authors' names or under the categories of origins of ideas).

- Note relevant information about sources used (note the name and call number of a library book for easy retrieval if needed again during the project).

Level 6 outcomes:

6.5 Explores different perspectives on complex issues through reading and viewing a range of texts, and constructs written and spoken responses relating these perspectives to personal understandings of the contemporary world.

6.6 Considers the contexts in which texts were or are created and how these are reflected in texts.

6.7 Compares linguistic structures and features of texts to highlight their similarities and differences in form and meaning.

6.8a Draws on a repertoire of strategies to maintain understanding through dense or extended texts.

6.8b Gathers, selects and organises information effectively for specific purposes.

LEVEL 5   Writing

Level 4 outcomes:

4.9 Uses writing to develop familiar ideas, events and information.

4.10 Adjusts writing to take account of aspects of context, purpose and audience.

4.11 Controls most distinguishing linguistic structures and features of basic text types such as stories, procedures, reports and arguments.

4.12a When prompted, uses a range of strategies for planning, reviewing and proofreading own writing.

4.12b Uses a multi-strategy approach to spelling.

Texts

At level 5, a student:

5.9 Uses a variety of text types for writing about familiar or accessible subjects and exploring challenging ideas and issues.

Evident when students, for example:

- Write about personal experiences (in letters, journals) with attention to detail, consciously using narrative structures to involve readers.

- Write a detailed description of a natural scene, an object, a place, choosing details to convey a specific impression of it to someone else (describe an agricultural show as either dirty or exciting by choosing appropriate details and structure).

- Write sustained narratives on familiar, possibly self-chosen, topics with attention to time order, characterisation, consistent narrative point of view, and development of a conclusion or point.

- Experiment with writing poetry in various specified formats (using simple metrical patterns; writing shape or concrete poems; using poetic elements such as imagery and rhyme to enhance meaning).

- Write informative texts for familiar but wide audiences, providing more than an exclusively personal perspective (write a newsletter article about a school event in such a way that both a wider school audience and the participants would find it interesting).

- Develop written arguments about ideas and issues for a general audience, stating and justifying a personal viewpoint, providing more than one argument and some relevant supporting details.

- Keep logs, journals or notes from teacher or peer discussions about writing, recording such things as ideas for future writing or aspects of their own writing that need more attention and reflections on personal experiences.

Contextual understanding

At level 5, a student:

5.10 Identifies the specific effect of context, audience and purpose on written texts.

Evident when students, for example:

- Discuss written forms such as advertisements and poetry in which the conventions of standard written English may be waived, the effects on audiences of varying these conventions, and experiment with controlling these effects (use a sentence fragment such as 'The very best' to make a strong point at the end of an advertisement or in a story, but understand that non-standard spelling and grammar are usually unacceptable in work intended to be read by others).

- Discuss the similarities and differences between talking to a friend about an event and writing to that friend about the same event (while much of the language is the same, the written version will probably be more organised).

- Consider the readability of presented work, taking into account context and purpose (use a word processor if available; set out a newspaper article using a real one as a model; use large print on posters so that they can be read from a distance).

- Understand that writers need to bring readers into the world of the text, and make efforts to set the scene clearly at the beginning of their own expository or imaginative texts.

- Understand that readers have expectations of certain text types and try to meet these (recognise the need to unify a story and make all details relevant; make topical relevance of a letter to the editor clear in the first paragraph).

Linguistic structures & features

At level 5, a student:

5.11 Controls the linguistic structures and features necessary to communicate ideas and information clearly in written texts of some length and complexity.

Evident when students, for example:

- Use suitable headings and sub-headings in sustained informational texts such as projects and assignments or accepted text divisions such as extra space accompanied by a short line to convey the passage of time in sustained narratives.

- Use paragraphs to indicate a sequence of ideas in informational and narrative texts.

- Control cause-and-effect sequences in narratives so that the reader is clear about what is happening and why.

- Understand and control basic grammar such as tenses and subject-verb and noun-pronoun agreement.

- Ensure that spelling and punctuation conform to standard Australian English, as demanded by the task.

- Experiment with rearranging sentences by transforming, expanding, rearranging and reducing them to achieve an intended meaning.

Strategies

At level 5, a student:

5.12 Draws on planning and review strategies that assist in effectively completing particular tasks.

Evident when students, for example:

- Take notes, select information, identify key ideas, and plan a sequence of ideas in the text.

- Select one or more planning strategies from a range including brainstorming, speed writing, circling main ideas in a topic, structured overviews, discussion with partner or group.

- Use writing to monitor and reflect independently on their own learning (use a reading journal to refine ideas about a text being read or viewed).

- Anticipate the likely expectations and needs of readers at every stage of composition, redrafting where necessary (readability, holding interest, need for explanations or definitions).

- Review writing to ensure that content and linguistic structures and features are consistent with text type (newspaper reports written in appropriate tenses, such as 'Last night … Enquiries are continuing').

- Carefully proofread successive drafts, using checklists and a multi-strategy approach to spelling.

Level 6 outcomes:

6.9 Conveys detailed information and explores different perspectives on complex, challenging issues through writing for specific and general audiences.

6.10 Predicts some of the likely characteristics and expectations of particular audiences and tries to accommodate or resist these expectations as appropriate.

6.11 Uses and experiments with a range of linguistic structures and features designed to influence audiences.

6.12 Revises own writing for meaning and effectiveness.

Earthworm environmental awards

Task

Three students chose to work as a team on a project based on the Earthworm Environmental Awards.

Background

Students considered the criteria on which the award would be judged, which included practicability, originality, clarity, and community involvement. They decided to focus on cleaning up their school. The finished project included a talk to about 450 students (scripted), a play put on for those students (unscripted; a transcript is provided), a song written and sung by the students, and a video produced with a university film and television school.

Organising the video entailed negotiations over the project and the fee, making appointments, and arranging permission slips and transport to the studio to mix the song.

The students each kept a record of the work. They ensured that tasks were shared and took part in brainstorming sessions. All three students were assessed as being at the same profile level.

Relevant outcomes:

Speaking and listening

5.1 Interacts with peers in structured situations, using a variety of text types to discuss familiar or accessible subjects involving challenging ideas and issues.

5.2 Identifies the specific effect of context, audience and purpose on spoken texts.

5.3 Discusses and experiments with some linguistic structures and features that enable speakers to influence audiences.

Writing

5.9 Uses a variety of text types for writing about familiar or accessible subjects and exploring challenging ideas and issues.

5.10 Identifies the specific effect of context, audience and purpose on written texts.

5.11 Controls the linguistic structures and features necessary to communicate ideas and information clearly in written texts of some length and complexity.

Summary comment

This project explores some challenging ideas and issues and demonstrates control over a variety of text types. The students' writing and speaking clearly demonstrate the ability to identify the specific effects of context, audience and purpose on texts. Linguistic structures and features are used effectively to influence the audience and indicate that the students are working at level 6.

Transcripts of students' project

Introduction to the video:

[1st speaker to camera]

A Starting to look after the world starts at home. We can't improve our world unless we improve our homes, our schools, our states, our countries, the world! [throws arms open]

[2nd speaker to camera]

We have realised that we are not only hurting ourselves through all this rubbish, but the environment around us. The wind blows the rubbish across the yard and into a nearby creek. This rubbish can cause harm and sometimes even death to our flora and fauna.

Address to assembly of students:

[1st speaker; reads with some mistakes and hesitations from notes without looking up]

B In Science we are involved in a science competition known as the Earthworm Environmental Awards. Our main aim is to clean up our school. We thought that starting in a small level would make people aware of the importance of helping looking after our school environment. What we propose to do is to remain — remind you of the responsibilities that *you* have, in part, of keeping our school clean. This is how we will do this.

[2nd speaker; reads fluently from notes and makes some eye contact with audience]

Every Friday starting today, you will be asked to participate in a weekly Emu Parade in which you will clean up your areas, as allocated by Mr Shadiac at the start of the year. We will record your progress on this chart.

[3rd student holds up colourful, hand-made chart and speaks directly to audience]

Help us clean up our school. How? It's easy. Just pick up rubbish through your weekly Emu Parade. Watch your progress go [indicates chart, which has a table of classes on it]. There's a prize for the best class. Are there any questions?

[Student in the audience asks, 'How does it get scored?']

[2nd student explains without referring to notes, then announces that there will be a short play]

(5.2) Understands needs of audience in terms of context and purpose; establishes purpose and calls for action (**A**).

(5.3) Control of linguistic structures and features necessary to influence audience: emphasis on the word 'you' (**B**).

(5.3) Understands how linguistic structures and features can be used to influence audience: tone of voice and vocabulary establish rapport with audience, for example, through identification and amusement (**C**).

(5.1) Understands how to choose text type to convey ideas and information: play shows attention to characterisation, dramatic tension is quickly established, and there is a fitting conclusion (**D**).

(5.3) Understands how linguistic structures and features can be used to influence audience: intonation and gesture confirm the meaning of the words and help listeners' comprehension (**E**).

(5.10) Understands needs of audience in terms of context and purpose: the whale example is used to appeal to and persuade the students (**F**).

(5.2 and 5.3) Rhythm and rhyme of the 'You see a paper' slogan are catchy and memorable and the slogan is repeated (**G**).

(5.2) Text type selected to effectively convey message that people will remember and which will provide background for the video (**H**).

(5.11) Demonstrates understanding and control of the features of this text type, with choruses (varying each time to extend the message), repetition of final lines, and verses (**I**).

(5.10) Understands the way grammatical conventions can be waived in some contexts: use of incomplete sentences to convey impressions (**J**).

(5.11) Control of imagery to clearly communicate ideas and ensure text's cohesiveness (**K**).

Play:

SCENE: A SCHOOLGROUND. TWO STUDENTS ARE WALKING TOGETHER. THEY ARE DRESSED PARTLY IN SCHOOL UNIFORM, PARTLY WITH RAGGED CHECK SHIRTS SLUNG ROUND THEIR WAISTS. A THIRD STUDENT, PROPERLY DRESSED, IS BENDING OVER AND PICKING UP PAPERS AND OTHER RUBBISH.

C STUDENTS 1 and 2: Oh, there's a nerd! (*They throw rubbish down on student 3*) *Student 3 picks up the rubbish.*

D STUDENT 1: Leave that paper there! It looks good to leave paper on the ground.

STUDENT 3: (*reluctantly*) OK. (*Throws paper back, then hesitates*) Hold on a minute. You see this area over here? (*gestures*)

STUDENT 2: I'm not blind, you know.

STUDENT 3: And you see this area over here?

E STUDENT 1: Oh <u>der</u>. [Laughter from audience]

STUDENT 3: Well, I don't want <u>this</u> area (*gestures towards clean area*) to end up looking like this area (*indicates rubbish*).

STUDENTS 1 and 2: We don't care!

STUDENT 3: Well, I do.

Pause.

STUDENT 1: I suppose she does have a point, you know.

STUDENT 2: Like what?

STUDENT 1: Well, if this area (*gestures towards clean area*) does look like this area (*indicates rubbish*) we'll be surrounded in rubbish. I'm joining <u>her</u>. (*Walks over to student 3*)

F STUDENT 3: (*to student 2*) Hey, did you know that Greenpeace found one whale with thirty plastic bags inside his stomach?

STUDENT 2: I don't care. That's only one whale. There's lots more out there in the ocean.

G STUDENT 3: But that whale too, and it died. Look: there's four easy steps to picking up rubbish. (*Demonstrates*) You see a paper; you pick it up; you walk to the bin; and you put it in. It's simple.

STUDENT 2: I don't care what you think. I'm not doing it.

STUDENT 1: Come on.

G STUDENTS 1 and 3 (*in unison, with matching actions*): See that paper; you pick it up; you walk to the bin; and you put it in.

STUDENT 2: Oh, I suppose you're right. But do it one more time with me, OK?

G STUDENTS 1, 2 and 3 (*in unison and working together*): You see a paper; you pick it up; you walk to the bin; and you put it in.

STUDENT 3: You see, it's simple. So now let's tidy up <u>this</u> area. (*All three bend down and do so*)

Song played during video (written and sung by the students): Attached.

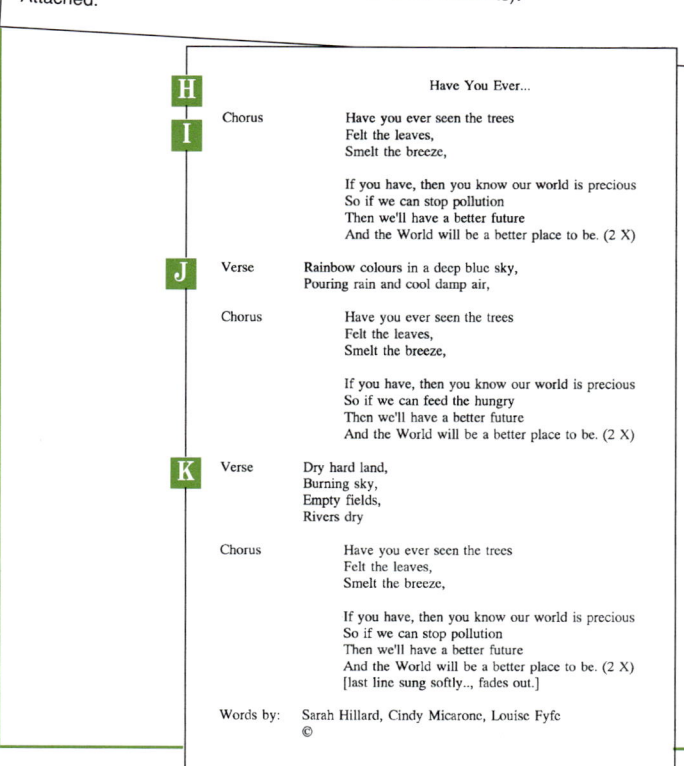

H I Have You Ever...

Chorus
Have you ever seen the trees
Felt the leaves,
Smelt the breeze,

If you have, then you know our world is precious
So if we can stop pollution
Then we'll have a better future
And the World will be a better place to be. (2 X)

J Verse
Rainbow colours in a deep blue sky,
Pouring rain and cool damp air,

Chorus
Have you ever seen the trees
Felt the leaves,
Smelt the breeze,

If you have, then you know our world is precious
So if we can feed the hungry
Then we'll have a better future
And the World will be a better place to be. (2 X)

K Verse
Dry hard land,
Burning sky,
Empty fields,
Rivers dry

Chorus
Have you ever seen the trees
Felt the leaves,
Smelt the breeze,

If you have, then you know our world is precious
So if we can stop pollution
Then we'll have a better future
And the World will be a better place to be. (2 X)
[last line sung softly.., fades out.]

Words by: Sarah Hillard, Cindy Micarone, Louise Fyfe
©

Window

Task

Students were required to use a list of set questions to write a detailed evaluation in essay form of a picture-book.

Background

Students undertook a three-to four-week picture-book unit on the theme of 'Journeys'. They read at least 12 picture-books from a selection provided by the teacher, kept a reading log and completed a checklist on each book read, reported to the class on the text they chose to evaluate, and wrote their own 'journey story'. Before doing the evaluation, students studied the notion of journeys in stories by reading together (in groups of two, three or four) a selection of Big Books and reporting to the class on the kinds of stories in those books. The teacher spent a lesson showing students a range of different kinds of picture-books. Students also spent two or three lessons reading and judging the picture-books shortlisted for the 1992 Children's Book Council of Australia Awards.

Relevant outcomes

5.5 Discusses themes and issues in accessible texts with challenging structures and ideas, and constructs responses interpreting these.

5.6 Recognises that texts are constructed for particular purposes and to appeal to certain groups.

5.7 Draws on knowledge of linguistic structures and features to explain how texts are constructed.

Summary comment

This evaluation gives an interpretation of the themes and issues in an accessible text with challenging structures and ideas. There is some recognition that texts are constructed for particular purposes and audiences, although this could be more explicit. The student understands the way the linguistic structures and features of the text construct meaning. Confident identification of themes and of the way linguistic structures and features contribute to meaning point to the work achieving beyond level 4. It is clearly not of the complexity required at level 6, however.

EVALUATION OF A JOURNEY BOOK

WINDOW - Jennie Baker 21/8

 A Window was based on one boy's life, journeying through the stages and changes of his surroundings and environment around him. It is written about real life happenings going on at the present moment. The journey was taken individually by the boy, although some animals did appear in it, but they didn't play any part in it.

Time was the use of transport during the journey. The journey taken through the stages of life.

The window frame shown in every picture during the journey, was fixed on one scene of the land and sky. The journey took part in the present time, for the whole story.

The journey was taken on behalf of us. Environment, **B** destroying humans. To hopefully make us realize just how much of our planet we are destroying.

There were no obstacles to be aware of during the boy's journey through life.

The journey started in a country scene, looking a window to the boys house. It finished, looking through the window of the once young man's house, who now had grown up, married and bought a house in a similar setting to the house he grew up in.

(5.5) The text is an accessible picture-book with challenging ideas (**A**); understands the text's main theme (**B**).

(5.7) Understands the link between the linguistic structures and features of the text and its meaning: identifies how the text's ending is linked with the theme (**C**).

C

D

The journey didn't complete unsuccessfully or successfully. It just finished with a closing paragraph, making us aware of the destruction we have caused to our once untouched planet, and if we don't look after or preserve our natural environment, there won't be any left for future generations to come. Only myths and legends.

I think the main character was unaware of the changes happening to the natural environment. I'm sure he was aware of the development of buildings, housing etc. He wasn't aware of the long term effect of destroying so much land and so many trees. It really made you stop and think about the existance of humans for the future years. I asked myself

"What will life be like in future years?"

"Will there be any trees, grass, soil for our children's children to look after?"

It also makes you feel a little bit selfish, in the way that there are a limited amount of resources left in the world, so why we destroy or use them all up now for ourselves, because sooner or later there isn't going to be any left, so why don't we be the ones to finish them off.

The book had most of its impact in its readers through the illustrations. They were so well presented, and thats the main thing I'll remember about the book.

(5.6) Understands that texts are constructed for particular purposes (**D**).

(5.7) Understands the link between the linguistic structures and features of the text and its meaning: identifies link between colour and theme (**E**).

E

From reading this I have learnt that, the amount of our natural environment we destroy daily, will gradually lead us to our graves.

Artistic Analalysig (Analysis)

The colours in the illustrations are very bold and bright. There was a large variety of colour used, but all the green's tended to dominate over most of the other colours. The use of a lot of different greens was a good idea to highlight the main problems. The colours are definately natural for the settings in the illustrations.

The collages used in the book, are one of the most "brilliant" arangement of collages I have ever seen.

Format

The illustrations were high in colour, very detailed, and the collages were very well done. Words are not used in the book, so you have to depend on your thoughts towards the illustrations to tell the story. She did a terrific job in doing that!

The front and back covers didn't tell anything about the storyline or much about the story. There are no white spaces on the illustrations.

The effect portrayed through the collage on the front cover is, of a small cottage in the country.

The illustrations told the whole story line all the way through the book.

Letter of complaint

Task

Students were required to write an argument about a subject of immediate concern to them and of which they had knowledge. Students who wrote letters of complaint were asked to prepare them to be sent and to check spelling, grammar and punctuation.

Background

The teacher showed examples of letters which put forward points of view. These were discussed in terms of their effectiveness. Students filled in a planning sheet before writing their first drafts. After the first drafts, the teacher spent time distinguishing between a letter of complaint and a letter presenting an argument. Formal letter layout was demonstrated. The teacher commented verbally and in writing on successive drafts. Two weeks were spent on the task, including some class time and some homework.

Relevant outcomes

5.9 Uses a variety of text types for writing about familiar or accessible subjects and exploring challenging ideas and issues.

5.10 Identifies the specific effect of context, audience and purpose on written texts.

5.11 Controls the linguistic structures and features necessary to communicate ideas and information clearly in written texts of some length and complexity.

5.12 Draws on planning and review strategies that assist in effectively completing particular tasks.

Summary comment

The letter successfully puts forward a point of view about a familiar subject, developing more than one argument and providing some relevant supporting details. The competence and detail of the letter indicate that the work goes beyond the requirements of level 4 but does not have the broader understanding of the issue expected of level 6 work. It does, however, display aspects of some level 6 outcomes (success in writing for a specific audience, and detailed revision of writing to make it more effective).

(5.10) Understands that readers have expectations of particular text types: letter uses accepted layout, using word processor to aid readability (**A**); understands context: provides reader with a clear introduction to the topic of the letter in the first paragraph (**B**).

(5.11) Uses linguistic structures and features that enable clear communication of ideas and information at some length: use of dot points (**C**).

(5.10) Understands context: council concerns (residents' health and safety of property) are targeted (**D**).

(5.11) Although 'it' is ambiguous in this sentence, essential grammar is well controlled (**E**); controls cause-and-effect sequences: consequences of action and lack of action are pointed out (**F**).

(5.12) Effective revision: the sentence was originally two sentences, which sounded less logical and less adult than the present version (**G**).

(5.10) Understands context: knows residents' needs must be weighed against costs (**H**).

(5.12) Effective revision: an abrupt 'Please reply' at the end of the first draft became the more polite and acceptable 'I would appreciate your reply' (**I**).

A

9 Solvay Court,
Surrey Downs, 5126
2/9/1992

Tea Tree Gully Council,
1020 North East Road,
Modbury, 5092.

Dear Sir/Madam,

B I am concerned about the state of the Council property behind the brush fences in Royal Admiral Place, Surrey Downs. The area is overgrown with grass and weeds and from Golden Grove Road it looks a mess.

I would like to bring the following points to your attention:

C - Mice, I know, are living in the grass, and snakes and lizards could also be living in it.

- It is potentially unhealthy having mice (and maybe other creatures) living there.

D - I and other residents living near the fences are hayfever sufferers and, in summer, when it is dry and some of the weeds have flowers, we are affected by the pollen.

- In summer, the grass could easily burn and, because the grass is right next to the brush fence, it too could go up.

E I would like to suggest that the grass be cut regularly, rather than poisoned, **F** because when it's poisoned the grass just dies, instead of being cut and taken away.

If the grass and weeds were cut regularly,

- they wouldn't grow to the point where they produce flowers,
- mice and other animals wouldn't have shelter there,
- there would be no fire risk in summer, and
- the area would look better.

G I know that there would be a cost involved, but it would be a lot less than the cost of a negligence claim against you for a person who was injured in a fire caused **H** by dry, uncut grass and weeds - let alone having to replace the brush fence and whatever else was damaged.

I suggest that, in the winter months, the grass should be cut monthly and fortnightly in the summer months.

I I would appreciate your reply.

Yours sincerely,

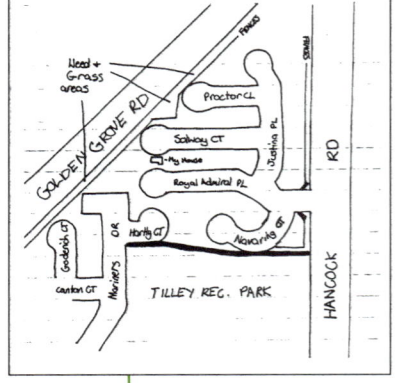

112

Task

Students were required to write a reflection on an experience.

Background

Students worked in small groups, telling their peers about something that had happened to them. They then discussed details of the experience, planned an approach to the task, and wrote a first draft for homework. The teacher wrote comments on the first drafts. The task was completed in class and at home. The class spends one period a week, usually devoted to writing, in the computer room.

Relevant outcomes

5.9 Uses a variety of text types for writing about familiar or accessible subjects and exploring challenging ideas and issues.

5.10 Identifies the specific effect of context, audience and purpose on written texts.

5.11 Controls the linguistic structures and features necessary to communicate ideas and information clearly in written texts of some length and complexity.

5.12 Draws on planning and review strategies that assist in effectively completing particular tasks.

Summary comment

The personal reflection is told with attention to detail and sequence, and is influenced by narrative structures which help to convey the events and ideas in an interesting way. These elements help distinguish it from level 4 work. The attention paid in the final version to linguistic structures and features (for example, text structure, correctness of spelling and punctuation) and the use of a word processor show awareness of the needs of readers. The sample also demonstrates effective use of planning and review strategies, some of which indicate achievement of outcome 6.12 in Writing.

(5.10) Understands that readers need to be brought into the world of the text through a succinct introduction (**A**).

(5.11) Controls linguistic structures and features necessary to communicate detailed information: paragraphs indicate a clear sequence of ideas (**B**).

(5.9) Explores challenging ideas: reflects on age difference, how it was perceived by others, and how the boys overcame it (**C**).

(5.11) Clear cause-and-effect-sequence (**D**); uses parallel structure ('I invited him over, he invited me over…') to suggest their developing friendship (**E**).

(5.12) Revises effectively: drafts show that the penultimate sentence here originally said only, 'I helped pack up the things in his room'. The addition helps us get a better picture of Richard and why he and the writer are friends (**F**).

(5.11) Complex sentence structure beginning with the most important element of the message, 'surprisingly' (**G**).

(5.9) Explores challenging ideas: notes in some detail the feelings that he has about Richard (**H**).

(5.4) Revises effectively: drafts show that the two penultimate sentences in this paragraph, which contribute significantly to the point of the piece of writing, were added later (**I**).

Draft 3.

MY FRIEND IS SHIFTING HOUSE!

BY Matthew

A It all began about three years ago when my brother, Alfred, introduced me to his friend called Richard. Richard was tall, Alfred's age and seemed friendly. Back then he must have thought I was a real idiot. I suppose it was just the way that I used to be.

B The age difference was a bit of a problem. I was nine and he was already thirteen. It wasn't that good to hang around with people in higher year levels, because their friends made you **C** feel a bit out of place. That's what it's like today. We mainly went to each other's house. That was and still is the best way.

D I started to get to know him better when Alfred, Richard and I went out somewhere e.g. the city, swimming, Highpoint. Alfred and Richard would decide that they were going out, and Mum agreed on one condition, that I would go with them. From then on we became friends. I invited him over, he invited me over and he **E** introduced me to comics, science-fiction, comedy and drawing.

We lived a five minute walk away from each other, so we got used to going to each other's house without that much difficulty. Then, something terrible happened. Richard's parents announced, without their children's consent, they were shifting house. This came as a bit of a shock to Richard, because he was used to one of his and my friends, Leigh, living two doors away. Most of the time when I went to Richard's house, Leigh was there. He was moving to Saint Bernard's estate, which takes about half an hour to walk to. We knew that this would mean that both Leigh and I would see Richard less. From then on we were counting the days **F** until Richard moved. Moving day was November the twenty ninth. Two days before he left, I helped him pack up all of the little things that he collected such as comics, models, books and more books. On November the twenty ninth he moved.

G Surprisingly, after he shifted we became better friends and we saw each other a lot more. I don't know what happened, but maybe it was because we lived further away and we just forgot about the distance and started riding to each other's house. He **H** has introduced me to so many things. I would have missed having someone to talk to about the things I was reading. Richard was **I** someone I could relate to. It was lucky that he didn't move to another suburb.

THE END!

LEVEL SIX

LEVEL 6 Statement

Students who have achieved level six can meet the literacy demands of the outside world. Their spelling, syntax and command of text structures are adequate for most expository and imaginative writing. They can grapple with the complex social issues they encounter in texts read, viewed and listened to, and they can talk and write about what these issues mean to them and their world.

Students take part confidently in both formal and informal situations where people speak. They listen for ideas and information and are alert to the way others speak to influence audiences. In conveying ideas and information themselves, students are mindful of suiting their language to purpose and audience.

Students use their growing understanding of the world and their increasing ability to interpret texts to read and view a variety of texts, including some adult texts. They recognise that texts have points of view, even when these are not explicitly stated, and with teacher assistance (for example, guided questioning and comparison of texts) identify and comment on them.

Students write in a variety of ways — expository, personal and imaginative — to explore complex issues. They increasingly recognise the importance of making their meanings clear for readers by using correct punctuation, spelling and grammar and by manipulating words and the structure of texts.

LEVEL 6
Table of outcomes

	Texts	Contextual understanding	Linguistic structures & features	Strategies
SPEAKING AND LISTENING	6.1 Conveys detailed information and explores different perspectives on complex issues through interacting with known social groups, principally peers, in structured and unstructured situations.	6.2 Identifies ways in which listeners' socio-cultural backgrounds, knowledge and opinions influence the meaning they obtain from spoken texts.	6.3 Experiments with knowledge of linguistic structures and features, and draws on this knowledge to explain how speakers influence audiences.	6.4 Critically evaluates others' spoken texts and uses this knowledge to reflect on and improve own.
	See page 118	See page 118	See page 119	See page 119
READING AND VIEWING	6.5 Explores different perspectives on complex issues through reading and viewing a range of texts, and constructs written and spoken responses relating these perspectives to personal understandings of the contemporary world.	6.6 Considers the contexts in which texts were or are created and how these are reflected in texts.	6.7 Compares linguistic structures and features of texts to highlight their similarities and differences in form and meaning.	6.8a Draws on a repertoire of strategies to maintain understanding through dense or extended texts. 6.8b Gathers, selects and organises information effectively for specific purposes.
	See page 120	See page 120	See page 121	See page 121
WRITING	6.9 Conveys detailed information and explores different perspectives on complex, challenging issues through writing for specific and general audiences.	6.10 Predicts some of the likely characteristics and expectations of particular audiences and tries to accommodate or resist these expectations as appropriate.	6.11 Uses and experiments with a range of linguistic structures and features designed to influence audiences.	6.12 Revises own writing for meaning and effectiveness.
	See page 122	See page 122	See page 123	See page 123

LEVEL 6 Speaking and Listening

Level 5 outcomes:

5.1 Interacts with peers in structured situations, using a variety of text types to discuss familiar or accessible subjects involving challenging ideas and issues.

5.2 Identifies the effect of context, audience and purpose on spoken texts.

5.3 Discusses and experiments with some linguistic structures and features that enable speakers to influence audiences.

5.4 Listens strategically and systematically records spoken information.

Texts

At level 6, a student:

6.1 Conveys detailed information and explores different perspectives on complex issues through interacting with known social groups, principally peers, in structured and unstructured situations.

Evident when students, for example:

- Explore ideas in discussions by comparing their ideas with those of peers and others, building on others' ideas to advance discussion, and questioning others to clarify their ideas.

- Identify the main ideas in both planned and unplanned spoken texts of some length and complexity (in a survey, interpret a long answer by a respondent in terms of the choices on the survey form; make accurate notes of main points while listening to a speech or group discussion).

- Identify a range of perspectives on contentious issues (listen to songs of social comment, speeches, interviews, debates, radio news programs, televised book and film reviews, and compare their perspectives).

- In informal groups, discuss and justify, with appropriate evidence, personal viewpoints on issues and texts (discuss opinions on the motives of characters in a novel and respond to others' views).

- Report formally on different perspectives on a complex issue, problem or point of view, and present their own opinion clearly and succinctly (present a summary of a problem and personal point of view to a student council meeting).

- Perform texts such as recitations, role play, and drama in front of familiar groups as a way of assisting the exploration of complex issues in a class.

Contextual understanding

At level 6, a student:

6.2 Identifies ways in which listeners' sociocultural backgrounds, knowledge and opinions influence the meaning they construct from spoken texts.

Evident when students, for example:

- Show understanding of the way different people react to spoken texts (roleplay themselves as various personae listening to an anecdote which might offend some people, such as one which relies for its humour on a stereotyped view of some group).

- Compare different responses to political speeches or interviews, exploring the extent to which differences might be the result of political allegiance, personal liking for or antipathy towards the politician, or the presentation of the speaker.

- Discuss the way vocabulary, accent and other aspects of speech reflect and are interpreted in terms of power relationships in our society (by examining the spoken texts of people in differing positions of social power).

- Experiment with the way different people interpret specialist vocabulary or specialised language constructions, and discuss the extent to which comprehension and interpretation depend on topic knowledge and understanding of context (of sports like cricket, occupations like wholesaling and retailing).

- Identify the kind of language conventions expected in formal spoken texts and understand how particular groups might react to alternatives (body language indicating boredom, long pauses which indicate uncertainty or having finished).

- Ask questions which show knowledge of the person being questioned and of the way language works (avoid questions like 'Have you stopped stealing?' because both yes and no imply that the respondent did once steal).

Linguistic structures & features

At level 6, a student:

6.3 Experiments with knowledge of linguistic structures and features, and draws on this knowledge to explain how speakers influence audiences.

Evident when students, for example:

- Note how presentation is adjusted according to size of group — in type of language, pitch of voice, pace — to maximise impact of the message (study the rhetorical devices in Martin Luther King's 'I have a dream' speech and comment on their emotional appeal to the audience).

- Identify the characteristics of varieties of spoken language such as colloquial speech and formal speech and identify and discuss the major features of formal texts (clearly demarcated introductions, main points and conclusions).

- Recognise the importance of clearly introducing and concluding formal spoken texts and using other staging cues to help audiences follow the speaker's train of thought (use words and expressions like 'Firstly...', 'Finally...' in formal spoken texts such as stories, anecdotes and speeches).

- Detect elements of persuasion and appeal in radio advertisements, commenting on the purpose and impact of pace, volume, tone, stress, music, as well as the images conveyed by vocabulary and ideas.

- Recognise that non-verbal elements may, intentionally or unintentionally, subvert the content of spoken presentations (the intentionally monotonous reading of a speech about how exciting life is will indicate that the speech is ironic).

- Note how speakers develop and clarify ideas by using analogies and other comparisons and attempt to do the same in spoken texts.

Strategies

At level 6, a student:

6.4 Critically evaluates others' spoken texts and uses this knowledge to reflect on and improve own.

Evident when students, for example:

- Note how speakers in formal situations recover from interruptions and attempt to use these techniques.

- Help to establish criteria for use by a class in evaluating spoken texts, and use these or others to evaluate their own and others' participation in group discussions and formal presentations.

- Plan for formal speech activities (draft complete speech, devise cue cards, read text aloud to themselves and others, tape record speech to check timing, anticipate expectations and needs of listeners).

- Use strategies to overcome self-consciousness (prepare thoroughly to maximise confidence, work with another student when possible, avoid looking at audience members likely to be disruptive).

- Notice the way speakers engage audiences and try to use similar techniques (speak with interest and personal enthusiasm, end texts with purpose and direction rather than allowing them to peter out).

- Evaluate success in conveying ideas and information to particular audiences and use this to develop speaking and listening skills.

Level 7 outcomes:

7.1 Works effectively with others in situations characterised by complexity of purpose, procedure and subject matter and a need for formality in speech and attitude.

7.2 Considers the interrelationships between texts, contexts, speakers and listeners in a range of situations.

7.3 Uses awareness of differences between spoken and written language to construct own spoken texts in structured, formal situations.

7.4 Uses a range of strategies to present spoken texts in formal situations.

LEVEL 6 Reading and Viewing

Level 5 outcomes:

5.5 Discusses themes and issues in accessible texts with challenging structures and ideas, and constructs responses interpreting these.

5.6 Recognises that texts are constructed for particular purposes and to appeal to certain groups.

5.7 Draws on knowledge of linguistic structures and features to explain how texts are constructed.

5.8a Uses knowledge of principal conventions of narrative texts to construct meaning from a range of text types.

5.8b Systematically finds and records information.

Texts

At level 6, a student:

6.5 Explores different perspectives on complex issues through reading and viewing a range of texts, and constructs written and spoken responses relating these perspectives to personal understandings of the contemporary world.

Evident when students, for example:

- Read and view novels and films, including accessible adult texts which raise complex social issues, such as Harper Lee's *To Kill a Mockingbird* or Charles Dickens' *A Christmas Carol*, and engage in guided discussion of the attitudes, concerns and themes underlying these texts.

- Read and view a variety of texts (including more than one text type) on an issue, noting the range of viewpoints, examining the selection, omission and emphasis of aspects of the issue depending on the text type and the view being expressed, and attempting to evaluate some of the arguments.

- Discuss orally and in writing texts read or viewed in relation to a point of view (refer explicitly to evidence in the text and demonstrate the ability to select the most effective evidence to support a stance for or against a proposition).

- Make some valid moral, psychological and philosophical generalisations about human behaviour based on evidence from texts read and viewed.

- Read newspaper articles on familiar topics, discuss the way different papers present the same topic, and compare this presentation with their own view and understanding.

- Respond both personally and in more detached and critical ways to texts, seeing both a personal and a wider significance.

Contextual understanding

At level 6, a student:

6.6 Considers the contexts in which texts were or are created and how these are reflected in texts.

Evident when students, for example:

- Recognise that authors choose particular text types for the purpose and audience of a communication, and suggest reasons for the choices (compare the expectations an author would have of an audience when recording or narrating a legend such as the legend of *Pygmalion*, the play *Pygmalion* (George Bernard Shaw), or the musical/film *My Fair Lady* (Shaw and Lerner and Loewe).

- Compare texts set in different times and places and account for some of their similarities and differences (compare the treatment of love and gang warfare in Shakespeare's *Romeo and Juliet* with a modern musical such as *West Side Story* or compare the treatment of the theme of change or transformation in Shakespeare's *A Midsummer Night's Dream* with Michael Gow's *Away* and the film *Dead Poets' Society*.

- Understand that both informational texts and fictional works represent a selection of information and data, and that what is left out is significant in understanding the attitudes and intentions of the author.

- Identify examples of symbols in books and films that have specific meaning to a culture (the elements of a film set that immediately identify the period).

- Understand that the construction and interpretation of images depend on the historical period in which they were made and the socio-cultural background of the target audience .

Linguistic structures & features

At level 6, a student:

6.7 Compares linguistic structures and features of texts to highlight their similarities and differences in form and meaning.

Evident when students, for example:

- Discuss the typical features or conventions of a range of text types (the use of imagery and stereotyping in advertising, the use of time lapse in novels and films).

- Transform short sequences of well-known stories such as Cinderella into various genres — horror, gangster, romance, adventure — by identifying specific characteristics of these genres, and discuss the effect of the genres on meaning.

- Detect thematic similarities in texts that differ in structure and language (a poem and a painting, for instance, compare a short story such as Henry Lawson's *The Drover's Wife* with Drysdale's painting on the same subject or a poem such as W.H. Auden's *Musée des Beaux Arts* with Brueghel's painting *Landscape and the Fall of Icarus*).

- Use knowledge of one text or text type to help interpret another (comment on the use of narrative techniques in non-fiction texts).

- Compare different text types, such as a short story and a film based on it or a drink-driving advertisement run on TV, radio and in newspapers, in terms of the demands, limitations and advantages of each form, noting differences in meaning and effect and examining the ways in which loss of advantages in one form has been compensated for by advantages in the other form.

- Evaluate information on the same theme or issue in different text types or media (in comparing a song and a play on the same theme, note selections and omissions, compare beginnings and endings, discuss which text is most effective in conveying a point of view or an idea).

Strategies

At level 6, a student:

6.8a Draws on a repertoire of strategies to maintain understanding through dense or extended texts.

Evident when students, for example:

- Compare their own experience and knowledge with characters, events, and values in texts to find points in common, especially when a text is set in an unfamiliar time and place.

- Cope with dense or difficult texts by highlighting important ideas, using cues provided by illustrations or tables, and making notes to record potentially confusing shifts in time and place in visual texts.

- Read aloud to establish the tone of a piece of writing (a newspaper editorial to hear its sarcasm).

- Use understanding of such things as relative pronouns and tense to maintain coherence when reading long or complex sentence constructions.

- Refer to their socio-cultural context to make inferences about texts

6.8b Gathers, selects and organises information effectively for specific purposes.

Evident when students, for example:

- Read and view selectively, recording only the most significant information.

- In supporting a point of view on a text, draft a list of supporting examples from the text and select the most effective and convincing.

- Define information requirements both before and during research, recognising when sources other than the school library are required.

- Use evidence from texts (both fiction and non-fiction) to confirm or challenge their own or others' points of view on an issue.

- Use efficient note-taking and note-making strategies (summarise information in own words, or write information verbatim, using quotation marks and noting page numbers, if it might be useful to quote directly in the final product).

- Ensure that sources are fully and accurately recorded (title, author, year of publication, page number).

Level 7 outcomes:

7.5   Constructs meanings from a range of texts, including those characterised by complexity of construction and subject matter, and justifies these with detailed and well-chosen evidence from the text.

7.6   Considers a variety of interrelationships between texts, contexts, readers or viewers and makers of texts.

7.7   Identifies and comments on the impact of techniques intended to shape readers' and viewers' interpretations of and reactions to texts.

7.8   Uses reading and viewing strategies that enable detailed critical evaluation of texts.

LEVEL 6 Writing

Level 5 outcomes:

5.9   Uses a variety of text types for writing about familiar or accessible subjects and exploring challenging ideas and issues.

5.10   Identifies the specific effect of context, audience and purpose on written texts.

5.11   Controls the linguistic structures and features necessary to communicate ideas and information clearly in written texts of some length and complexity.

5.12   Draws on planning and review strategies that assist in effectively completing particular tasks.

Texts

At level 6, a student:

6.9 Conveys detailed information and explores different perspectives on complex, challenging issues through writing for specific and general audiences.

Evident when students, for example:

- Construct sustained and unified narratives that attempt to do more than present action and events (stories have more than one complication for characters to overcome; plots, even if derivative, provoke thought about people's lives).

- Construct a written argument for a general audience, featuring a clear introduction to the topic, supporting examples to justify the writer's opinion, awareness of alternative opinions, suggestions for action if appropriate, and a suitable closing statement.

- Write extended expository texts using information from different sources, referring to suitable text models for help with organisation and language, and expressing a clear point of view.

- Write formal letters that convey detailed information or a point of view (to a newspaper or a potential employer).

- Write an accurate account within a structured format requiring close attention to detail and sequence (a tax return, an insurance claim or an accident report).

- Write real or mock newspaper articles about issues and events, trying to write as a journalist rather than with the omniscience of an author of a fiction text (arranging material according to the inverted pyramid formula of news reports).

- Explore different perspectives in narratives by experimenting with writing in different ways (telling a story first from one character's viewpoint, then from another's; using flashbacks, parallel plots, ironic twists; putting forward a point of view about an issue in a story rather than a formal argument).

Contextual understanding

At level 6, a student:

6.10   Predicts some of the likely characteristics and expectations of particular audiences and tries to accommodate or resist these expectations as appropriate.

Evident when students, for example:

- Realise that people judge writers by the surface features of their writing as well as its content, proofread their own writing carefully, especially where writing to impress readers (writing for publication or to a potential employer).

- Experiment with designing a text for one audience, then altering its content and style for another (a drink-driving advertisement aimed first at teenage drivers and then at the general public).

- Select words and images to provoke positive or negative responses in readers (use 'slim' rather than 'skinny' or vice versa, depending on the desired effect).

- Try to subvert stereotypes (portraying women as workers outside domestic settings, Aboriginal workers as professionals, disabled people as professionals).

- Ensure that written instructions are targeted at the intended audience and comprehensive because readers cannot ask questions.

- Use relevant examples to support opinions, recognising that readers need to be convinced by thoughtful argument rather than simple assertions.

Linguistic structures & features

At level 6, a student:

6.11 Uses and experiments with a range of linguistic structures and features designed to influence audiences.

Evident when students, for example:

- Use suitable setting-out and standard Australian English when writing texts such as letters for formal purposes.

- Show awareness of the function of synonyms by choosing suitable alternative words to avoid clumsy repetition.

- Adopt structures for the way they could influence readers ('A minority claims that… However, most people acknowledge that…').

- Select information to influence readers' responses to a text (in developing a point of view about an issue, in arousing suspense in a narrative, in creating humour).

- Experiment with ways of sequencing information (ordering arguments in an expository text on the basis of priority, chronology or some other kind of order; sequencing ideas in narratives or poetry in unconventional or non-chronological ways).

- Distinguish between active and passive voice, and experiment with both to judge their usefulness in various contexts.

Strategies

At level 6, a student:

6.12 Revises own writing for meaning and effectiveness.

Evident when students, for example:

- Proofread punctuation and grammar so that meaning is clear (ensure that placement of commas conveys the intended meaning, that word order and use of pronouns have not created ambiguity).

- Use strategies to overcome lack of confidence in revising effectively (workshop writing in small groups or with a partner).

- Try to read their own work from the perspective of another reader and make revisions (manipulate text structure to make the writing as interesting or intriguing as possible).

- Ensure that all elements in a piece of writing are relevant (check expository writing for relevance to the topic; check that all incidents in a narrative are relevant to the development of plot and character).

- Add new ideas during revision to make writing more effective (clarify a sequence of events, describe a character more fully, perform extra research to provide more convincing reasons for an argument).

- Use strategies to improve sequence and coherence in writing (cut and paste paragraphs using either paper or a word-processor).

Level 7 outcomes:

7.9   Writes sustained texts characterised by complexity of purpose and subject matter and a need for formality in language and construction.

7.10   Selects text type, subject matter and language to suit a specific audience and purpose.

7.11   Controls spelling, syntax and text structures to meet the demands of most expository and imaginative writing.

7.12   Critically evaluates others' written texts and uses this knowledge to reflect on and improve own.

A guide to writing a children's book

Task

Students were required to study an agreed topic of personal interest during a five-week block. This student wanted to write a children's picture book, but found during the initial research that there was little guidance available and decided instead to produce a guide to writing a children's book. The audience specified was 'any English student wanting a guide, however it would be aimed at grade 7 and 8 students'.

Background

The student spent five weeks of class and homework time in discussions with peers and teacher and in producing three drafts and this final version.

Relevant outcomes:
Reading and viewing

6.6 Considers the contexts in which texts were or are created and how these are reflected in texts.

6.7 Compares linguistic structures and features of texts to highlight their similarities and differences in form and meaning.

6.8b Gathers, selects and organises information effectively for specific purposes.

Writing

6.9 Conveys detailed information and explores different perspectives on complex, challenging issues through writing for specific and general audiences.

6.10 Predicts some of the likely characteristics and expectations of particular audiences and tries to accommodate or resist these expectations as appropriate.

6.11 Uses and experiments with a range of linguistic structures and features designed to influence audiences.

6.12 Revises own writing for meaning and effectiveness.

Summary comment

This guide conveys detailed information on a challenging topic for a specific audience. Pertinent information has been gathered, sifted and organised. The student considered a number of aspects of the creation of picture books, including authors' intentions and use of linguistic structures and features. The work shows evidence of an effort to meet the requirements of its intended audience (for example, in the linguistic structures and features used) and of effective revision.

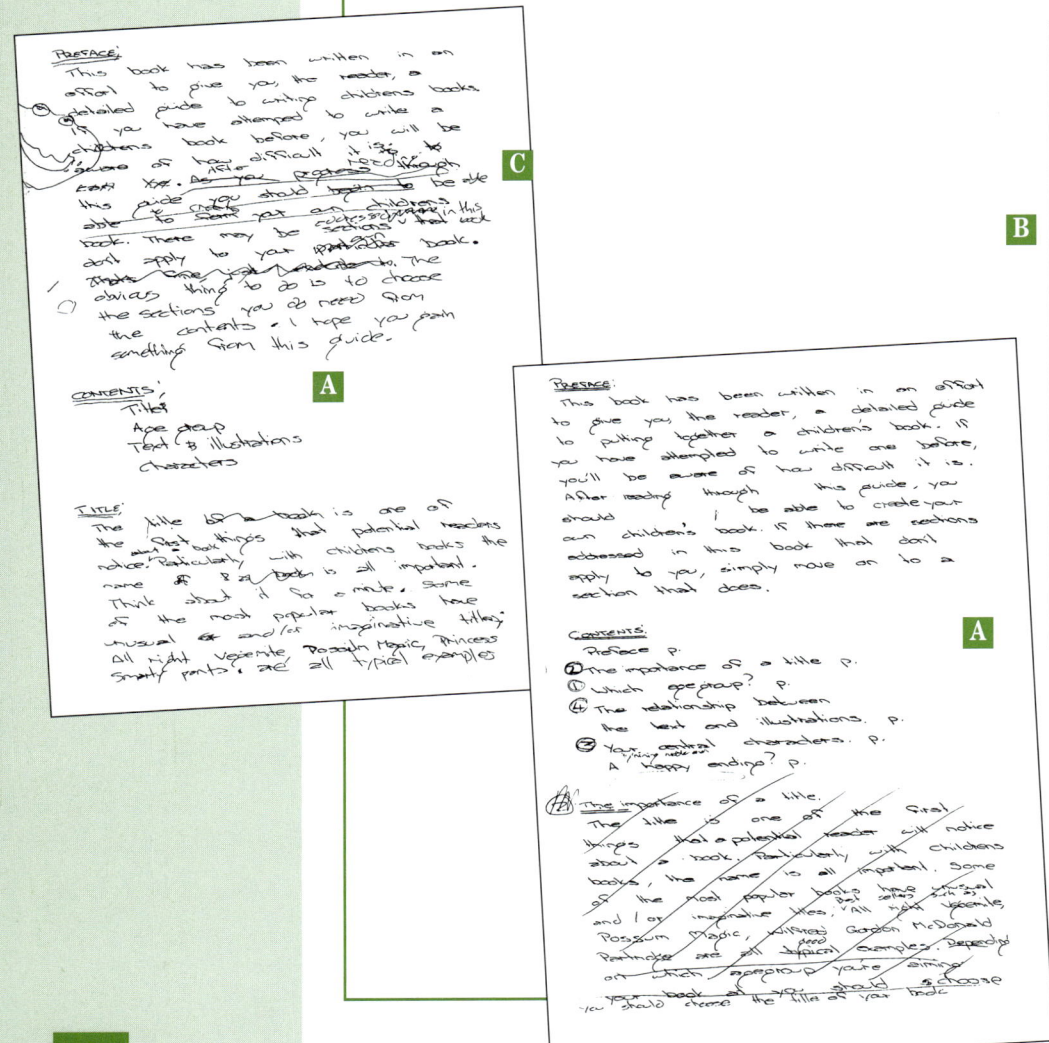

(6.8b) Thoughtful organisation: sequence is logical and drafts reflect attention to importance of this, as sections 1 and 2 were originally reversed (**A**).

(6.10) Thought about expectations and needs of readers (**B**).

A GUIDE TO WRITING A CHILDREN'S BOOK

CONTENTS
Preface
Which Age Group?
The Importance Of A Title
Your Central Characters
The Relationship Between The Text And The Illustrations

PREFACE

B This booklet has been written in an effort to give you, the reader, a detailed guide to putting together a children's book. If you have attempted to write one before, you will be aware of how difficult it can be. After reading through this guide, you should be able to **C** create you own children's book. If there are sections addressed in this booklet that do not apply to you, simply move on to one that does. I hope this guide will aid your writing.

WHICH AGE GROUP?

D The whole structure of your book depends upon which age group you are writing for. You must have a clear idea before you commence writing of what type of book you wish to produce. If your illustrations are to convey much of the story with only a few words per double page, you are looking at creating a picture book.

Picture books are generally read to or by children aged zero to five. Choose a topic which will capture their attention and which will be readily understood by them. Obviously the topic you choose should have the potential to produce effective illustrations as these will be the focus of the reader's attention

---

If you wish you book to contain a little more text, you should aim it at slightly older children, say from five to seven years old. This is the format most true children's books take. The text should play as important a part as the illustrations, if not more so. The readers will be focusing most of their attention on the text, so keep the story interesting.

E You may choose to write for an older audience. In this case it would be wise to make more of the story. The book may include some illustrations, but they should not be so detailed as to take **F** away from the text. The plot may be more intensive and intricate, the characters may have more detailed personalities and the text may take up more content than the illustrations.

B It is important to go through this process before you begin to form your book. In this way you can set yourself tasks according to the age group you have chosen and end up with a suitable book. The alternative is to have a book which doesn't cater for any age group and so has no specific audience.

If you wish to look through some books to get an idea of the age group you want to write for and how to go about it, have a look through some of the following books.

Zero - Five: Mr Men books, Grug books, Little Golden books.

Five - Seven: Dr Seuss books, Beatrix Potter

Seven and over: Enid Blyton, Trixie Beldon

THE IMPORTANCE OF A TITLE

The title is one of the first things that a potential reader will notice about a book. Particularly with children's books, the name is all important. Some of the most popular books have unusual and/or imaginative titles. Best sellers such as *All Right Vegemite*, *Possum Magic* and *Wilfred Gordon McDonald Partridge* are all **G** good examples.

H You should choose the title of your book according to the age group you are writing for (see chapter one). If you wish to pitch **F** you book at infants, the title should be simple to say, catchy and interesting. Infants like to repeat phrases, so if you title is catchy **I** and sounds nice, you book will catch children's attention. Many people say that you shouldn't choose a book by it's cover, however this is quite often how children choose their books.

The other aspect of a title you should consider is the actual presentation. The title may be catchy and correct for your audience but if it is dull and boring to look at then you will lose potential readers, as many children pick out their own books. If you have access to some younger children, have a look through their bookcase and observe which books are their favourites. More often than not the title will be colourful and eye-catching as well catchy.

YOUR CENTRAL CHARACTERS

Characters play an important part in any book but particularly in children's books. This is because children focus most of their attention on personalities rather than plots. Stories such as *Little Red Riding Hood* have two obvious main characters - Little Red Riding Hood and The Big Bad Wolf - and three background characters, the mother, the grandmother and the woodcutter. This gives the children who are reading the book two characters to focus their attention on, and three other less significant characters to fill in the story. Obviously, the older the audience, the more characters you can successfully include.

F The personalities of the people in your book should not be too intricate as you don't want to confuse your younger readers. Particularly with small children, you should make your characters' personalities easy to discern. As with *Little Red* **E** *Riding Hood* the characters are either good or bad. The older the readers of your book are, the more complex you can make your **F** characters. Age really is the deciding factor in most aspects of story writing.

Decide upon the type of personalities you want your characters to have. For example, a nasty snake and a good little church mouse. Try also to be consistent with the images of characters. For instance, you wouldn't put a snake who eats mice as a nice guy. Although this is typecasting it makes the easier for young children to follow. If your audience is older this rule needn't apply to the same degree, as children of a more mature age are more able to make judgements of their own about characters.

THE RELATIONSHIP BETWEEN TEXT AND ILLUSTRATIONS

For some books, illustrations can be crucial, others do not rely upon them that much. Most children's books, however, include both text and illustrations. It is important to include both so the child who is reading it has visual stimulation as well as mental. Illustrations can tell a story all of their own or else aid the text in telling the story. If the latter is the case it is important to have pictures that convey the message you wish to be sent to the reader.

Remember too that you don't necessarily have to have corresponding illustrations. You may want your illustrations to tell another story, or you may like to put in a hidden story or message in the pictures.

As you can see, there are many variations of the relationship between text and illustrations. There is no right or wrong way to set up the illustrations or text, just be sure that the format suits the age group you are writing for and the type of story you are creating. In this way you can set up the relationship in a way that suits you and your book.

(6.12) Revised for greater effectiveness: 'you should be able to create your own children's book' originally read 'as you progress through this guide you should begin to be able to form your own children's book' (**C**).

(6.6) Aware of the effect on form of purpose and audience (**D**); aware of the effect that intended audience has on the text construction (**E**).

(6.7) Able to compare texts in terms of linguistic structures and features to highlight their differences in meaning (**F**).

(6.12) Revised for greater effectiveness: drafts indicate that titles were carefully selected from a wider range (**G**).

(6.11) Language is tailored for intended audience: use of second person pronoun, straightforward sentence structure (**H**).

(6.12) Revised for greater effect: 'your book will catch children's attention' was originally 'your book is likely to be a hit with children' (considered by the student to be too colloquial), and later, 'your book is likely to be popular' (the student decided 'is likely' was vague and imprecise) (**I**).

Who dares to love

Task

Students were required to write a play exploring an issue of their choice. The task called for a description of the setting, a plot outline, and a script.

Background

After reading a short play and then watching two students perform it, students wrote a one- or two-page script to practise the conventions of scriptwriting and to focus on the need for conflict in drama. Follow-up lessons were designed to increase students' awareness of setting, of audience and purpose, and of the concept of conflict in drama (many had thought only of physical conflict). Students spent two weeks of class and homework time drafting the plays (eight x 60-minute lessons). This is the second and final version. The student received little individual help from the teacher, but worked with other students, who offered support and opinions.

Relevant outcomes

6.9 Conveys detailed information and explores different perspectives on complex, challenging issues through writing for specific and general audiences.

6.10 Predicts some of the likely characteristics and expectations of particular audiences and tries to accommodate or resist these expectations as appropriate.

6.11 Uses and experiments with a range of linguistic structures and features designed to influence audiences.

6.12 Revises own writing for meaning and effectiveness.

Summary comment

The play explores different perspectives on a complex, challenging issue in a way that communicates successfully with its intended audience. It is an imaginative, unified narrative with a didactic purpose; although it is somewhat cliche'd and predictable, it is a significant personal statement about the issue. Audience needs and characteristics are understood and met, and linguistic structures and features are carefully used to advance point of view.

WHO DARES TO LOVE

BY KYM

THE PLOT:

A university student from Australia named Joanna Michaels comes to the southern American city of Atlanta and stays with a white family in a mixed community. Joanna, a white third year medical student meets Matt Daniels, a black twenty year old house painter when Matt is hurt in a fight with two white boys who believe that blacks should be servants. Through Joanna's kindness, Matt realises that he has feelings for Joanna. Joanna yearns to know more about Matt. They fall in love and have to face the town's continuing racist attitudes. Will their love survive?

THE SETTING:

Atlanta, George, 1937. A little town on the outskirts of Atlanta where everyone knows everyone else's business. It is a small farming district, the main export of which is wheat. Each day, the men go out into the fields, while the women stay at home and look after the children and cook. The older girls and boys hang around the corner store flirting with each other, after school.

The corner store is a small hardware and food shop. There is also a post office, a library, a drugstore and a newspaper shop. There is a local pool in the centre of the town, with a barbed wire fence around **[A]** it. There is graffiti on the door, stating NO BLACKS. The council have painted over the writing many times, but the message keeps re-appearing.

The main street, or main drag, as the locals call it, is lined with shops and a large park. A number of streets branch off the main drag.

The average house has a small frontyard, three bedrooms, one bathroom and a small kitchen and lounge. Most of the houses have a small orchard or vegetable garden out in the backyard. Blacks and whites live in harmony, but it is only skin deep.

SCENE ONE: A rickety old truck makes it's way down the main drag, people take interest in the truck as it stops in front of a newspaper shop. Joanna Michaels steps out of the truck and makes her way to the back, where the luggage is placed. John Edwards helps get Joanna's luggage off the truck.

Joanna:	Thank you very much. [smiling]
John:	You're welcome, honey. [patting Joanna on the back]

[Joanna and John make their way into the small shop, struggling with the weight of the bags.]

John:	Mary Lou, Maureen! Where are you? [shouting]

[Mary Lou and Maureen enter and rush over to John]

John:	Joanna this is Mary Lou, my daughter, [pointing to a girl about 17 years old] and this is Maureen, my wife. [pointing to a burly woman, about 50 years old]
Mary Lou:	Well, we're all glad to meet you! [spoken in a southern accent] **[B]**
Maureen:	Come in and make yourself at home. That long boat ride must have been terrible. [She puts her arm around Joanna and sits her down.] Would you like a cup of coffee or anything to eat? Here, put your feet up. [She gets a smaller stool and places it under Joanna's feet.]
John:	[Putting his hands up] Ladies, ladies! Now you'all stop **[C]** fussing over Joanna! The poor girl probably just wants to go to bed. Now you two go and prepare Joanna's bed. O.K.? Go'on!
Maureen:	[Upset] Well, sorrrie! We just wanna make Joanna feel at home! Don't we, honey? [looking at Mary Lou]
Mary Lou:	Yeah! [putting her hand on her hips and pouting] And **[D]** what about my friends? I told them she was a coming today and they all could meet her. [Turning to Joanna] What's it like living in Australia?
Joanna:	Well…um. It's great!!
Mary Lou:	Man, she talks funny.
John:	No, she talks like an Australian!
Mary Lou:	You mean they all talk like that?

(6.11) Uses linguistic structures and features designed to influence audiences: details of setting contribute to impression of a town where there is only superficial harmony **(A)**.

(6.10) Understands audience's background knowledge and expectations: stereotyped version of hospitality in American South used to provide a contrast to the way people behave to Matt when he is injured **(B)**.

(6.11) Experiments with linguistic structures and features designed to influence audiences: approximation of Southern accent helps readers' or listeners' involvement in the world of the play and the culture of the South **(C)**; uses linguistic structures and features designed to influence audiences: female protagonist being Australian highlights the culturally based nature of the community's racism and

John: Yes.

Maureen: Where exactly do you live?

Joanna: In Newcastle, near Sydney.

Mary Lou: Do they have any good looking men there?

Maureen: Mary Lou!! [looking shocked]

Mary Lou: What? I was just asking!

Maureen: [turning to Joanna] Don't worry about her, child. She's man crazy at the moment!

John: We can ask Joanna questions tomorrow. Right now I think Joanna would like to get to sleep, so hurry up and get her bed ready! [Mary Lou and Maureen exit]

John: Sorry about them. They get overexcited!

Joanna: Thank you I really need a rest.

John: Right this way. (John leads Joanna out)

SCENE TWO:

John, Maureen and Mary Lou are at the breakfast table, eating breakfast. Joanna comes in and sits down next to Mary Lou.

All: Good morning.

John: Sleep well?

Joanna: Yes, thank you.

[C] Maureen: Well, dig in honey! Breakfast is the best meal of the day. [Pause]

Mary Lou: How old are you? [looking at Joanna]

Joanna: Nineteen.

Mary Lou: Wow! I'm eighteen, but I will be nineteen next spring.

John: What career are you interested in pursuing?

Joanna: I am studying to become a doctor. I've done two years of study out of four.

Mary Lou: Why so many? I couldn't do...[A yell interrupts Mary Lou mid-speech. Everyone rushes through the house, into the shop and out into the main drag]

Joanna: Oh my God! [A black man is lying in the middle of the road clutching his right arm. Further down the street two white boys are running away. Silence. Everyone, but Joanna and Mary Lou go inside]

Joanna: We've got to help! [Mary Lou grabs Joanna's arm]

Mary Lou: Don't! He's black!   **[E]**

Joanna: [Pulls her arm away from Mary Lou and rushs to the black man's side] Are you O.K? What's your name?   **[F]**

Matt: Matt! [looks surprised] [Mary Lou goes back into the shop]

Joanna: Hi Matt. I'm Joanna. Do you know who did this? [Looking at his arm]

Matt: [Looking down, whispering] No.

Joanna: [looking at him, disbelievingly. Pause] It looks like a shallow knife wound. What were you doing?

Matt: I was just walking down the street and... [sentence uncompleted]

Joanna: Ahh, yes. Do you have something to bandage your arm?

Matt: No, but I do in my house. Thank you for everything. I will be O.K. now.

Joanna: I am sure you will but I would prefer to come with you, to make sure.

Matt: Suit yourself. [Matt and Joanna walk down a nearby street to Matt's house]

Matt: This is it. [They go inside and Matt finds a bandage and they sit on the chairs at the kitchen table. Joanna expertly dresses and bandages the wound]

---

encourages empathy and sympathy from an Australian audience (**D**).

(6.9) Recognises different perspectives on the issue (**E**).

(6.11) Characterisation of Joanna makes it clear that she has humanitarian instincts, which would appeal to some Australian readers or viewers (**F**).

(6.10) Matt's fear that no relationship can begin between him and Joanna makes readers feel the injustice of the situation (**G**); understands the nature of the audience being written for: use of derogatory expression 'black boy' is offensive and reinforces readers' and viewers' sympathy for the protagonists' plight (**H**).

(6.12) Revises own writing for effectiveness: stage directions originally more detailed but less effective (**I**).

Joanna: [mesmerised by his beautiful brown eyes] You should wash it every day and keep it clean.

Matt: [Matt looks touched by her kindness] Thank you, thank you very much.

Joanna: I'd like to see you again...I mean, your cut, of course. [Joanna goes red with embarrassment]

[G] Matt: [smiles, then frowns] Don't...it's not proper.

Joanna: I really should go. Do you know a doctor who could dress you arm?

Matt: No.

Joanna: So there. I will meet you outside the newspaper shop tomorrow.

Matt: [giving up] O.K. But not outside the newspaper shop!

Joanna: 9.30am sharp! [Getting up to leave] Outside the newspaper shop! Bye.

[Joanna leaves. Matt sighs and looks at his bandaged arm.]

SCENE THREE:

Matt is waiting outside the newspaper shop and two white boys come up and abuse him.

[H] First boy: Hey black boy, how ya going? [He pushes Matt. Matt stumbles but quickly recovers]

Second boy: [He touches Matt's right arm. matt ignores him but winces in pain.] Oh well looky here. What happened to you black boy? Did someone jack you up? [Joanna comes out of the shop, sees what"s going on and puts her hands on her hips. The boys stop pushing Matt and stare at Joanna]

Joanna: What's going on here?

First boy: A black party. Do you wanna join in?

Joanna: No I don't. Could you please leave! Go and play cars or whatever you little boys do over here.

[The two boys turn to leave but call out behind them] We'll see you round black boy. [The boys exit]

Matt: Thank you...again.

Joanna: Your'e welcome. [silence] Um...How's your arm? Is it still sore?

Matt: Yeah, abit. I've washed it twice today already. [He smiles]

Joanna: [Smiles too.] That's good. [There is a long pause as they look into each other's eyes. Joanna is the first to look away. Maureen and Mary Lou come out of the shop into the street.]

Joanna: Hi! Maureen, Mary Lou. How are you? [Maureen and Mary Lou walk straight past Joanna and Matt, ignoring them] Maureen, Mary Lou! [speaking louder. Pause.] Maybe they didn't hear me.   **[B]**

Matt: Maybe I should go.

Joanna: Wait! I'll walk you to the corner.

Matt: [Hesitant] Are you sure?

Joanna: Yes. [They start walking down the street.]

Matt: [Shyly.] Thanks for your help. You don't know how much this means to me. [They stop in front of Matt's street]

[I] Joanna: Don't forget to keep that cut clean to stop infection. [Pause] Well, I had better be going. [She turns and leaves. Matt calls after her]

Matt: See you later. [Matt looks longingly after Joanna.]

Matt: She would be easy to love. [Looking up to the sky] God!! Why does the colour of one's skin matter so much? Why do we have to dare to love? [Matt walks towards his house]

The Caine Mutiny

Task

Students were required to write a formal essay on Herman Wouk's novel *The Caine Mutiny* in answer to the question: 'Do you think that the "mutiny" was justified? Argue the case one way or the other and support your view.'

Background

Students had read *The Caine Mutiny*, written answers to questions on the incidents and characters, and viewed the 1950s film of the book. During class discussion of the requirements of formal essays, students were reminded that they should present an argument supported by relevant evidence. They were asked to plan their essays at home and to write the first draft in class in 40 minutes. Students were given another period to look over their drafts and discuss them with peers before writing a final version in class.

Relevant outcomes

6.5 Explores different perspectives on complex issues through reading and viewing a range of texts, and constructs written and spoken responses relating these perspectives to personal understanding of the contemporary world.

Summary comment

This essay is closer to level 6 achievement than to level 5 because of the complexity of the issues it tries to grapple with, the length and complexity of the text itself, and the degree of organisation of the response. It is clearly not yet approaching level 7 work, principally because of the way the topic is partly lost sight of half-way through the essay, moving the focus from whether the mutiny was justified to what caused it. With help from peers or the teacher, the student might have been able to correct this.

ESSAY

Do you think that the "MUTINY" was justified? Using details from the book to support you view.

A It is hard to decide whether the mutiny was justified because there are many points that could be argued for or against the mutiny, but my view is that the mutiny was uunjuustified.

B The captain wasn't very popular on the caine because from the moment he stepped aboard the ship he harshly enforced rules and regulations upon the men, which they weren't used to on the caine. The reaction to Queeg passed from irritation and disgust to dislike and hatred. Queeg fussed about the tiniest details eg. Whether a shirt tail was hanging out. If this was the case the person involved would have to write a report stating why the shirt tail wasn't tucked in and the morale officer would have to write a report stating why he had neglected to notice the shirt tail hanging out seeings that was the job of the morale officer. None of these activities and others of this sort, can be used to conclude that the captain was paranoid. Sure, when the action was getting rough, he kept to the protected areas of the ship, but then even the bravest **C** people get scared once in awhile. I don't think these things made his judgements wrong, whilst he was in command of the ship.

C Captain Queeg did make a few errors from my point of view, but then again everyone makes mistakes and his mistakes didn't injure anyone.

C The final cause of the mutiny was caused by the situation when the caine was in the heart of the typoon. I think Maryk got scared in the heat of the storm and wasn't thinking straight, not that ianyone could think straight in the middle of a typoon.

All through the typoon thoughts of Keefer bringing up the idea that Queeg was mentally unsound. This idea was ppicked up by Maryk. This is why he started keeping a secret diary of all the captain's unreasonable acts and unprofessional behaviouur. All these thoughts were refreshed in Maryk's mind as they passed through the typoon. All of which led him to the extent of mutiny.

Maryk thought that if Queeg was to captain the ship through the typoon the ship would be lost at sea.

In the great storm, the sea took control of the ship being lost because of the way Queeg was handling it was the final cause of the mutiny.

(6.5) Tackles an issue recognised as complex: aware that it is not easy to say whether the mutiny was justified (**A**); response to the essay topic is organised, with a clear introduction and an emerging argument that Queeg's unpopularity does not mean that his judgements were necessarily wrong (**B**); relates the situation on the ship to a personal understanding of the contemporary world (**C**).

LEVEL SEVEN

LEVEL 7 Statement

Students who have achieved level seven are aware of their audiences and purposes for communicating with others and are able to cope with the formal style and language required by some situations. They listen to, read, view and respond to a wide range of complex and demanding texts dealing with social, personal and philosophical issues.

Students are alert to the assumptions and inferences in what people say. They try to speak fluently and confidently in formal and more casual and familiar situations, always being aware of why and to whom they are speaking.

Students read and critically view a wide range of text types, and justify their interpretations of and views about texts with detailed evidence. They evaluate rhetorical techniques for their effectiveness and legitimacy.

When writing, students try to match text type, structure, tone and vocabulary to the demands of situations. They express themselves precisely when writing for often complex purposes, and they explore ideas about texts and issues in an organised and precise way.

LEVEL 7
Table of outcomes

	Texts	Contextual understanding	Linguistic structures & features	Strategies
SPEAKING AND LISTENING	7.1 Works effectively with others in situations characterised by complexity of purpose, procedure and subject matter and a need for formality in speech and attitude.	7.2 Considers the inter-relationships between texts, contexts, speakers and listeners in a range of situations.	7.3 Uses awareness of differences between spoken and written language to construct own spoken texts in structured, formal situations.	7.4 Uses a range of strategies to present spoken texts in formal situations.
	See page 132	See page 132	See page 133	See page 133
READING AND VIEWING	7.5 Constructs meanings from a range of texts, including those characterised by complexity of construction and subject matter, and justifies these with detailed and well-chosen evidence from the text.	7.6 Considers a variety of interrelationships between texts, contexts, readers or viewers and makers of texts.	7.7 Identifies and comments on the impact of techniques intended to shape readers' and viewers' interpretations of and reactions to texts.	7.8 Uses reading and viewing strategies that enable detailed critical evaluation of texts.
	See page 134	See page 134	See page 135	See page 135
WRITING	7.9 Writes sustained texts characterised by complexity of purpose and subject matter and a need for formality in language and construction.	7.10 Selects text type, subject matter and language to suit a specific audience and purpose.	7.11 Controls spelling, syntax and text structures to meet the demands of most expository and imaginative writing.	7.12 Critically evaluates others' written texts and uses this knowledge to reflect on and improve own.
	See page 136	See page 136	See page 137	See page 137

LEVEL 7 Speaking and Listening

Level 6 outcomes:

6.1   Conveys detailed information and explores different perspectives on complex issues through interacting with known social groups, principally peers, in structured and unstructured situations.

6.2   Identifies ways in which listeners' socio-cultural backgrounds, knowledge and opinions influence the meaning they obtain from spoken texts.

6.3   Experiments with knowledge of linguistic structures and features, and draws on this knowledge to explain how speakers influence audiences.

6.4   Critically evaluates others' spoken texts and uses this knowledge to reflect on and improve own.

Texts

At level 7, a student:

7.1 Works effectively with others in situations characterised by complexity of purpose, procedure and subject matter and a need for formality in speech and attitude.

Evident when students, for example:

- Make significant contributions to independent work groups (by helping to establish clear purposes, procedures, and schedules; conveying complex information and ideas; checking work for relevance; reflecting on and if necessary modifying their own behaviour — for instance, being aware of dominating discussions).

- Assist discussion groups towards a group response to texts or issues (by refining the question or task, accurately synthesising information from a number of contributions, reflecting group conclusions).

- Interview an adult, demonstrating sound preparation (background research, intelligent ordering of questions), flexibility (improvising questions to follow up unexpected responses), and an organised approach to recording the interview (use of tape recorder, note pad).

- Participate in formal meetings, adhering to meeting procedure while listening and speaking (comment through the chair, refrain from speaking when others have the floor).

- Participate in debates, demonstrating team spirit during the preparation, anticipating the other team's position, and selecting key elements of the opposition's argument for reply.

- Listen critically to detect values and assumptions in other people's language (recognise the use of loaded terms such as 'the Aboriginal problem').

Contextual understanding

At level 7, a student:

7.2 Considers the inter-relationships between texts, contexts, speakers and listeners in a range of situations.

Evident when students, for example:

- Comment on why style and content of spoken language vary in different contexts (listen critically to the style and language of two radio news programs and analyse their similarities and differences; compare and contrast everyday language with that of television soap operas).

- Observe the specific ways in which the tone and manner of speakers alter depending on whether they are speaking in public or in private (recognise that political opponents blustering about each other on television might talk much more reasonably in private).

- Show understanding of the need for agreed procedures in meetings (that comments should be made through the chair to maintain order and fairness).

- Recognise that selection, omission and ordering as a result of editing influence interpretation (understand that the 30-second grab shown on TV news or broadcast on radio might not sum up or show the complexity of the opinion of the person recorded).

- Take into account audience diversity in terms of such things as background and opinions, and try to ensure that this is acknowledged in the content and language of their own speech (that a talk about sport to a general audience should not use examples exclusively from male sports).

- Frame questions to elicit particular information, showing understanding of the purpose of the task and of the person being addressed (ask children one question at a time; frame questions so they are unambiguous and do elicit the required information).

Linguistic structures & features

At level 7, a student:

7.3 Uses awareness of differences between spoken and written language to construct own spoken texts in structured, formal situations.

Evident when students, for example:

- Select aspects of a written research assignment for presentation in speech, making necessary adjustments (simplifying sentence construction to make the material clearer for listeners).

- Choose less formal and complex language for speech than for written work on the same topic, and use such aids as body language, intonation, handouts.

- In formal speech, stress key words to ensure audience attentiveness and use pauses to emphasise important points.

- Recognise importance of written prompts, preparing speech cue cards and overheads and handouts to help audience concentration and understanding.

- Take advantage of the flexibility of spoken texts by being alert to indications of audience confusion or boredom and respond by attempting to clarify ideas, skipping planned items, pitching the voice differently.

Strategies

At level 7, a student:

7.4 Uses a range of strategies to present spoken texts in formal situations.

Evident when students, for example:

- Use the language and conventions expected in formal settings (suitable vocabulary and manner, rhetorical devices, visual aids).

- Plan effectively by preparing notes, cue cards, visual aids and layout of physical space of prepared speeches or by jotting notes and ordering them in a situation such as a meeting where there is little time to plan.

- Use notes unobtrusively while maintaining eye contact and fluency.

- Structure material imaginatively to interest an audience in material that has no inherent interest.

- Use time well, judging material and audience attention span and pacing own speech effectively.

- Use some recovery techniques in response to disruptions of formal presentations (waiting, recapping, or reading notes).

Level 8 outcomes:

8.1 Interacts responsively, critically and confidently with both familiar and unfamiliar audiences on specialised topics in formal situations, and consistently achieves a variety of purposes in speech.

8.2 Shows sophisticated understanding of the power and effect of spoken language when speaking and listening.

8.3 Analyses how linguistic structures and features affect interpretations of spoken texts, especially in the construction of tone, style and point of view.

8.4 Uses listening strategies which enable detailed critical evaluation of texts with complex levels of meaning.

LEVEL 7 Reading and Viewing

6.5 Explores different perspectives on complex issues through reading and viewing a range of texts, and constructs written and spoken responses relating these perspectives to personal understandings of the contemporary world.

6.6 Considers the contexts in which texts were or are created and how these are reflected in texts.

6.7 Compares linguistic structures and features of texts to highlight their similarities and differences in form and meaning.

6.8a Draws on a repertoire of strategies to maintain understanding through dense or extended texts.

6.8b Gathers, selects and organises information effectively for specific purposes.

Texts

At level 7, a student:

7.5 Constructs meanings from a range of texts, including those characterised by complexity of construction and subject matter, and justifies these with detailed and well-chosen evidence from the text.

Evident when students, for example:

- Read or view literature texts and discuss layers of meaning created by means of such things as allegory, parable, analogy (consider how parable is used in the Gospels or Bunyan's allegorical methods in *The Pilgrim's Progress*).

- Detect values and assumptions in what characters in fiction say and do, and comment on characters' development of self-knowledge and understanding (for instance, consider whether King Lear gains in self-knowledge in Shakespeare's *King Lear* or whether Emma really changes in Jane Austen's *Emma*).

- Explore a text by entering imaginatively into the lives of characters, justifying the characters' actions by assuming their point of view in describing events and interactions (write a chapter, prologue or epilogue of Emily Brontë's *Wuthering Heights* from Heathcliff's point of view or create a dialogue about ambition and power between current political figures using the exchanges between Macbeth and Lady Macbeth in Shakespeare's *Macbeth* as a basis).

- Recognise the complexity of construction of some apparently straightforward texts (explaining the significance of the ideas underlying apparently simple stories and poems about everyday events, the carefully constructed nature of film texts, the role of minor characters in narratives, the principles behind the selection and ordering of information in short newspaper reports).

- Produce more than one interpretation of a text (in interpreting a play for performance, making judgements about the implications of particular lines and stage directions).

- Organise information and ideas from texts read and viewed so that they provide compelling evidence for a clear point of view.

Contextual understanding

At level 7, a student:

7.6 Considers a variety of inter-relationships between texts, contexts, readers or viewers and makers of texts.

Evident when students, for example:

- Consider how a reader's or viewer's sociocultural identity may influence the interpretation of a text (compare and suggest possible reasons for different views of controversial texts like the film *Romper Stomper* or arguments on issues like smoking).

- Discuss the concentration of expression and language in poetry (for instance, consider poetry such as that of John Donne, Andrew Marvell, Gwen Harwood, Sylvia Plath, Margaret Atwood from these perspectives) and the extent to which poetry can thus be interpreted differently by different people.

- Use knowledge of the contexts in which texts were created to interpret them (comment on the significance of the conflict between loyalty and betrayal in the film *High Noon*, made in America during the McCarthy period).

- Make links between social issues and the production and circulation processes of media texts (examine the proposition that the popular media represent the dominant culture and that minority groups are often ignored or misrepresented).

- Examine the role of the media in creating or promoting causes such as UN military action, a campaign against the road toll, or the election of a particular political party.

- Recognise particular stereotypes as serving the interests of some groups in society at the expense of others (dole recipients being characterised as bludgers).

Linguistic structures & features

At level 7, a student:

7.7 Identifies and comments on the impact of techniques intended to shape readers' and viewers' interpretations of and reactions to texts.

Evident when students, for example:

- Comment on the way texts such as documentaries or current affairs programs of commentary and interviews on a current issue are structured to present a particular point of view, and explain how the same facts might be used to support different points of view.

- Note the way the rules of and expectations about genres can be manipulated for effect (giving ironical instructions such as 'How to write an F essay').

- Comment on the effect of words in positioning an audience to respond to a text in a particular manner (in a newspaper headline such as 'Strike $5b flop' or in poetry).

- Describe and comment on different narrative styles such as the telling of a story from a naive narrator's point of view, as in Graham Greene's short story *I Spy*, Daniel Keyes' short story *Flowers for Algernon* or Glenda Adams' short story *Lies*, and discuss whether equivalents are possible in films such as *Careful, He Might Hear You*.

- Discuss how aspects of language choice and style provide insight into texts (explore reasons why Golding chose to write *The Inheritors* from the point of view of the Neanderthals rather than using an omniscient narrator or the impact of Shylock's plea for mercy in Shakespeare's *The Merchant of Venice*; note the use in films of long-shots to signify both real and metaphoric isolation).

Strategies

At level 7, a student:

7.8 Uses reading and viewing strategies that enable detailed critical evaluation of texts.

Evident when students, for example:

- Recognise that a text is an entity and respond to it as a whole and not just to fragments (in analysing a character in a novel, take into account the whole of the character's experiences, for example, consider Tess's murder of Alex in the light of other events in Hardy's *Tess of the D'Urbervilles*).

- Acquire a vocabulary that can describe variations in tone (aggressive, enthusiastic, insolent, passionate, matter-of-fact, sarcastic, whingeing).

- Recognise that, because they have been deliberately constructed, all parts of texts are significant (analyse the way a title might tie together main characters, events and themes).

- Compare endings of texts with their beginnings to detect themes and points of view.

- Reflect on what their own responses to texts reveal about their personal values and attitudes.

- Use knowledge of argument and persuasive techniques to identify fair and unfair use of generalisations and facts.

- Critically compare information in different texts, such as primary and secondary sources, to check for accuracy, omission and bias.

Level 8 outcomes:

8.5   Analyses and criticises in a lucid way texts produced for a range of purposes and audiences, including popular texts and linguistically demanding texts which may involve varied narrative perspectives and subtle subtexts.

8.6   Analyses texts in terms of the sociocultural values, attitudes and assumptions that they project and reflect.

8.7   Analyses how linguistic structures and features influence interpretations of texts, especially in the construction of tone, style and point of view.

8.8   Uses reading and viewing strategies that enable detailed critical evaluation of texts which may have complex levels of meaning.

LEVEL 7 Writing

Level 6 outcomes:

6.9 Conveys detailed information and explores different perspectives on complex, challenging issues through writing for specific and general audiences.

6.10 Predicts some of the likely characteristics and expectations of particular audiences and tries to accommodate or resist these expectations as appropriate.

6.11 Uses and experiments with a range of linguistic structures and features designed to influence audiences.

6.12 Revises own writing for meaning and effectiveness.

Texts

At level 7, a student:

7.9 Writes sustained texts characterised by complexity of purpose and subject matter and a need for formality in language and construction.

Evident when students, for example:

- Write a range of texts, including stories, plays and poems to reflect on attitudes, values and issues in ways that, while not necessarily fresh and original, are interesting and thought-provoking.

- Write imaginative texts using a persona (convincingly adopt a persona different from themselves in age, conceptual capacity, cultural background).

- Write precise, accurate, clear and carefully organised task instructions involving a complex sequence of events or for a task which is difficult to describe.

- Write sustained reports on complex subjects, attempting to evaluate as well as inform (write a biography of a parent which explicitly or implicitly comments on that parent's life as well as giving factual details).

- Maintain a generally consistent point of view about complex and abstract issues throughout expository texts.

- Demonstrate control of content, substantiating views on issues and texts in an organised way, seeing distinctions between arguments or positions on an issue and between texts which deal with similar events and issues.

Contextual understanding

At level 7, a student:

7.10 Selects text type, subject matter and language to suit a specific audience and purpose.

Evident when students, for example:

- Experiment with subject matter and language to challenge stereotypical plots and characterisation (write a science fiction story which alters stereotyped or predictable sex roles).

- Adopt a voice to suit purpose and audience (choose to write with obvious conviction, using emotive examples from personal experience, rather than in a more dispassionate style, recognising that this could make the ideas in the text clearer and more appealing to particular readers).

- Revise work to meet the demands of specific writing tasks and audiences (check spelling in a job application; ensure that writing is as clear as possible given the constraints of specialised vocabulary and concepts).

- Choose writing techniques designed to persuade particular audiences on an issue (choose from text types such as formal argument, parody, narrative, poetry, dialogue and drama).

- Write task instructions to suit an intended audience's linguistic and conceptual capacities (using diagrams and symbols for non-English speakers; using humour to spice up dreary subject matter).

- Write relevant introductions to such texts as formal letters, essays, recognising that readers need to be quickly and efficiently introduced to the reasons for writing.

Linguistic structures & features

At level 7, a student:

7.11 Controls spelling, syntax and text structures to meet the demands of most expository and imaginative writing.

Evident when students, for example:

- Spell, punctuate and use words with acceptable accuracy so that errors do not detract from a reader's understanding or from the text's fluency or authority.

- Use linguistic structures and features to attempt to influence audiences (rhetorical questions used to engage readers' attention at beginning of expository texts; simple analogies or metaphors to illustrate or prove a point).

- Construct coherent and logical texts about abstract subject matter (essays with thesis statement, thesis development, and ideas marshalled at end; paragraphs in expository texts consisting of ideas related to a topic sentence).

- Generally use grammatically complex sentences without major syntactic errors (sometimes write 'the group in which he was a part of…' rather than 'the group of which he was a part', but are able when prompted to correct such errors).

- Write dialogue set out, punctuated and constructed in such a way that the reader does not have to struggle to identify speakers (write dialogue that sounds authentic; begin each person's dialogue on a new line).

- Record sources accurately and fully in footnotes and bibliographies, using an academic referencing system.

Strategies

At level 7, a student:

7.12 Critically evaluates others' written texts and uses this knowledge to reflect on and improve own.

Evident when students, for example:

- Note how writers achieve particular effects, such as suspense, lyricism and sarcasm, and try to use these techniques (describe the way staccato sentences create impact).

- Note the way endings in texts such as stories, poems and anecdotes often convey important information about the theme and point of the material, and experiment with writing such endings.

- Examine how writers try to engage audiences and experiment with these ideas (write with evident interest and personal enthusiasm; begin texts in unusual or interesting ways).

- Evaluate the amount and type of information in expository texts and use this understanding in own expository texts (write at sufficient length to clearly convey ideas and information, select information carefully to convey a convincing point of view).

- Help to establish criteria for use by a class in evaluating written texts, and use these and other performance indicators to evaluate their own and others' work.

- Evaluate degree of success in conveying ideas and information to particular audiences and use this to develop their own skills in writing for specific audiences.

Level 8 outcomes:

8.9 Writes convincingly and expressively on specialised topics and complex, often abstract, ideas, and consistently achieves a wide variety of purposes in writing for both specific and general audiences.

8.10 Makes critical choices of tone and style to suit different purposes and to influence audiences.

8.11 Manipulates linguistic structures and features for specific effect so that meaning is conveyed expressively and concisely.

8.12 Revises writing of self and others for cohesion, impact and meaning.

The year of living dangerously

Task

Students were required to present a three-to five-minute speech on a character from a novel studied. This student chose *The Year of Living Dangerously* by Christopher Koch. Students could speak about a character, 'become' a character, or, while in role as one character, talk about another.

Background

Students had practised similar talks. Little teacher assistance was provided. The student chose to take on the persona of the character Billy Kwan, who kept dossiers on all his friends and contacts, including Guy Hamilton, the journalist he helped. Billy would begin and end the speech typing up the latest information for his dossier on Guy. In between, Billy would deliver a monologue setting the scene for his reflections in the dossier. The speech was given in an empty room to teacher and a tape recorder.

Relevant outcomes:

Speaking and listening

7.1 Works effectively with others in situations characterised by complexity of purpose, procedure and subject matter and a need for formality in speech and attitude.

7.2 Considers the inter-relationships between texts, contexts, speakers and listeners in a range of situations.

7.3 Uses awareness of differences between spoken and written language to construct own spoken texts in structured, formal situations.

7.4 Uses a range of strategies to present spoken texts in formal situations.

Reading and viewing

7.5 Constructs meanings from a range of texts, including those characterised by complexity of construction and subject matter, and justifies these with detailed and well-chosen evidence from the text.

7.8 Uses reading and viewing strategies that enable detailed critical evaluation of texts.

Summary comment

The student shows the ability to enter imaginatively into a text of complex construction (it shifts in time and narrative perspectives) and subject matter, and to do this by taking on yet another narrative viewpoint. Evidence from the text is detailed and well-integrated and there is successful use of reading strategies and of strategies to present spoken texts in formal situations. The student manages the complex purpose of the speech capably, and shows an awareness of the inter-relationships of texts, context, speakers and listeners in constructing a text purportedly partly written and partly spoken but which in reality is all spoken. Neither the original text nor the student's response show the complexity typical of level 8 work, and the student would be expected to communicate more crisply at that level.

Type and read

A July 28 You are apparently too stupid - or too vain - to have realised what the lady wants from you. You proceed **B** to use and neglect Jilly. You continue to chase Vera - no doubt for her body, money, or both. FOOL Guy - how can you be such a FOOL.

C **Look through files**

Type and Read

D Still you continue to be neglect Jilly, You are different to what I thought. Why can't you learn to give,......Why can't

E you learn to love.........Maybe I tried too hard.......Maybe I created you.

Name: Guy Hamilton

F **Nationality:** Technically Australian, regards himself as British.

Born: 1936, under the sign of Capricorn.

G **Remarks:** A hybrid Saxon-Celt, of attractive appearance, Moderate to conservative in politics. Somewhat 'correct' for a man of his 'generation'. A gentleman. His danger is to shut himself off, ruling neat rules around himself, making a fetish of his career, and making all his relationships temporary. He must learn to give… He must learn to love…

(7.1) Complex purpose: student has to 'be' Billy Kwan and pretend to type dossier while reading a prepared response to the text (**A**).

(7.2 and 7.3) Somewhat formal language shows that student is aware of difference between normal language of speech and language of a report, however personal, and that this is influenced by context (**B**).

(7.4) Careful consideration of how to present the information about Billy and the other characters: begins in the present, writing up the latest portion of the dossier, then uses the file to explore past events from Billy's point of view, then returns to the present to conclude (**C**).

Level 7
WORK SAMPLE

**Speaking
and
Listening**

**Reading
and
Viewing**

I He is myself! I should have been him. Why not, God? Why not?

I remember the first night that he arrived. Alone. He was working on his first foreign posting for the Australian Radio and Television Corporation. I knew from the moment I saw him we would make a good partnership. So I jumped at the opportunity to give him a good start. Guy's predecessor, Potter, had neglected his job, and as a result left Guy without any contacts. It is hard enough for a new correspondent on their first foreign appointment, almost impossible without contacts, but I knew Guy could do it, I knew he was capable of success.

Guy said little that first night. He kept his senses open and took everything as it came, just prompted us with brief questions. I saw it as my duty to give Guy some contacts. I lined up an interview for him **J** with Sukarno the next day. Nothing special but it was a start.

The interview didn't work well. Wally O'Sullivan had much more prestige with Sukarno and he took charge. This made Guy realise how hard it was going to be. Although he had failed that day, he remained patient and planned on doing better the following day. That was one thing about Guy, he always took pride in his job, and he was very ambitious and capable of success. I mentioned to Guy that I could get him an interview with Audit the leader of the communist Party. It had been impossible for anyone to get interviews with Audit and Guy considered it a stupid remark.

Well, the interview did work out. Guy got world coverage from his report and received respect from the other journalists in Jakarta, which was not an easy task. This also marked the beginning of our partnership. He did the words, and I was his eyes.

Guy turned out better than I expected. This led me to believe he was the perfect man and as a result I set him up with my Jilly. But this is where Guy started to turn cold. He took advantage of her, he didn't give her <u>any</u> love. This was my mistake. I found out that Guy was capable of numbing his feelings and ignoring everybody else's feelings in the process. I made the matter worse by encouraging the relationship and giving Jill and Guy the use of <u>my</u> bungalow for <u>their</u> **H** love-making. I started to wonder if things were going to turn out for the best.

Maybe if Guy hadn't got involved with Vera the situation could have been a lot better. I can't bear the thought of Guy spending the night with a <u>Russian</u> diplomat. I don't know whether Guy loved her or just wanted her <u>body and money</u>. It affected him in a negative way. This was also the time that Guy found out about Jill's pregnancy which she chose not to tell him. I suspect he searched through my bungalow and found the information in her dossier.

Guy became unstable after finding out about Jilly's pregnancy. He became selfish and neglected the feelings of everyone around him. **K** This led to yet <u>another</u> 'fantasy' trip with Vera at Bandung. I can't bear the thought of what happened their. After this I new it was the end of Guy for me.

Guy tried to mend his mistakes by regaining my friendship, but there was no way that I was going to be ever be friends with him. I gave **L** him a good start, and now he turns into a <u>traitor</u>. He is a <u>selfish</u> and <u>cold person</u>, who shows <u>no love or respect to others</u>. Especially my Jilly.

(7.5) Careful construction of meaning based on the text, including comment on what character has learnt (**D**).

(7.8) Uses reading strategies to enable detailed critical evaluation of texts: refers to important details revealed at the end of the text and uses these to reflect on other parts of the text (**E**).

(7.3) Uses strategies to present formal spoken texts: preparation of cue cards (**F**).

(7.8) Student notes important details scattered throughout the text, integrating some here in Guy's dossier (**G**).

(7.3) Underlines key words to remember to emphasise them (**H**).

(7.3) Understands differences between spoken and written language: change of tone from the written dossier to the spoken outburst that begins the reflection on recent events (**I**).

(7.3) Incomplete sentence used to give flavour of reflective talk (**J**).

(7.5) Constructs meaning with close attention to detail: understands significance of the minor character, Vera (**K**); musters detailed information and organises it to logically reach this point (**L**).

The media and the environment

Task

Students were required to write an argument in prose on an issue they were interested in.

Background

The original essay was handwritten. Spelling, punctuation and expression have been preserved.

Relevant outcomes

7.9 Writes sustained texts characterised by complexity of purpose and subject matter and a need for formality in language and construction.

7.10 Selects text type, subject matter and language to suit a specific audience and purpose.

7.11 Controls spelling, syntax and text structures to meet the demands of most expository and imaginative writing.

7.12 Critically evaluates others' written texts and uses this knowledge to reflect on and improve own.

Summary comment

Essay is a sustained piece of formal writing dealing with complex subject matter in a logical and coherent way. Spelling, syntax and text structures are controlled and generally accurate. The sophistication and control of content, language and structure indicate that the work has exceeded the requirements of level 6. It does not have the expressiveness and depth of understanding that characterise level 8 work.

How effectively can the media be used in promoting environmental issues?

A Environmental issues — how did we become aware of these? Mainly through the media, which has publicised intensively the condition of our world. There are segments on the radio, television and in newspapers and magazines, educating the public on the degradation of our earth. Means to save the planet have been explored and examined, but how effective can the media be, in getting the public to take action?

B The media are the link between the local, state and federal government and people of society. They are used as vehicles for the government to educate, make the public aware of the state our earth is in and hopefully get them to take action. But the media can, and they have, been the initiator in bringing change. They have exposed and manipulated the government and large companies' treatment of the environment, to the public, leaving them no choise, but to change their policies.

C People's consciousness of environmental issues can be raised, but the aim is to change their habits. For years, the media promoted smoking to society. People responded to the media exposure and there was an increase in the percentage of the population who took up the habit. When the effects of smoking was discovered, the media publicised the issue intensively and now there **D** are more non smokers than smokers. If the media has that much power over the public, then they can change people's habits towards the environment. Only recently, there was coverage on beached whales. The media received a huge response from the public, and despite the bitter cold, many people went down to save the beautiful animals. As a result only thirteen out of the forty-nine whales died.

E The media reports many stories which shock the public. The stories stir up interest from society and, in this state, society can be encouraged to take action. However, it is rare to have a follow up to the story. To keep interest flowing and action continuing, the media should inform the public about the progress or lack of progress of environmental issues.

Television, is probably the most effective way for the media to promote issues. Visual imagery makes more of an impact on people. When the media showed people helping the whales, it sent shivers down my spine, to **F** know people can come and work together to try and save them. It put tears in my eyes seeing whales that had died and made me wish I was there helping.

Newspapers and magazines are read by a large percentage of society. They are not as effective as television as people can easily 'flick' through the paper and miss environmental articles. However, even if you have pictures like the cartoon boy who is environmentally friendly, that will remind readers about the environment.

Radio is another way the media can promote issues. How many people listen to the radio when they are in the car? The media would be especially effective in promoting environmental issues on the radio in peak hour traffic. I found the handy hints they used to have on **F** the radio interesting and they were little things which helped the environment. For instance, if you drive on tyres that are firmly pumped up, you will save on petrol and reduce exhaust emmission, than if you have slightly flat tyres.

D The media is a part of society, a part of people's lives. As Darwin is isolated from the metropolitan areas of Australia, it is the media who keeps us up with the awareness, education and action in environmental issues. It is the media who can encourage the public to take **G** action in saving our earth.

(7.12) Understands how writers attempt to engage audiences: provides essential background ideas, use of rhetorical questions (**A**).

(7.10) Introduction quickly and efficiently introduces readers to the reason for writing (**B**).

(7.9) Controls content and shows ability to see distinctions between different elements of issue (**C**).

(7.11) Understands how linguistic structures and features might influence readers: the 'if…then' structure and use of repetition for emphasis in the conclusion (**D**); logical progression through essay: moving from looking at the media generally to examining the potential contribution of each medium in turn (**E**).

(7.12) Writer has noted how writers use evidence from personal experience to achieve particular effects and attempts to use this technique (**F**).

(7.11) Conclusion has sense of purpose (**G**).

LEVEL EIGHT

LEVEL 8 Statement

Students who have achieved level eight communicate confidently with teachers, peers, and other adults in the school and local community. They strive to be perceptive and analytical and to make sophisticated adult judgements about complex social, environmental and political issues. They are aware not only of the function of language but also of its drama and power.

Students strive to speak confidently, both formally and informally, inside and outside the school, and to be critical listeners. They have been taught to understand the needs of their audiences and so are able to attempt to manipulate their responses (to emotionally move them, persuade them, or make them laugh, for instance).

Students at this level are critical and reflective readers of all kinds of texts, both written and visual. They attempt to convey their ideas about texts in lucid and compelling ways. They compare texts with other texts and with the society around them. They discuss and analyse style and tone and account for their effectiveness in particular situations. They also challenge the assumptions and values expressed in texts. Aware of the influence of the mass media, they are particularly analytical readers of both written and visual mass media.

Level eight students strive to write with an assurance, precision and vitality that will testify to their social competence. They explore complex themes and issues in a variety of styles that compel readers' interest and attention and are capable editors of both their own and others' writing.

LEVEL 8
Table of outcomes

	Texts	Contextual understanding	Linguistic structures & features	Strategies
SPEAKING AND LISTENING	8.1 Interacts responsively, critically and confidently with both familiar and unfamiliar audiences on specialised topics in formal situations, and consistently achieves a variety of purposes in speech.	8.2 Shows sophisticated understanding of the power and effect of spoken language when speaking and listening.	8.3 Analyses how linguistic structures and features affect interpretations of spoken texts, especially in the construction of tone, style and point of view.	8.4 Uses listening strategies which enable detailed critical evaluation of texts with complex levels of meaning.
	See page 144	See page 144	See page 145	See page 145
READING AND VIEWING	8.5 Analyses and criticises in a lucid way texts produced for a range of purposes and audiences, including popular texts and linguistically demanding texts which may involve varied narrative perspectives and subtle subtexts.	8.6 Analyses texts in terms of the sociocultural values, attitudes and assumptions that they project and reflect.	8.7 Analyses how linguistic structures and features influence interpretations of texts, especially in the construction of tone, style and point of view.	8.8 Uses reading and viewing strategies that enable detailed critical evaluation of texts which may have complex levels of meaning.
	See page 146	See page 146	See page 147	See page 147
WRITING	8.9 Writes convincingly and expressively on specialised topics and complex, often abstract, ideas, and consistently achieves a wide variety of purposes in writing for both specific and general audiences.	8.10 Makes critical choices of tone and style to suit different purposes and to influence audiences.	8.11 Manipulates linguistic structures and features for specific effect so that meaning is conveyed expressively and concisely.	8.12 Revises writing of self and others for cohesion, impact and meaning.
	See page 148	See page 148	See page 149	See page 149

LEVEL 8 Speaking and Listening

Level 7 outcomes:

7.1   Works effectively with others in situations characterised by complexity of purpose, procedure and subject matter and a need for formality in speech and attitude.

7.2   Considers the inter-relationships between texts, contexts, speakers and listeners in a range of situations.

7.3   Uses awareness of differences between spoken and written language to construct own spoken texts in structured, formal situations.

7.4   Uses a range of strategies to present spoken texts in formal situations.

Texts

At level 8, a student:

8.1 Interacts responsively, critically and confidently with both familiar and unfamiliar audiences on specialised topics in formal situations, and consistently achieves a variety of purposes in speech.

Evident when students, for example:

- Convey a sense of genuine communication with a variety of audiences on formal occasions (by sounding relaxed and spontaneous during a carefully rehearsed speech).

- Use talk to explore complex concepts and ideas to clarify their own and others' understanding (try out metaphors and similes to explain abstract ideas).

- Respond quickly and appropriately to people and situations to maintain an overall purpose (modify content and approach when speaking to an unresponsive audience or when a new time limit is unexpectedly imposed; confidently and good-humouredly handle diversions and unexpected questions; interact competently on the telephone with strangers, conveying information succinctly and clearly and responding relevantly and decisively).

- Identify, challenge and justify interpretations of the underlying assumptions, points of view and subtexts in spoken texts (identify when what is said seems contrary to what the text itself suggests and justify that interpretation with evidence from the text).

- Negotiate agreements in groups where there are disagreements or conflicting personalities, managing the discussions sensitively and intelligently and concluding them with positive summaries of achievement.

- Assert sustained points of view or ideas to both familiar and unfamiliar audiences with determination and conviction but without aggression, condescension or disrespect.

Contextual understanding

At level 8, a student:

8.2 Shows sophisticated understanding of the power and effect of spoken language when speaking and listening.

Evident when students, for example:

- Critically examine their own reactions to spoken texts (are alert to their own vulnerability to emotional and other seductive appeals and can dispassionately analyse the personal and linguistic reasons for this).

- Examine the way interpretation is influenced by style of presentation (analyse the tones of news bulletins on 'serious' and youth-oriented stations, and how these might affect the intended audiences).

- Analyse spoken texts in terms of the socio-cultural values, attitudes and assumptions they convey (examine texts for subtexts, significant inclusions or exclusions; discuss the power of language to reinforce or change values and attitudes; use non-sexist and non-racist language and ideas and information).

- Analyse the characteristics of intended audiences and demonstrate psychological and interpretative insights in choosing approaches that suit audiences (choose language calculated to appeal emotionally to specific audiences; decide not to begin a speech with a joke based on a common stereotype; use cajoling or more authoritarian language when negotiating within a group).

- Anticipate likely disagreements between themselves and listeners, and structure material to minimise or overcome this (during negotiations or a mock election speech).

- Understand that people respond to both non-verbal and verbal elements of spoken language and work on enhancing interpersonal skills to improve communication with others.

Linguistic structures & features

At level 8, a student:

8.3 Analyses how linguistic structures and features affect interpretations of spoken texts, especially in the construction of tone, style and point of view.

Evident when students, for example:

- Identify characteristics of a speaker's tone and style of presentation (what makes it bombastic, humorous, reasonable).

- Analyse the way non-verbal factors in spoken texts influence people's judgement of speakers (as trustworthy or untrustworthy, ironic or naive).

- Discuss reasons for particular stylistic techniques (the way a politician might end sentences with a pronounced downward inflection to convey 'the final word'; repeated use by an interviewee of a media interviewer's name to convey intimacy and sincerity).

- Discuss the way rhetorical devices such as the triptych ('of the people, by the people, for the people') sustain audience interest by involving listeners in powerful language, rhythms.

- Explore the way that analogies, imagery and other comparisons affect the tone and mood of spoken texts and provide insight into the speaker's motives and opinions.

- Analyse features such as the use of the word 'we' or of the passive voice by public figures seeking to deflect or deny blame for alleged wrongdoing.

Strategies

At level 8, a student:

8.4 Uses listening strategies which enable detailed critical evaluation of texts with complex levels of meaning.

Evident when students, for example:

- Do research before listening so that evaluation is based on knowledge of the topic and of perspectives on the issue.

- Use linguistic knowledge to pick up cues to assist in the interpretation of complex texts (in detecting irony and point of view).

- Compare spoken texts on an issue to analyse them critically (compare two interviews given by a public figure to detect selections, emphases and omissions that signal changed views or policies).

- Infer meaning by using socio-cultural understanding of the purposes of particular text types and media and the motivations of individuals such as public figures (know that vested interests may colour some individuals' views and listen carefully for clues to the subtext; know that the impartial appearance of current affairs program items may be bogus and listen critically for bias).

LEVEL 8 Reading and Viewing

Level 7 outcomes:

7.5   Constructs meanings from a range of texts, including those characterised by complexity of construction and subject matter, and justifies these with detailed and well-chosen evidence from the text.

7.6   Considers a variety of interrelationships between texts, contexts, readers or viewers and makers of texts.

7.7   Identifies and comments on the impact of techniques intended to shape readers' and viewers' interpretations of and reactions to texts.

7.8   Uses reading and viewing strategies that enable detailed critical evaluation of texts.

Texts

At level 8, a student:

8.5 Analyses and criticises in a lucid way texts produced for a range of purposes and audiences, including popular texts and linguistically demanding texts which may involve varied narrative perspectives and subtle subtexts.

Evident when students, for example:

- Approach with confidence the reading and understanding of visually forbidding texts written for adult audiences (long and densely written material such as extended analyses in 'quality' newspapers, extracts from poetry and prose of previous centuries such as Homer's *Iliad*, Swift's *A Tale of a Tub* or Milton's *Areopagitica*).

- Construct sophisticated readings of popular texts such as children's adventure stories, fairytales and cartoons (examine the social values implied in Bugs Bunny cartoons or in Enid Blyton stories).

- Offer interpretations of texts from different theoretical perspectives (offer both a feminist reading and a more traditional interpretation of Chaucer's 'The Wife of Bath's Tale' or Mukherjee's *Wife*).

- Draw conclusions from synthesising material read and viewed, making generalisations based on patterns and trends (the formula to which Mills and Boon books are written; distinctions within and between texts in terms of characters, themes, inferred authorial intention).

- Make connections that show insight between their own reading experiences and the way others might react to texts in order to explore the significance of aspects of texts ('Vivian's genuine, caring approach to life wins and holds audience support. The audience finds delight in her struggle to come to terms with a world that is foreign to her, reacting with joy when her tormentors get their just desserts.').

- Explore a text through an imaginative response that implies an analysis of or a point of view about the text (composing a letter from Ophelia to Hamlet written just before her 'mad' scene drawing from material in Shakespeare's *Hamlet*).

Contextual understanding

At level 8, a student:

8.6 Analyses texts in terms of the socio-cultural values, attitudes and assumptions that they reflect and project.

Evident when students, for example:

- Make sophisticated connections between the characters, people and ideas portrayed in texts and the socio-cultural values the texts project (the implication in television science programs that science is progressive and helps solve problems).

- Explain the impact of an author's own views and values on a text (infer an author's values from a text and analyse their effect on the text's content and construction).

- Read and view texts set in other times, recognising that societies' values change over time (after viewing 1940s newsreel footage of women in the Australian Land Army, comment on society's views of women then and now).

- Dispute a common reading of a text, providing evidence from the text and citing other relevant factors (argue that a cartoon or advertisement depicting a woman as an incompetent driver is sexist rather than amusing).

- Parody text types such as a sixteenth century sonnet sequence or the nineteenth century Gothic novel to make a point about the values, attitudes, beliefs and reading practices that underpin such texts (use the sonnet form to satirise Elizabethan attitudes towards love, or write a melodrama in rhyming couplets using scenes from Charlotte Brontë's *Jane Eyre* as a basis).

- Analyse texts in terms of the cultural values suggested by what they omit (a television documentary or book about Australia's past that does not mention Aborigines; or a television soap opera that features only well-off people).

Linguistic structures & features

At level 8, a student:

8.7 Analyses how linguistic structures and features influence interpretations of texts, especially in the construction of tone, style and point of view.

Evident when students, for example:

- Write about the effect of production design on films (the way black-and-white footage implies documented truth; the way set design subtly suggests aspects of a character's socio-cultural context, as the peacock-tail pattern in the wallpaper behind the main character in the film *My Brilliant Career* offers a perspective on Sybylla's struggle to break free from society's expectations regarding feminine beauty).

- Discuss the way interpretation is influenced by variations of rhythm and pace (by modifying established metres in poetry and by editing in films).

- Explain the specific effects of sound imagery (alliteration in poetry and headlines).

- Analyse the factors, such as certain sentence structures, that contribute to the narrative voice in imaginative texts (the factors which make the Peter Porter poem *Your attention please* sound like a government warning, or the factors which contribute to the macabre qualities of Emily Dickinson's poetry).

- Analyse the use of techniques — such as characterisation, wit, cynicism and irony — designed to position readers and viewers to take particular views ('By giving Edward vulnerable qualities, the film-maker does not allow him to alienate the audience as his associates do.').

- Describe the tone of various texts, using a widening range of adjectives such as 'indignant', 'arrogant', and justifying judgement by close reference to the text (discuss the way the writer of a letter to the editor seems to feel about the topic or describe and analyse Pope's attitude to vanity in his poem *The Rape of the Lock*).

Strategies

At level 8, a student:

8.8 Uses reading and viewing strategies that enable detailed critical evaluation of texts which may have complex levels of meaning.

Evident when students, for example:

- Use recognisable features, familiar concepts and knowledge of genre to construct meaning from linguistically complex texts (interpret a Shakespeare sonnet using knowledge of genre, identifiable symbols and recognisable concepts).

- Compare the purposes of different texts in the understanding that an author's purpose(s) is an important part of the meaning-making process (compare a newspaper editorial with a news report in the same newspaper, noting selection, omission, emphasis and implied viewpoint and relating these to text type and audience expectations).

- Understand characters' feelings in narratives without necessarily sharing them, and bring psychological insight to bear on characters' thoughts and experiences (consider the narrator's point of view in some of Browning's dramatic monologues or Clegg's point of view in John Fowles' *The Collector*.

- See puzzles in texts as sources of intellectual pleasure, and accept that imaginative texts will not necessarily end neatly and offer solutions to issues.

- Realise that fiction communicates ideas powerfully because it can flesh out abstractions otherwise difficult to discuss and analyse (Swift's presentation of political satire through his narrative of a fantastic journey in *Gulliver's Travels*).

- Make connections between responses to texts and identity (by comparing their personal responses and interpretations with those of other people and considering what the results might indicate).

LEVEL 8 Writing

Level 7 outcomes:

7.9 Writes sustained texts characterised by complexity of purpose and subject matter and a need for formality in language and construction.

7.10 Selects text type, subject matter and language to suit a specific audience and purpose.

7.11 Controls spelling, syntax and text structures to meet the demands of most expository and imaginative writing.

7.12 Critically evaluates others' written texts and uses this knowledge to reflect on and improve own.

Texts

At level 8, a student:

8.9 Writes convincingly and expressively on specialised topics and complex, often abstract, ideas, and consistently achieves a wide variety of purposes in writing for both specific and general audiences.

Evident when students, for example:

- Write narratives and poems which highlight complex and abstract themes or issues in fresh and imaginative ways through action, setting, imagery, characterisation.

- Write fiction which requires careful inferential reading ('Sometimes there are voices in my head, telling me to do things. But I never do them. I just go to sleep in the inky blackness and when I wake up the voices have gone. They said I killed someone. But I know I didn't. I was asleep when it happened.').

- Write specialised texts accurately and convincingly (general interest newspaper feature and 'colour' stories which use typical journalistic tone and text structures; drama and film scripts focusing on significant moments of conflict and featuring correct setting-out).

- Write expository texts acknowledging the complexity of issues or subject matter, showing mature understanding of socio-cultural context, developing paragraphs and the whole text, and conveying a clear sense of the writer.

- Write vividly, confidently and with conviction in a personal voice about topics of personal interest and concern with the intention of engaging, moving or entertaining the intended reader.

Contextual understanding

At level 8, a student:

8.10 Makes critical choices of tone and style to suit different purposes and to influence audiences.

Evident when students, for example:

- Analyse the characteristics of intended audiences and show some psychological and interpretative insights in choosing between different approaches for an audience (compel newspaper readers' attention by beginning a feature article on an important but abstract issue with a human interest angle; use language calculated to make an emotional appeal to specific audiences).

- Demonstrate mature judgement in deciding on the style and tone of a piece designed to influence or appeal to a particular audience (whether to write a letter of complaint with a coldly rational or highly emotive tone).

- Convey abstract information effectively (use metaphors appropriate to an audience to make complex and abstract notions more understandable).

- Employ prose rhythms to suit purposes (natural speech rhythms in first-person narration to enhance realism and to encourage empathy between narrator and reader; rhetorical cadences for effect in expository texts).

- Use imagery to enhance meaning in both expository and imaginative texts ('the term "easy rider" roared into our lexicon in the early seventies'; 'on the issue of the ordination of women as Anglican priests there are as many experts as there are parish churches.').

- Deliberately leave reader to fill in 'gaps' in imaginative texts which have complex levels of meaning or which demand the active involvement of the reader for their full effect, relying on a common linguistic and socio-cultural understanding (in writing a story or poem from the point of view of a persona).

Linguistic structures & features

Strategies

At level 8, a student:

8.11 Manipulates linguistic structures and features for specific effect so that meaning is conveyed expressively and concisely.

Evident when students, for example:

- Use a variety of punctuation devices — dashes, semi-colons and ellipsis marks — to convey precise information about the rhythm, meaning and tone of a text (use quotation marks to distinguish between own and others' views within texts: 'Fashion magazines promote the "beautiful" female figure.').

- Draw on a variety of words and grammatical and syntactic structures to convey meaning economically and precisely (use subordinate clauses rather than several sentences; use and correctly punctuate parenthetical remarks; avoid tautologies; choose between subtly different words and phrases for maximum effect).

- Use a range of stylistic features (symbolism, imagery, understatement, irony) to illustrate ideas in both expository and imaginative writing.

- Deliberately contravene some linguistic conventions, especially in imaginative writing, to shock or otherwise manipulate the reader (use incomplete sentences, no punctuation, 'florid' prose).

- Use linguistic structures and features appropriate to particular personae and situations in imaginative writing (use naive language and ideas in writing first-person narrative by a child).

- Deliberately order points in an argument to cumulatively build up to a convincing conclusion.

At level 8, a student:

8.12 Revises writing of self and others for cohesion, impact and meaning.

Evident when students, for example:

- Read their own writing from an outsider's perspective and identify gaps and inadequacies, especially in logic and completeness.

- Imaginatively rearrange information in a narrative or argument to increase the impact of the piece on a designated audience.

- Critically evaluate their own writing (in discussion with peers, teacher or other adult, show willingness to discard, delete and take new directions).

- Present work appropriately and with regard for impact (understand which layout options will increase readability and impact).

- Read peers' writing critically and, in offering advice, focus on particular areas such as content, grammar or proofreading (note the sequence of main ideas in a piece of expository writing and point out unexplained leaps of reasoning or lack of consistency in plot).

Antony and Cleopatra

Task

Students were required to present a five-minute speech on any aspect of the literature texts studied over the year, and to use a prop associated with the text.

Background

Students were given guidelines prepared by the school. They were aware that they were being assessed on their grasp of content, thoroughness of analysis, relevance, originality, oral presentation skills, and the use of the prop.

The student and the teacher discussed ways of making the message of the speech clear to all the students in the audience. The speech was delivered to about 15 students and two teachers from behind a desk on which stood three beakers. One contained water, one was empty, and the third was full of earth.

Relevant outcomes:

Speaking and listening

8.1　Interacts responsively, critically and confidently with both familiar and unfamiliar audiences on specialised topics in formal situations, and consistently achieves a variety of purposes in speech.

8.2　Shows sophisticated understanding of the power and effect of spoken language when speaking and listening.

Reading and viewing

8.5　Analyses and criticises in a lucid way texts produced for a range of purposes and audiences, including popular texts and linguistically demanding texts which may involve varied narrative perspectives and subtle subtexts.

8.7　Analyses how linguistic structures and features influence interpretations of texts, especially in the construction of tone, style and point of view.

8.8　Uses reading and viewing strategies that enable detailed critical evaluation of texts which may have complex levels of meaning.

Summary comment

The student presented a conceptually sophisticated analysis of a complex text in a lucid and compelling way. Confidence in a formal situation was evident from voice and body language and minimal reliance on notes, suggesting a thorough understanding of the material and diligent rehearsal. Important to the student's analysis was the effect of linguistic structures and features on a reader's interpretation of a text. The selection and arrangement of material shows a sophisticated understanding of the power and effect of spoken language. Clearly, a variety of reading strategies have enabled the student to work in sophisticated ways with texts with complex levels of meaning.

NOTE:
Attached are the student's notes and a transcript, below, of part of the speech.

[Picks up glass of water] Water is the most fascinating and the most powerful of all the elements. And don't let the calm **A** of this still glass of water fool you, because the serenity of water can so often be deceptive. [Puts glass down] From the gentle snowflake that drifts from the heavens to the vapour that forms a cloud in the bathroom ceiling when you **B** step out of the shower to the huge tidal wave that submerges an entire nation, all of these are the various forms of water, in its various guises. . .

This power and changeability renders it very appropriate **C** that in *Antony and Cleopatra*, the protagonist, the Queen of Egypt, has her element as water. This is a woman who we find it very hard to classify and characterise because so **B** often her behaviour and her attitudes are constantly changing, just like water. In only one scene, in the third Act — um, in the third scene in the first Act, she explores the entire range, the entire spectrum of emotions — from loneliness to fury, to confusion to sadness, and hurt and bitter scorn. Both water and Cleopatra, then, are **D** unpredictable, unbiddable and incredibly powerful.

(8.1) Confident, responsive approach: direct communication with audience in use of 'you' and the imperative form (**A**).

(8.2) Sophisticated understanding of language's power to involve an audience which is less familiar with the content and ideas of the speech than the speaker: use of familiar examples, use of 'we' (**B**).

(8.8) Uses reading strategies for the close analysis of complex texts: understands importance of setting in understanding of character (**C**).

(8.5 and 8.2) Lucid synthesis of an idea on the text, and a clear summary of the logic so far to help listeners follow the argument (**D**).

E Now the play *Antony and Cleopatra* is basically about two different worlds, the world of Rome and the world of Egypt. And if we say that Egypt is characterised by water, then it is logical to

F assume that the opposing world of Rome would be symbolised by an opposing element, which is earth. The absorption of Antony in Cleopatra is, quite simply, the absorption of earth in water. The merging of the two elements gives us a higher awareness of the conflict between the two worlds, which is so important as a concern of *Antony and Cleopatra*.

G Now this isn't just an arbitrary idea, an arbitrary comparison that I've thrown up because I've seen the similarities between the characters and the respective elements. No indeed, these ideas of earth and water, and mud and vapour, which is water in its various forms, these go right to the heart of the play and create a strong current of imagery which sweeps throughout *Antony and Cleopatra*. . .

For example, the first time we see a portrait of Cleopatra is by a description by Enobarbus, where she is floating down a river on a barge. Immediately we see, we recognise, Cleopatra as being inextricably linked with water. She identifies with it, and we relate water as being her element.

H On the other hand, Antony twice loses in his Roman wargame. Twice he elects to fight at sea rather than on land, and twice he suffers defeat in the face of battle. He has been leaning towards this watery world of Egypt — on the most superficial level the imagery is consistent.

Now at this point of time in the play an anonymous Roman soldier interposes and pleads to Antony: 'Noble emperor, do not fight by sea. Let th' Egyptians and Phoenicians go a'ducking; we have us'd to conquer standing on the earth and fighting foot to foot'. Now what this soldier does is convey to us the imagery of earth as being linked with the Roman mindset, that kind of heavy solidity of earth and the Roman world…

(8.2) Sophisticated understanding of language's power to demarcate sections of a text: use of the introductory 'now' accompanied by appropriate vocal inflection (**E**).

(8.5) Insightful analysis of a linguistically demanding text (**F**).

(8.1 and 8.2) Demonstrates both a well-expressed conviction and an awareness of the importance of emphasising that the interpretation is a valid one, supported by the whole text (**G**).

(8.5) Compelling evidence for point of view (**H**).

(8.7 and 8.8) Uses reading strategies for detailed analysis of a complex text, aware of the effect of linguistic structures and features on the text's meaning: having established the metaphors for Antony and Cleopatra, student follows this to a logical conclusion with implications for plot and theme, for example, '"Let Rome in Tiber melt" [implies] power to absorb even strength of Rome' (**I**).

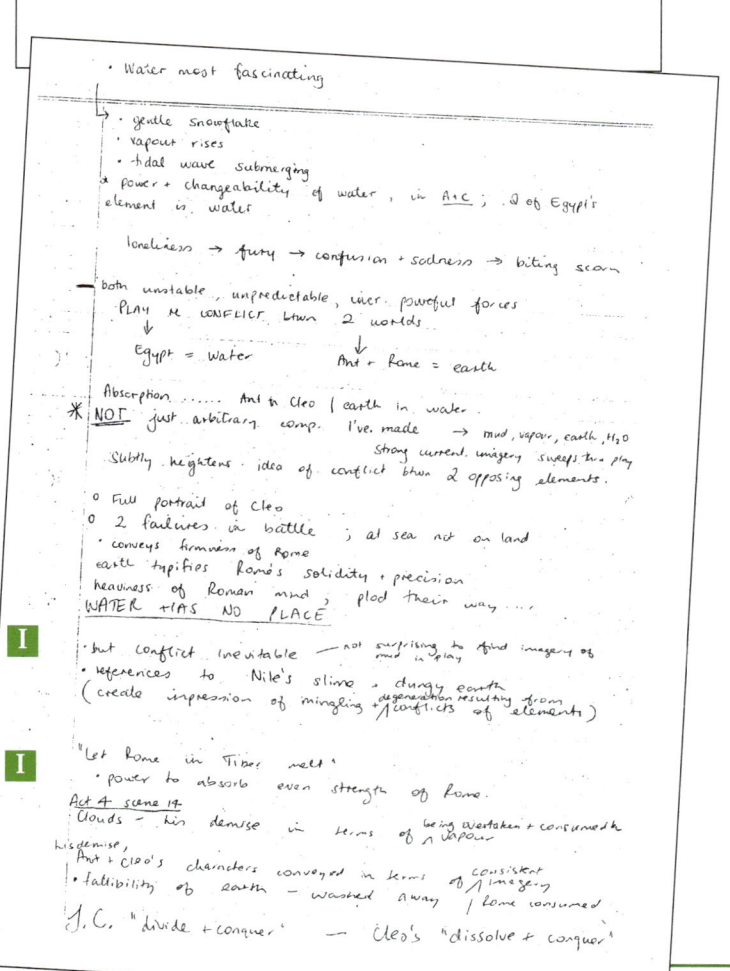

Gallipoli

Task

Students were required to examine the ways texts represent and comment on human experiences and ideas, and analyse the ways in which views and values are expressed in texts.

Background

Students studied the film *Gallipoli* in class, exploring the way it portrays and comments on Australian involvement in the First World War. Students could negotiate with their teacher to write an essay on any aspect of the film.

Relevant outcomes

8.6 Analyses texts in terms of the socio-cultural values, attitudes and assumptions that they reflect and project.

8.7 Analyses how linguistic structures and features influence interpretations of texts, especially in the construction of tone, style and point of view.

Summary comment

This essay presents a lucid analysis of a popular film which has subtle subtexts. The analysis focuses on the social and cultural values, attitudes and assumptions that the film reflects and projects. It discusses ways that linguistic structures and features, such as selected images and characterisation, work to promote the film's desired interpretations. The degree of analysis is the key feature distinguishing this work from level 7 achievement.

(8.6) Understands the text's values and attitudes, and connection between these and the film's purpose and audience (**A**); understands that selection and omission of detail contribute a reader's interpretation of the socio-cultural values of the text (**B**).

(8.7) Analyses the way characterisation influences the tone and point of view of the text (**C**); analyses the way selection of detail positions the film's viewers to accept its attitudes and values (**D**).

VIEWS AND VALUES

GALLIPOLI

How and why has Peter Weir distorted the history of "Gallipoli"?

As a commercial filmmaker, Weir has an obligation to present images that the public find appealing, and in line with their views and values. It is this sentiment that justifies the distortion of real events in making a box office hit but it isn't a disclaimer for the part Weir, and even Gammage and Bean played in the making of this film.

The film going public of the early 1980's were a group with a diminished sense of national identity and pride. No longer were they able to identify with the British Empire as home, because Australia had followed the United States into televised war in Vietnam. Television and the political events of 1975, where the Federal Government was dismissed by the Governor-General, served to taint the national innocence. A recession that was the worst since the 1930's Depression also served to eat into the security of these people. They were looking for an identity that, while still being unfamiliar to them, was tangible. Portraying heroic actions by Australians at Gallipoli served to revive a pride the general population had lost touch with - the stage direction for **A** Archy's death is that "he is hit by a machine gun blast but it appears as though he has just breasted an invisible tape, combining the action of victory with Australian heroism".

Examples of selective referencing to support the "Australian hero' theme abound in the making of "Gallipoli". Weir manages to have the fraction of a second shrapnel burst the right colour, but **B** can somehow remain ignorant of the fact that New Zealanders were present at Gallipoli.

A lack of justification of action also exists in the film. Even the British commanders, who are portrayed as unfeeling and unyielding masochists, wouldn't have decided to send Army Corps halfway around the world to have a blind stab at a cliff without it having some strategic gain. The Gallipoli Peninsula offensive, centred at Anzac Cove, Suvla Bay, and the point is barely mentioned; Robinson says "Not just diversions, Major. Vitally important diversions." Robinsons confession is brief and the 'secrecy' element allows for a film almost completely free of justification, and the film viewer hoping to see a glorified image of Australia would easily dismiss this important point.

An anti-British sentiment prevails throughout the film most evidently when the Infantry are in Cairo and Frank, Billy, Barney and Snow demonstrate their disrespect by impersonating two English Officers, assuming British accents when calling "Tallyho!" after them. Australians of 198.. wanted to see that the nation had been right in turning **A** away from the 'mother country'. <u>Gallipoli</u> provides justification for this turn by revealing only a negative side to the English soldiers. At one point in the climax of the battle, the British, meeting no opposition at Suvla are, according to a Radio Operator "just sitting on the beach drinking cups of tea". Also adding to the negative view of the British is the portrayal of Colonel Robinson as an **B** Englishman, rather than the Australian who his part was modelled on, and a particularly unfeeling one at that: when told of the grave implications of continuing the assault on the NCK Robinson says "I said push on".

C Characterization was manipulated in order to uphold an Australian identity that film goers were ready and willing to accept. They craved the innocence of early twentieth century Australians and by enforcing the 'rural myth' the

---

larrikinism and innocence of the perceived 'Australian character' was captured. Archy, the central character, is a naive, but virtuous person, who runs miles barefoot over rough ground towards the start of the film in order to defend his, and his Aboriginal friend Zac's honour. Victorian Lighthorsemen were at Gallipoli, but by giving central characters Western Australian backgrounds, a less **C** urban collective identity was achieved. Frank Dunne is the only character who is from a town background, but he is found in the outback and is accepted by Archy, a stockmans son, implying that Frank does have a rural identity of sorts. He does meet criticism when it is revealed he doesn't ride: one of the new Lighthorsemen advises Frank of the stationary horse upon which he sits for his riding test "he won't bite mate" to the laughter of the crowd.

Nowhere in the film is the famous Anzac blood thirstiness, **B** of men writing home expressing disappointment because war hadn't fulfilled their ideas of bloody battle on open ground, in fact, in one scene, "Frank looks ill" as a result of the action of shaking an exposed corpses' hand by soldiers as they passed. The film viewing public wanted to see Gallipoli Anzacs as the virtuous, blameless victims they'd been educated to see.

Historians have always tended to romanticise Anzacs, even Bean, the official historian, was accused of perpetrating the rural myth and of being somewhat bloodthirsty, glorifying battle scenes and the like. In writing a preface to <u>The Story of Gallipoli</u>, Gammage inadvertently discredits his work in appraising the film - he says

---

everything was made to be 'right', and although a slight disclaimer exists in acknowledging the fiction of the film, he ignores the lack of context "Gallipoli" occurs in.

Peter Weir distorted the history of Gallipoli by avoiding using all facts about the action. No actual lies are passed off as fact, but the action of leaving out, and **D** underemphasising other facts of the crusade dramatically distorts the film. Weir was presenting an image of Australia that the public wanted to see - this is proved by the fact that the film won so many awards and was seen by so many people. The Australian image was glorified in <u>Gallipoli,</u> and the history of the battle was distorted to give Australians an opportunity to revive a faith in themselves that was in danger of disappearing.

Bibliography

Dermody, S & Jacka, E <u>The screening of Australia</u> Currency Press Pty Ltd 1988

Kitson, J <u>Gallipoli - How the Film-Makers Twisted History to Market a Myth</u>

Lohrey, A <u>Gallipoli: Male Innocence as a Marketable Commodity</u> Island Magazine No 9/10 March 1982

White, R <u>Inventing Australia, Images and Identify 1688-1980</u> George Allen & Unwin Australia Pty Ltd 1988

Cold water surfing

Task

Students were required to negotiate with the teacher over the choice of a writing topic and their approach to it.

Background

Not available.

Relevant outcomes

8.9 Writes convincingly and expressively on specialised topics and complex, often abstract, ideas, and consistently achieves a wide variety of intended purposes in writing for both specific and general audiences.

8.10 Makes critical choices of tone and style to suit different purposes and to influence audiences.

8.11 Manipulates linguistic structures and features for specific effect so that meaning is conveyed expressively and concisely.

Summary comment

Although not an abstract topic, the experience of surfing was difficult to describe well. The text is expressive and interesting, thus achieving its purpose. Tone and style are well chosen to suit the purpose and to convey the experience to an audience unfamiliar with the sport. The writer maintains linguistic control throughout, doing some manipulation for special effect, making sure that meaning is conveyed concisely and clearly.

A **B** **C**

D

COLD WATER SURFING

By Allan

Saturday, 6 am. It's a cold July day in southern Tasmania – midwinter in the 'holiday isle'. I open my eyes. It's still dark. By a feat of will power that would have turned an indian fakir green with envy, I kissed my warm bed goodbye and – get this – had a cold shower to prepare myself for the cold.

By 7 am I'm in the car, speeding toward South Arm. The car is loaded with my surfboard, wetsuit and other items necessary for a surf trip. The weather the night before had promised a good solid swell of 4–5 metres for southern waters. It should be big.

Our car heater's blocked, dammit. I'm almost shivering already! As we bounce over the speed humps before the south Clifton beach car park, I start to hear the muffled roar of the surf. Then we grind to a halt and I leap out and take a quick jog over the sand dune for a squizz. A shiver runs up my spine, and not entirely due to the spectacular sight of a huge barrel charging it's way in to the beach.

As my cheuffer bumbles towards me quite unnecessarily carrying my gear for me, I realise that this is the biggest surf I'd ever witnessed first-hand. Having no second thoughts, I grabbed my surfboard off the car.

Slowly easing on my wetsuit, I check out who else is here. There are only two others in the water, nobody I know. I'm by myself today, although usually I have a packed car. Today nobody could or would come, so I get a free surf for once. Reaching down, I wax my board, and finally put my leg rope strap on. Then I pick up my board and slowly scan the waves with a look of great concentration on my face. This might have looked like I was searching for the best break, but I was really just procrastinating, delaying the time when I would have to immerse myself in the turbulent water. I did my careful-examination-of-the surf bit for a moment longer, decided I was only prolonging the agony, and walked down to the waters edge.

(8.11) Uses present tense in many places to increase the immediacy of the experience (**A**).

(8.10) Wry style adopted and maintained: contrast of midwinter and 'holiday isle' to create humour and empathy (**B**); intimate, 'chatty' tone to enable direct contact with the reader (**C**).

(8.9) Expressive writing, using convincing detail, on a specialised topic (**D**).

(8.10) Consideration for potential reader's lack of specialised knowledge: concise explanation of the art of paddling out (**E**).

I had learned the hard way never to go in slowly, so I hesitated, then marched straight in. I won't go into detail about the heart-stopping cold and the icy numbness that crawls from your boots to your groin area, but I will say that it reminded me of the stories I'd heard of when Hitler had forced certain prisoners in Siberia to line up outside in sub-zero temperatures while he considerately made his servants pour water over them until they froze solid.

Shrugging of my morbid thoughts, I paddled swiftly over the first wave and headed for a nice left-hander.

E I was half way out, and so far I had managed to paddle over most of the stuff that came my way. This may not seem like any big deal to the reader, but paddling out in huge surf requires a lot of skill, agility, timing, and luck. That I had managed to paddle over most of the waves that came my way was pretty lucky, too. for usually you have to duck-dive waves, which, without going into **C** too much detail, means that you get your head wet. So? Well, when you get your head, and, more specifically, your hair wet, it results in a large body heat loss, in other words, you get colder a lot quicker.

'This isn't so bad', I thought, feeling pretty pleased with myself. My wetsuit was warming up, I was still fairly unchilled, and I was nearly behind the breaking waves. Then a large unbroken wave reared up in front of me. I decided to paddle over it, sure that I would make it. Sure enough, I paddled over it, but only to find another wave doubled up behind it. I went instinctively to duckdive it, but it was too late, and it picked me up and hurled me backwards, burying me in a mountain of whitewash. The saying: **F** 'Pride comes before a fall' flicked abstractly through my mind as I was tumbled around under the surface like a piece of washing in a tumble dryer. Finally, just when I was beginning to forget which way was up, and my lungs felt like they would explode, I clawed my way to the surface. I gasped, and not just for air, although that was the main reason. The water was excruciatingly cold, and my head ached as if I had been hit in the temple with a hammer. Treading water, I pulled my board toward me, pulled myself on, and flicked my cold, wet fringe out of my eyes.

'This sucks', I thought, and paddled back out. The wave had knocked all the water out of my wetsuit, and it took a while to warm up again. I didn't worry any more about going over waves, so I duckdived the few waves that got in my way.

F As I sat out the back waiting for a good set, I reflected on how cool it was, sitting here, just behind the breaking waves, with the sunrise still frozen over the hills as it dragged itself slowly off the sky. The waves were perfect. They peeled away perfectly, in long straight **G** sets, displaying wide growling barrels and sharp, meaty lips. All was well with the world, and for a brief moment there was peace.

Enough gooey poetic stuff. My wave was beckoning me, an I paddled hard, exempt from the cold, to distraction, even to the fear of sharks that constantly haunts most people surfing by themselves. I caught it. This was without the largest wave I'd ever caught, and the drop down it's face was almost verticle. Slowly I straightened out from my crouch, pushing out with my right leg (I'm a natural-footer, which means that I have my right leg at the back of the board. The opposite is goofy-footed). As I came out of the bottom turn I urged my board high up the wave to generate as much speed as possible. Making sure I had plenty of room, I buried my rail and came around so that I was facing the white water. As I came out of the carve I headed back up the wave, and as I reached the lip I buried the other rail and executed a cutback, the white water coming over me until I was completely inside the barrel. I pushed down on my back foot, the barrel muttering obscene things at me. Just when it looked like I would make it, the barrel closed out on me, and I was pounded down into the waiting arms of the sand-bank below. This time I was too stoked to care.

H After an hour and a half in the water, I had had enough. It was 9:15 and there were a few more surf fanatics on the beach and in the water. Too exhausted to care, I let the waves push me towards the beach. I stumbled out of the water and on to the beach, and headed toward my gear, clutching my board and tripping over my legrope. Unco? No, just mega cold. My feet were numb. My hands were numb. My whole body felt as if it had been recently anaesthetized.

(8.11) Uses imagery to convey meaning expressively and concisely **(F)**; thoughtful use of vocabulary: specialist words (barrel, stoked, closed out) are used in such a way that meaning is conveyed expressively **(G)**; understands way sentence length and construction can be varied for effect: use of short sentences and repetition to emphasise the cold **(H)**.

After a few mugs of coffee from the thermos, half of which splattered onto the sand – my hands felt like those of a man with Parkinson's disease – I began to feel a little warmer. I had peeled of my wetsuit, thankful for the guy who invented rip cords and plastic zips. After I had my dry clothes back on, my feet began to thaw out, and the chilblains hit with sadistic vengeance. I left my shoelaces undone since I could not perform the intricate manoevre of tying them, and stumbled back up the beach towards the car park, where my chauffeur was most likely sitting in our vehicle knitting.

"Hey!"

It's Jonathon, a friend of mine from Taroona High.

"Any good?" He asks.

"Not bad. Pretty cool." I mutter casually through blue lips.

"In more ways than one, eh?" He smirks, and cruises off down the beach cackling hysterically at his cleverly veiled wit. I'm so cool I laugh on the inside, so I didn't follow his example and laugh my head off when I thought of him staggering out off the water in a few hours later just as cold, unco and numbed as I.

On the drive back, as I gorge myself on a bag of greasy chips bought from a corner shop, I reflect our reasons for getting up early in the morning in the middle of winter in Tasmania and going surfing in the icy water. Most people looking on would no doubt gain the impression that we were either schizophrenic cot-cases, or devout maochists.

Many people would have trouble understanding why we do it, and, indeed, I don't quite understand myself sometimes. But I do recall thinking to myself that morning, 'that was definately worth the hassle".

Easy rider

Task

Students were required to choose an area of interest about which to write an argumentative piece of prose.

Background

Not available.

Relevant outcomes:

8.9   Writes convincingly and expressively on specialised topics and complex, often abstract, ideas, and consistently achieves a wide variety of intended purposes in writing for both specific and general audiences.

8.10 Makes critical choices of tone and style to suit different purposes and to influence audiences.

8.11 Manipulates linguistic structures and features for specific effect so that meaning is conveyed expressively and concisely.

Summary comment

This essay tackles the complex area of gender stereotypes and images with confidence, conviction and expressiveness. The writer's choice of tone and style have a high probability of influencing an audience in the way intended. The essay's major strength is its control of linguistic structures and features for specific effect; this in particular distinguishes it from level 7 work.

easy rider

by Tanya

Wild thing   She's standing in the doorway of the drugstore, hands on hips, her black leather jacket heavy with chains, the visor of her authentic Harley Davidson cap tilted sullenly over one eye. She's trouble. This old gub, see, he doesn't want his store smashed up, so he walks right on up to her and asks, conciliatory like, "What you rebelling against?". She gives him a long cool look, mean and appraising. There's a silence you could drive a Norton through. And then she speaks, her eyelids not flickering once, her voice smooth as brake oil: "What you got?"

That scene, or something like it, was written for Marlon Brando in his 1954 debut film, The Wild One. It was not written for a woman. Women do not belong in bikie movies, except as faithful girlfriends or free-living "tramps" to be passed around like reefers. In 1954, when Brando slouched onto the scene. it was inconceivable that a biker could be anything but a man. (Forget that women handled beast-like motorcycles perfectly throughout the Second World War.) The popular image of a biker's girlfriend, as interpreted in the cinema, was a neat brunette, a Natalie Wood type, looking concerned for her man's safety in a pink frock with a cardigan hung over her thin, vulnerable little shoulders.

In the early seventies, when the term Easy Rider roared into our lexicon and brought with it a whole saddle bag of new cliches, the archetypical "bikie's moll" had become a supposedly sexually liberated, long haired blonde in bell bottoms, a girl so amenable (or out of it) she stood by her man through all kinds of neanderthal rituals including girlfriend swapping and bizarre initiation rites.

In our cinema, and therefore in our popular culture, women rarely ride motorbikes, except in porn movies, where they ride a lot of other things, too. In bikie movies, and bikie life,

(8.9) Vivid, confident expression of ideas (**A**).

(8.10) Chooses language and ideas likely to appeal to and influence an audience which, while not specified, can be assumed to be similar to the writer — interested in the issue, probably female, and educated enough to understand the vocabulary, terminology and syntax used (**B**); shows mature judgement in deciding on opening paragraph: portraying a woman in Marlon Brando's role to subtly emphasise a range of ideas, one being the rarity of such a role for women (**C**); effective communication of abstract ideas through use of examples and potent images (**D**).

they're regulated to the role of mere convenience, receptacle, unworthy of the amount of attention it takes to get the chrome Harley insignia polished and gleaming. The motorcycle has been appropriated by man as the supreme phallic symbol for himself, the extension he has when he's not having an extension. Motorcycles are tough: girls are not. Girls sigh on the sidelines **E**

Oh yeah? Post Thelma and Louise, we have a new inclination. Enough of this sighing, already. We wanna take control. No longer shrinking violets or bimbos deflecting blonde jokes, the nicest compliment that can be paid us is "What a tough cookie!" Who would we most like to emulate? Audrey Hepburn? Jackie O? Nah! Arnold Schwartzeneger. We pout, we snarl, we kick butt. Our collective consciousness has been raised. Victims no more, we're vixens with vroom vroom. When someone asks us what it is we are rebelling against, we say, "Plenty!" **F**

Girls are the wild ones this year, leaving men in their dust. (The men have their own agendas, kissing and hugging each other and finding their masculinity in therapy sessions in the bush.) We have appropriated Brando's swagger, stolen his clothes. The black leather jacket, periodically resuscitated into fashion, most recently with a punkish proclivity, is a classic. So are blue jeans. Together with the leather cap they have been the provenance of groups as diverse (or perhaps not so) as Nazi lieutenants, punk rockers and Greenwich Village leather queens. Perhaps it is this combination of Sal Mineo, Sid Vicious and the Stormtrooper that makes black leather so appealing for the modern girl. When you are taking over the world, a bit of S&M never goes astray. **G**

Right on the button, M. Lagerfeld has interpreted the bikie look his way for Chanel, combining some "un-tough" fabrics such as silk and delicate colours such as pink with motorcycle leathers and boots. As necessary additions to this, shall we say, unexpected look, are enough heavy silver and gold chains, belt buckles and enormous pendants to make the outcome of a battle with the Comancheros decidedly in the wearer's favour. (Oh, and don't forget the camellia tucked into the leather bustier.)

Other designers have been equally loose in their interpretation of le tough. Versace likes his biker to wear short, pleated skirts with the black leather. Fishnet tights go under Michael Kors's Gestapo-ish black leather trench. Mean machine from Yves Saint Laurent's sequined georgette evening

dress. Issac Mizrhai likes fluffy feather sleeves atop his Triumph.

What the looks have in common are a few key pieces: the leather cap, the leather jacket, the heavy chains and enormous jewellery borrowed from rap, the whips. And, just when you've parted with your straight leather skirt, guess what's back? The rest is purely inspirational . Chiffon at 200 kilometres per hour? Sure! Pearls at pit stop? Why not? **H**

Okay. It's get-real time. No-one's going to be throwing a leg over a Harley in a trillion dollars worth of Chanel silk, now are they? What we have here is not very far from what we had before. Fishnets, short leather skirts, open jackets revealing bustiers, saucy caps, the indispensable pout - does this not remind you of, dare I say, a bikie moll? If girls wanna take control, they have to take control of the images they give out. The truth is unavoidable: the one accessory you won't find at the Chanel boutique is the one you must have . . . a motorbike. **I**

(8.11) Sophisticated use of punctuation: parentheses, colons, points of ellipsis (**E**); range of sentence lengths and structures used to convey meaning expressively, as in this paragraph (**F**); uses a wide formal and informal vocabulary depending on purpose: 'wanna', 'un-tough', 'appropriated', 'punkish proclivity'—note choice of 'proclivity' for alliteration (**G**); argument is subtle but effective: penultimate paragraph leads reader to the realisation that 'nothing really has changed' and thus to writer's final point (**H**); uses range of stylistic features: imagery, irony (**I**).

Appendix

National collaboration in curriculum

National collaboration on curriculum began in June 1986 when the AEC resolved to support the concept of a national collaborative effort in curriculum development in Australia to utilise to maximum effect scarce curriculum resources and to ensure that unnecessary differences in curricula from State to State be minimised.

By 1987, the AEC had identified five priority areas for collaborative activity: science, numeracy, literacy, languages other than English (LOTE), and English as a second language (ESL).

Three initiatives

The AEC took three significant initiatives in 1988. First, it 'establish[ed] a working party to develop a discussion paper for a national approach to monitoring student achievement ... which takes cognisance of the programs already in place or under development at the State and Territory level'.

Second, it decided to develop a statement of the national goals and purposes of education in Australia.

Third, it set up a project to map the mathematics and general curriculum in all States and Territories through a study of their curriculum documents. The project was managed by the Directors of Curriculum, comprising the senior officers responsible for curriculum in the States and Territories as well as senior officers in the Commonwealth and the non-government systems. These maps were completed in early 1989.

Landmark decision

In April 1989, the AEC saw the second initiative come to fruition when it endorsed the *Common and Agreed National Goals for Schooling in Australia*.

It also agreed to 'strengthen further the effective collaboration which has occurred to date to enable greater effectiveness and efficiency in curriculum through the sharing of knowledge and scarce curriculum development resources across systems' and 'remove unnecessary differences in curriculum between systems'.

Building on the work on the third initiative, the AEC decided to develop a statement on mathematics which would include, within the framework of the agreed national goals, 'the knowledge and skills to which all students are entitled' and the 'agreed areas of strength in curriculum development which might be shared and built upon'. It also decided to set up three more mapping projects, this time in technology, science and English literacy.

Widening scope of activity

In October 1989, the AEC widened the scope of national collaborative curriculum activities to include a mapping of the social sciences, an audit of environmental education materials and a map of the environment as a cross-curriculum study. In May 1990, it decided to include, as one of the terms of reference for the writing of curriculum statements, the principles and objectives of the *National Policy for the Education of Girls*. It also asked for an audit of Aboriginal education curriculum materials. This was followed in December 1990 by approval for statements to be developed in English, technology and science.

Profiles

In mid-1990, the working party set up in 1988 under the first AEC initiative presented its report. It recommended the development of profiles to describe students' learning outcomes at a number of levels. In December 1990, the AEC endorsed the development of two profiles — English and mathematics — by the Australasian Cooperative Assessment Program (ACAP). The profiles would 'provide a framework which can be used by teachers in classrooms to chart the progress of their students, by schools to report to their communities and by systems' reporting on student performance as well as being amenable to reporting student achievement at the national level'.

Eight areas of the curriculum

In April 1991, the AEC launched the projects in their final form by deciding that statements and profiles would be developed for eight broad learning areas, forming a template of the knowledge and processes to be taught and learnt in Australian schools. Most States and Territories had already adopted their own sets of key learning areas, which generally clustered around the eight areas of learning adopted by the AEC.

Project management

Until August 1991, the projects to develop statements were being managed by the Directors of Curriculum and the profiles by ACAP. This structure did not assist the establishment of a close nexus between statements and profiles and so was replaced by the AEC Curriculum and Assessment Committee (CURASS), which managed all projects to completion.

CURASS' two major responsibilities were for consultation and the progressive approval of draft statements and profiles through consensus. States, Territories and the Commonwealth had up to two representatives each on CURASS. Non-government systems and sectors were also represented, as were the government and non-government teachers' and parents' organisations. In June 1992, a secretariat was established to support CURASS.

The committee developed a series of guideline papers that set out its position on issues important to the projects. The papers described the nature of statements and profiles, dealt with the roles and functions of the committee itself, set out its processes of consultation, dealt with issues relating to inclusivity and explored pedagogical implications.

Career education in Australian schools

In 1989 the AEC established a Working Party on Career Education and by December 1990 career education within the schooling sector had become the major focus of its activities. The Working Party prepared a document *Career Education in Australian Schools: National Goals, Student, School and System Outcomes and Evaluative Arrangements* which the AEC referred to CURASS in June 1992 'to inform its consideration of career education components within the national collaborative curriculum and assessment framework ...'

CURASS decided that career education in general and the document *Career Education in Australian Schools* in particular should be 'taken into consideration in the development of statements and profiles' especially in health and physical education and studies of society and environment.

Inclusivity

In 1992, CURASS decided to undertake two supplementary projects — one for students of English as a second language and the other for students with disabilities. These projects developed the national ESL Scale and the Towards Level 1 section in the profiles and helped ensure that these students had access to the profiles.

In addition, the Commonwealth funded two initiatives aimed in part to achieve high levels of inclusivity in national collaborative curriculum activities.

The first of these was the National Aboriginal and Torres Strait Islander Studies Project, made up of five sub-projects. The first led to the development of the *National Philosophy and Guidelines for Aboriginal Studies and Torres Strait Islander Studies, K–12*. The second secured the inclusion of Aboriginal studies and Torres Strait Islander studies and perspectives within the national statements and profiles. The other three sub-projects aimed to assist teachers in incorporating Aboriginal studies and Torres Strait Islander studies in their programs.

The second Commonwealth-funded project was the Gender Equity and Curriculum Reform Project. This had as one of its components the appointment of a gender equity consultant to each of the national collaborative curriculum projects to ensure that the principles and objectives of the *National Policy for the Education of Girls in Australian Schools* were incorporated into the design briefs, statements and profiles.

The statements and profiles was completed in their present forms in 1993. In July 1993, the AEC referred the documents to States and Territories.